P9-CDV-405

The Role of Domestic Courts
in the International Legal Order

*THE PROCEDURAL ASPECTS OF
INTERNATIONAL LAW SERIES*

RICHARD B. LILLICH, *editor*

JX
4173
, F3

The Role of Domestic Courts
in the International Legal Order

RICHARD A. FALK

SYRACUSE UNIVERSITY PRESS 1964

128864

Library of Congress catalog card: 64-16924

Copyright © 1964 by Syracuse University Press
Syracuse, New York

ALL RIGHTS RESERVED

Manufactured in the United States of America
by the Vail-Ballou Press, Inc., Binghamton, New York

FOR MARIA

3124/66   TB   4.34

FOREWORD

THIS BOOK is the third volume in the Procedural Aspects of International Law Series prepared under the auspices of Syracuse University College of Law's International Legal Studies Program and published by Syracuse University Press. The first full-length book by Professor Richard A. Falk, Woodrow Wilson School of Public and International Affairs, Princeton University, it assays the dual status of domestic courts as national institutions and as agents of an emerging international legal order. Challenging "the contemporary tendency to give foreign policy precedence over international law in domestic courts," (p. 4, n.5) he makes a powerful plea for a judiciary unwilling to subordinate the outcome of lawsuits to the vagaries of executive policy, but also willing to play a passive role in those areas "where there is no consensus among national units." (p. 111) The high calibre of the analysis and argument in this book is established by a single observation: the author's main thesis, first advanced in a 1961 article constituting Chapter V of this study, was adopted lock, stock, and barrel by Mr. Justice Harlan writing for the Supreme Court in *Banco Nacional de Cuba v. Sabbatino*.

The bulk of the book considers the act of state doctrine, an old rule of judicial self-restraint which Professor Falk supports for new reasons. Joining issue with international lawyers, including this writer, who have urged the courts to reject the doctrine and assume a more active role in the application and creation of international law rules, he contends that "rules of deference applied by domestic courts advance the development of international law faster than does an indiscriminate insistence upon applying challenged substantive norms in order to determine the validity of the official acts of foreign states." (pp. 6–7) "Rather than risk the bias of decentralized review," he argues, "it is preferable to insist upon deference, relying upon diplomatic pressure and supranational review for the application of substantive standards of international law." (p. 106)

The author appends two major qualifications to his arguments for judicial deference. "First, deference is inappropriate if the subject matter of dispute is governed by substantive norms of international law that are adhered to by an overwhelming majority of international actors." (p. 9) Only in matters of "legitimate diversity," situations where "there is no global consensus in favor of making universal a single substantive standard," (p. 127, n.29) should courts apply the act of state doctrine. The majority opinion in *Sabbatino* reflected this thinking by acknowledging that "the greater the degree of codification or consensus concerning a particular area of international law, the more appropriate it is for the judiciary to render decisions regarding it. . . ."

The second qualification, according to Professor Falk, "is that judicial deference to executive authority—internal deference—must not be achieved by sacrificing judicial independence." (p. 10) His thesis here, he notes, "runs against the current of American judicial practice that has tended to treat international law issues almost as if they were political questions and thus more suitable for executive than judicial settlement." (p. 136) Only by separating national policy from the application of international law in domestic courts can the prestige of international law as a legal order be enhanced. (p. 11) It is worth noting that the Supreme Court in *Sabbatino* did not pass upon the validity of the so-called *Bernstein* exception, thus maintaining its independence in act of state cases.

Among the many other topics receiving fresh treatment from the author's dual perspective, space permits mention only of sovereign immunity. He strongly criticizes the tendency by courts "to play dead whenever the executive chooses to act," (p. 160) trenchantly calling the rationale in *Mexico v. Hoffman* "a notion developed by men who are skeptical about the role of law as a regulator of international matters, for what could be more embarrassing to the development of the habits of law than a bland endorsement of an inconsistent pattern of disposition?" (p. 161) Attacking recent efforts to justify executive intervention in sovereign immunity cases on the ground that the doctrine is one of "comity" rather than law, the author aptly observes that "the word 'flexibility' is a euphemism for the liberation of the executive from standards and rules, even those of his own fashioning." (p. 154) His plea, here again, is for the judiciary to free itself from self-imposed subservience to the executive and adopt "the policy of extending law to cover in an orderly and just fashion as many controversies involving international law as possible." (p. 167)

In sum, it is a rare book that has as many fresh insights into old problems as this volume contains. It deserves to be read by all international lawyers and by all persons concerned with the procedural problems of building an international legal order. The product of five years of research, thought, and writing, it is a significant contribution to the literature in this area of international law and a distinguished addition to this Series. After reading the book, re-read the Supreme Court's opinion in *Sabbatino* to see Professor Falk's jurisprudence in action.

RICHARD B. LILLICH

Syracuse University
June, 1964

PREFACE

THE ROLE of domestic courts in the development of international legal order has become, rather unexpectedly, a matter of controversy and excitement for both attorney and academician. Interest has centered upon the extent to which domestic courts in the United States should give deference to official acts of foreign states and, especially, whether deference is owed to the official acts of those states that adhere to an alien social, political, and economic philosophy. The character of such an inquiry is a reflection of the wider conflict in world affairs between the liberal democratic states of the West and the communist states of the East. The inquiry is influenced, as well, by such other features of international relations as the danger of nuclear war and the appearance, ambition, and outlook of the new states. A main argument of this book is that an awareness of this international context has a radical effect upon an analysis and appraisal of domestic courts in international law cases. Among the most pervasive effects of this awareness is a doubt about the adequacy of the nation-state as the basic organizing unit for mankind.

Two sets of considerations dominate my interpretation of the proper role for domestic courts to play. First, international law exists in a social system that possesses weak central institutions. As a result, international tribunals are not consistently or conveniently available to resolve most disputes involving questions of international law. Domestic courts can help to overcome this structural weakness in the international legal system. Also, since no international institution is endowed with legislative competence, it is difficult to change old rules in response to changes in the composition and character of international society. If international law is to develop into a universal basis of order, then it is necessary that divergent attitudes toward the content of law be treated with respect. The older states must put forth a special effort to broaden international law enough to make it compatible with the values of socialist and anticolonial states. It is of no value to insist upon the old rules developed when all of the active international actors accepted *laissez-faire* economics at home and imperialism abroad. Domestic courts in the older states can help adapt international law to the modern world by developing principles that express tolerance for diverse social and economic systems.

Second, domestic courts must struggle to become their own masters in international law cases. The executive must not be allowed, and must certainly not be invited, to control the outcome of judicial proceedings by alleging the precedence of foreign policy considerations. The courts are not good vehicles for the promotion of foreign policy; moreover, the independence of courts from national political control is essential if international legal order is to be upheld and developed. A legal tradition depends upon the autonomy of its method and the saliency of its governing principles. Only an independent judiciary can establish such a tradition.

Although discussion of these matters is confined to the situation in the United States, the interpretation advances a general conception of the optimum participation of domestic courts in the international legal system. I am animated by the conviction that it is sensible and necessary for states, regardless of their history or orientation, to allow national courts increasingly to serve the cause of world order without regard to national affiliation. The immediate objective is to make judicial outcomes in international law cases as independent as possible of the nationality of the adjudicating tribunal. Of course, it will be argued that this is unrealistic. My reply is that the peace and order of the world rest upon such a precarious basis that action must be taken to make proposals like this one realistic. The transformation of international society cannot take place by itself. To avoid a traumatic transformation impelled by global tragedy, it is necessary to assume the risks of appearing foolish by dedicating ourselves to the tasks of peaceful transformation. This book is intended to illustrate the character of peaceful transformation. As such, it intends to be radical.

RICHARD A. FALK

Princeton, New Jersey
January, 1964

ACKNOWLEDGMENTS

RICHARD B. LILLICH, Director of International Legal Studies at Syracuse University College of Law, encouraged me to write this book. I am grateful for his initiative and, even more, for his wise suggestions about how to improve the manuscript. Professor Lillich's interest and sympathy seem most meritorious because he strongly takes issue with my position on a number of crucial points.

I am very indebted to Mrs. Barbara Yount. She has helped me to get a disorderly manuscript under some measure of control. Her patient concern with details of style and form would excite the envy of every bodhisattva I have known. In short, Mrs. Yount's editorial and research assistance has been an undisguised blessing.

As usual, I have asked too much, too often, too urgently, of Mrs. Jean McDowall. But, as usual, she has supervised with skill and imagination the various typings and retypings, managing always to surprise me with the finished product by the time I need it. As well, I thank Mrs. Constance Ducey for doing all the initial typing during the hottest part of last summer and Miss Priscilla Bryan for enduring many pages of footnotes this fall.

I wish also to thank Klaus Knorr, Director of the Center of International Studies at Princeton, for allowing me to use the fine facilities of the Center while I was working on this book.

Finally, I wish to thank *Temple Law Quarterly, Rutgers Law Review,* and *Howard Law Journal* for permission to use my material initially published as articles. An earlier version of Chapter VI was first circulated as an occasional paper by the Center of International Studies which has given permission for its use here in a somewhat revised form. Similarly, the American Society of International Law has given me permission to use as the basis of Chapter IV an article that first appeared in its *Proceedings.*

CONTENTS

Foreword vii

Preface xi

Acknowledgments xiii

I. Domestic Courts and World Legal Order: A Statement
of Purpose and Outlook 1

II. Domestic Courts, the Modern State, and World Legal
Order 14

    The Position of the State in Contemporary World
    Politics 14

    The Impact of the State upon the Courts . . . 19

III. International Jurisdiction: Horizontal and Vertical
Conceptions of Legal Order 21

    The Basic Horizontal Emphasis of International
    Legal Order 24

    Observation on the Delimitation of Legal
    Competence by the United States 27

    Some Aspects of a Horizontal Idea of International
    Legal Order 39

    Conclusion 50

IV. The Relevance of Contending Systems of Public Order
to the Delimitation of Legal Competence 53

V. Toward a Theory of the Participation of Domestic
Courts in the World Legal Order: A Critique of *Banco
Nacional de Cuba v. Sabbatino* 64

    Nuclear Weapons, the Cold War, and Socialism . . 67

    Exposition 77

    Critical Commentary 84

    The Argument Concluded 112

VI. The Further Search for Principles in the *Sabbatino* Case . 115

    Judge Waterman's Opinion 118

A Note of Commendation 123

Sabbatino and the Restatement 129

Sabbatino and the "Solicitor General's Memorandum Recommending U.S. Supreme Court Review" 131

The *Sabbatino* Brief for the United States as *Amicus Curiae* 132

Conclusion 137

VII. Sovereign Immunity: A Discourse on Recent Havoc . . 139

Sovereign Immunity and Act of State: A Policy Contrast 139

Rich v. Naviera Vacuba, S.A.: The Status of Sovereign Immunity in Domestic Courts Today . 145

Some Comments on the Commercial Exception to the Rule of Immunity: Doctrine and Policy . . 158

Persons, Things, and Claims 164

Sovereign Immunity and World Order 167

VIII. Domestic Courts and World Legal Order: Concluding Comments 170

Index 179

The Role of Domestic Courts
in the International Legal Order

Chapter I

Domestic Courts and World Legal Order:
A Statement of Purpose and Outlook

IT IS no longer necessary to apologize for presenting a study of
international law that, in the process of examining the law as it is,
develops an argument for what the law should be. This happy state
of affairs is not, however, evidence of a revived natural law. Proposals to evaluate law need not entail an insistence upon the relevance of moral norms to law nor need they advance claims about
the discovery of special access to truth. Evaluations can be based
upon the study of the character of the social system within which
law is expected to function. It is this that I hope to do in the course
of working out a theory about the use of domestic courts in the international legal system. The study of international society, its structures and processes, provides the data for the recommendations that
are made. The analysis of this data yields an evaluative standard
against which the behavior of domestic courts can be measured.

But the analysis itself is carried on within a normative framework, of which the most relevant element is a belief in the need for
and value of an expanding and improving system of world legal
order. This bias against international anarchy enjoys verbal support
from most leadership groups in the world today, but it does not
always get itself translated into appropriate action. The conduct of
domestic courts in the United States usefully illustrates the distance
that separates a verbal commitment to world legal order from its
realization in acts. I hope to be able to set forth an approach that will
encourage the ideal to become the deed.

The reason that it is unnecessary to apologize for, or scarcely to
explain, the orientation that has been just outlined is a tribute to
the pioneering excellence of Roscoe Pound and the more recent
achievements of Harold Lasswell and Myres S. McDougal. These
men have created in the United States a scholarly *ambiance* in which
it is taken for granted that the social system, as an object of study,
generates criteria by means of which the work of law may and should
be evaluated. This new encouragement of evaluation has created

1

some special problems, problems reminiscent of those that prompted the attacks of earlier centuries upon natural law.

The remarriage of description and evaluation in legal scholarship is a hazardous venture that must be embarked upon with great caution. The jurist resents being kept in the wings when so much action takes place on stage. There is hence a great temptation for the scholar to preach in the costume of the legal scientist and to present his own private version of what the law should be. He does this in the guise of conveying the only thing that he is particularly competent to do: a clarification of the law as it is.[1] Thus one finds all varieties of ephemera—especially the residues of patriotism and bias—obstructing the scholar's vision of social reality.[2] This is obviously not the kind of evaluation that deserves commendation. When the positivists insisted upon the divorce of law from morals, they were partly reacting to the damaging tendency of natural lawyers to present moral or national aspirations as already contained within existing law. The gap between "the law" as so conceived and the behavior of states naturally engendered cynicism about the claims made on behalf of international law. The positivists partially closed this gap by restricting the province of law to the restraints that were

[1] My enthusiasm for Professor McDougal's work is moderated by criticism on this account. See Falk, Book Review, 8 NATURAL L. F. 171, 175–84 (1963).

[2] The legacy lingers on, tormenting the endeavor of international law. It is still frequently maintained that international law is little more than a rationalization for national interests. The partisan commentary on the legality of the 1962 quarantine imposed upon shipping bound for Cuba could confirm the suspicion that international lawyers within and without government confound the distinction between legal analysis and national interest. E.g., Chayes, The Legal Case for U.S. Action on Cuba, 47 DEP'T STATE BULL. 763 (1962); Law and the Quarantine of Cuba, 41 FOREIGN AFFAIRS 552 (1962); Meeker, Defensive Quarantine and the Law, 57 AM. J. INT'L L. 515 (1963); Cristol & Davis, Maritime Quarantine: The Naval Interdiction of Offensive Weapons and Associated Material to Cuba, 1962, id. at 525; Fenwick, The Quarantine Against Cuba: Legal or Illegal?, id. at 588; MacChesney, Some Comments on the Quarantine of Cuba, id. at 592; McDougal, The Soviet-Cuban Quarantine and Self-Defense, id. at 597; Mallison, Limited Naval Blockade or Quarantine-Interdiction: National and Collective Defense Claims Valid Under International Law, 31 GEO. WASH. L. REV. 335 (1962); Crane, The Cuban Crisis: A Strategic Analysis of American and Soviet Policy, 6 ORBIS 528 (1963). Cf. Rousseau, Le blocus américain de Cuba et le droit international, Le Monde, Oct. 24, 1962. My criticism is aimed at those who make use of international law to rationalize foreign policy rather than to establish a universal system of common restraint. International lawyers within the scholarly community have a special responsibility, it seems to me, to engage in detached analysis of legal issues in order to provide their own society with an accurate view of what international law permits and what it prohibits.

actually accepted as operative in the behavior of states. This was a genuine contribution, causing to emerge a more realistic appreciation of what international law could and could not do. We must not sacrifice this realism in the course of attempting to enlarge the scope of juristic inquiry beyond traditional limits. We wish, of course, to maintain our discipline and yet have the opportunity to appraise and recommend, as well as to describe and analyze. It would appear that the positive value of an insistence upon specifying law by reference to operative restraints remains an essential element in any adequate approach to international law. But the identification of what are the restraints that are operative can no longer be achieved by positing rules about the process by which valid law is created, a process known in the international system as the study of the sources of international law. We need to substitute social observation for formal rules as the method by which to specify the scope of operative restraints upon national behavior.

The positivist conception identified the content of international law as those rules generated by the accepted sources of law: treaties, state practice, general principles prevailing in municipal law systems, judicial decisions, and the teachings of the most highly qualified publicists. My argument, then, is for a wider conception of sources and for a more processive image of the nature of law in world affairs. Accordingly, this book conceives of international law as embracing all normative phenomena that create stable expectations in the life of international relations. Special attention is given to those norms that are generated by national judicial institutions but that never attain either the formality of an international agreement or even the lesser explicitness of international custom. The general problem of improving the normative environment of international relations presents social and political questions, as well as those of a legal nature. The study of international law can proceed most fruitfully at this stage of the development of international society if the status of law is granted to norms that have emerged from sources additional to those enumerated in Article 38; [3] agreement among states or au-

---

[3] Article 38 of the Statute of the International Court of Justice reads as follows:

    1. The Court, whose function is to decide in accordance with international law such disputes as are submitted to it, shall apply:

    a. international conventions, whether general or particular, establishing rules expressly recognized by the contesting states;

    b. international custom, as evidence of a general practice accepted as law;

thoritative national practice can no longer provide a useful conception of international law.[4] My attitude toward international law and its sources establishes the jurisprudential setting for this study of the proper functioning of domestic courts, both in their role as agents of the international legal system, as well as in their more orthodox role as national institutions.[5]

I admit that this blurs, although it does not obliterate, the distinctions among law, morality, custom, prudence, and self-interest. Some of the clarity achieved by the methods of analytical jurisprudence about the concept of law is voluntarily surrendered. This makes it difficult to define "law" in a satisfactory manner and, therefore, to distinguish the legal norm from the nonlegal norm. But why should we strive so hard to have a clear concept of law? We must keep in mind that the enterprise of law is less concerned with the purity of language and clarity of concepts than with the regulation of human behavior under a variety of recurring conditions.[6] The development

---

c. The general principles of law recognized by civilized nations;

d. subject to the provisions of Article 59, judicial decisions and teachings of the most highly qualified publicists of the various nations, as subsidiary means for the determination of rules of law.

2. This provision shall not prejudice the power of the Court to decide a case *ex aequo et bono,* if the parties agree thereto.

This instruction to the court expresses the usual understanding of the formal sources of international law. Throughout this book, a wider conception of sources is used and defended. The defense rests on the need to have a conception of law that is wide enough to describe the operative content of norms in international life. Such an argument assumes that Article 38 excludes norms from the scope of international law that are proper and useful to include— norms that I have identified elsewhere as the horizontal content of international law. See especially Chapter III.

[4] A more complete account of the reasoning that supports this conclusion, now stated summarily to suggest quickly my outlook, is given later in Chapter I.

[5] Domestic courts are generally understood to be national institutions even when called upon to apply law emanating from extranational sources in private and public international law cases. It is also understood, but not often articulated, that domestic courts function as part of the international legal system: in applying and developing its norms and in giving them effectiveness, publicity, and prestige. It is this latter set of functions, especially in the context of public international law, that serves as a focus for this series of inquiries and appraisals of domestic courts and of world legal order. Among other priority scales to be challenged is the contemporary tendency to give foreign policy precedence over international law in domestic courts.

[6] A helpful consideration of the role of definitions, and the limitations of this role, is contained in FRIEDRICH, MAN AND HIS GOVERNMENT—AN EMPIRICAL THEORY OF POLITICS 3–4 (1963).

of norm-oriented behavior is the central social objective of those seeking the growth of legal order in world affairs, and this objective can only be satisfied by the adoption of a phenomenological jurisprudence of international law.[7]

This statement of outlook has been thus belabored because it seems crucial to argue for a conception of law that incorporates a wider view of normative phenomena than has been traditional among international lawyers. It is necessary, first, to make law more relevant to the study and the conduct of international relations in the contemporary world; second, to compel a sharper appreciation of how order can be introduced into a social system that is as decentralized as world society; third, to connect up law with its roots in social ethics and political action and, thereby, to stress the visible behavioral contours rather than the posited formal constituents of a definition.

The extension of law in international relations should not be identified, as it is so often in studies of domestic judicial practice, with the maximum application of universal substantive standards.[8] The

[7] There are, no doubt, pedagogical advantages that derive from adopting a concept of law that enables a sharp demarcation of subject matter. Clear boundaries encourage clear thinking about what goes on within them. But the delimitation of law achieved by analytical jurisprudence not only separates law too sharply from its social and political milieu but also is inappropriate for the study of order in a social system that must operate with weak central institutions. The most fertile source of rules in international affairs is the subtle process by which national behavior is transformed by official acts into community standards. This is a process of ordering and disordering that cannot be easily located in time or space. Nevertheless, it dominates the efforts of public officials to develop stable expectations in international life. A plea for a constructive use of this ordering process in the context of the United States domestic courts is the major task set for this book. Chapter III makes a more concerted attempt to present the conception of law that animates my understanding of these problems.

People may ask, "Why call this law"? An adequate response must deal with several factors: first, the need to make public officials more aware of order-creating potentialities; second, the consequent usefulness of classifying rules and processes as being within "the law," that is, as being within the vocational competence of those who deal with disputes between states; third, the tendency of public officials to give more respect to restraining rules once they are considered part of the governing law; and, fourth, the deeper understanding of law that comes from the adoption of functional criteria for its identification and from the idea of the conscious creation of stable expectations by competent officials as a functional criterion that serves well both the interests of study and the development of international law.

[8] The criticisms made of the act of state doctrine by KENNETH CARLSTON in his important book LAW AND ORGANIZATION IN WORLD SOCIETY at 192, 264–70

allocation of legal authority to prescribe substantive rules—the jurisdictional task—is a part of international law that is peculiarly
relevant to the proper functioning of domestic courts. It is at least
as important to determine what shall not be decided as it is to identify what shall be decided. The use of rules of deference—by which
a court forecloses inquiry into the validity of challenged action by
validating action simply because the actor was a foreign state—is
an important technique to standardize what should not be decided.[9]
It is essential to be explicitly aware of the need to decide certain
kinds of cases by deferring to the legal policy of those foreign states
with antagonistic social and political systems. No service is rendered
to international law when officials act upon the pretense that a shared
community of policy, interest, and value underlies the contemporary
network of global relations and is hence available for implementation
by each national actor. This pretension supports the treatment of
national policy, interest, and value as if they were universal. Such behavior invites retaliation, engenders distrust, and undermines those
actual and potential claims of international law to make stable the
relations among the entire community of states.

In a divided world, there will be a divided law.[10] Under such
conditions, rules of deference applied by domestic courts advance
the development of international law faster than does an indiscrim-

---

(1962) illustrate this unfortunate identification: "But for the so-called act of
state doctrine of Anglo-American private international law, the forum state
would be free to establish the paramountcy of international law in attributing
legal effect to foreign acts of state." (p. 192.)

[9] This is, of course, an ancient task for legal institutions called upon to apply
law to foreign events. The quest for a uniform method of performing this task
has been of central concern in the field of conflict of laws. Not only must common rules of deference (or reference) to foreign law be adopted, but also the
basis for deference must be explicated. A succinct summary is found in Note,
The Act of State Doctrine—Its Relation to Private and Public International Law,
62 COLUM. L. REV. 1278, 1282–83 (1962). There is the related problem of the
extent to which these common rules of deference as they have developed in the
international system are prescribed by international law; states certainly possess
some discretion, but the common restraints that limit discretion on the national
level require further clarification. For a notable attempt, see Stevenson, *The
Relationship of Private International Law to Public International Law*, 52
COLUM. L. REV. 561 (1952).

[10] For a useful depiction, see Lissitzyn, *International Law in a Divided World*,
INT'L. CONC. (March, 1963); for a more theoretical analysis, see Hoffmann,
International Systems and International Law, in 14 WORLD POLITICS 205
(1961).

inate insistence upon applying challenged substantive norms in order to determine the validity of the official acts of foreign states.[11] Such a traditional doctrine in the practice of the United States—and now under attack for a variety of provincial reasons that are justified by a false appeal to the ideal of a universal law[12]—offers a very useful context in which to study this entire issue of jurisdictional self-restraint. Those who yearn for a greater willingness to make jurisdictional self-assertions often either overlook the significance of the challenge directed at the homogeneous historical basis of the older international law or regard the challenge as an occasion for "protracted conflict." This latter position requires a state either to treat its values as authoritative for purposes of law or to submit to an implacable enemy that will act as if its outlook is authoritative, regardless of what others do.[13] According to such interpreters of the

[11] The relationship between national and international legal authority is a theme that is relevant to all aspects of an analysis of the role of domestic courts. International law has always taken into account the delicate connection between national policy and international insistence. Thus, in such crucial areas as recognition or immunity, the international prescription supplies only minimum standards or limiting conditions, and national authority is given considerable residual discretion. For example, premature recognition is forbidden and absolute immunity for an ambassador is mandatory, but a state is entitled to withhold recognition as long as it wishes or to grant or not to grant immunity from domestic process to a foreign-state trading vessel. One of the factors that should enter into an analysis of the extent of this residual discretion is the absence or the presence of domestic uniformity. A world divided on matters of policy can only support legal order if it allocates authority in a manner that confirms the distribution of power.

[12] It is relevant to observe that rules of deference, such as the act of state doctrine, developed and prospered during a period when the actors in world affairs shared a common outlook. With the disappearance of this common outlook, there has been an increasing attempt to insist upon the application of a universal standard. So long as a single policy viewpoint prevailed among international actors in economic matters, the ritual of deference was not obstructive. Now, however, when diversity in fact exists, there is strong pressure to restrict deference and to assert as binding a set of substantive norms that had been shared at an early period in international relations. Deference can be defended as being a formal basis of allocation that acknowledges the importance of states in international relations; deference can also be defended, as it is in the text, as a way of institutionalizing respect for diverse social and economic policies, thereby affirming the possibilities of law—in the sense of stable expectations— amid antagonism.

[13] This view has been given forceful expression by McDougal & Lasswell, *The Identification and Appraisal of Diverse Systems of Public Order*, in Studies in World Public Order 3–42 (1961); the opposite emphasis is dominant in Jenks, The Common Law of Mankind (1958) and in Northrop, The Taming of Nations (1952).

international scene, domestic courts should assert substantive norms as perceived by national perspectives for several alternative reasons: because they are "the law" as a consequence of the past, because they are "right" by conforming to some objective account of social values, or because there is occurring the kind of inevitable struggle for supremacy that renders any self-restraint a case of self-denial tending toward suicide. Advocates of this last view ask that the pragmatics of the cold war and the frustration of the new states be given precedence in domestic courts. This historicosocial analysis of law and politics is directly opposite to the understanding of the contemporary world that underlies my interpretation of the role that is proper for domestic courts to play.

It is, of course, possible that either an acceptance of objective values or a belief in the irreconcilability of the East-West conflict would lead to a more fruitful understanding of the desiderata of world order. The validity of first principles, however, is outside the scope of this study. There is, however, an obligation to identify one's point of departure. In this vein, I will assume that the particular rules of international law depend for their validity upon a relevant consensus and that the content of the law should be shaped to express the prevailing distribution of power and authority.[14] The absence of effective central institutions in a deeply divided world will inevitably lead to considerable territorial control over operative national policy. If this decentralization in action is confirmed by symbolic acts of deference on the part of domestic courts, then there exists some possibility of developing a stable international legal order, based on patterns of reciprocal self-restraint, and hegemonical conflict is not considered a necessary attribute of diversity.

The defense of the rules of judicial deference has sometimes formed a part of an argument in favor of a national or internal consolidation over the subject matter of foreign relations.[15] In this kind of analysis, the emphasis is upon the inadequacy of litigation as a means of resolving those disputes with international implications. Deference, then, is defended as a way of getting the controversy

---

[14] Chapters III and IV are, however, somewhat equivocal on this issue in the presence of special factors and circumstances.

[15] This argument is persuasively developed by Metzger, *The Act of State Doctrine and Foreign Relations,* in INTERNATIONAL LAW, TRADE, AND FINANCE: REALITIES AND PROSPECTS 66–77 (1962).

out of the courts and into the foreign office. The executive has a flexibility in the negotiating context that enables consideration of special circumstances, whereas the judiciary is confined by craft and by tradition to a narrow definition of the legal problem. Executive solutions can cover a category of cases rather than a single controversy. The diversity of alien social systems can be tacitly respected by the executive official without arousing domestic passions and special interest groups. The privacy of the executive process and the control over timing offer additional reasons in support of internal deference. Thus, the foreign office seems to be better endowed than a court to adjust legal relations between and among nations with diverse social and economic systems.[16]

Judicial deference, then, has both an external and an internal aspect. In external relations, deference allocates among states a competence to take account of the distribution of value, policy, interest, and power existing in the world today, and thereby discloses the special character of international law as well as the continuing primacy of jurisdictional rules for a social system that is both decentralized and divided. As a consequence of this delineation of judicial function, the internal function of deference is to transfer responsibility for the settlement of disputes from the courts to the foreign office, thereby acknowledging the superior opportunities that exist for legal settlement on the executive level of interaction between and among diverse states.[17]

Judicial deference is not advocated in an unrestricted form. Two major qualifications are asserted. First, deference is inappropriate if the subject matter of dispute is governed by substantive norms of international law that are adhered to by an overwhelming majority of international actors. In other words, where there is a firm social support for a substantive standard of law, then a domestic court

[16] Rules of deference, it should be underscored, do not validate the contested foreign behavior from the viewpoint of substantive international law. Rather, a decision to defer is a way of explaining that a domestic court is not a suitable forum within which to make the determination of validity. In this respect, the act of state doctrine resembles the doctrine of *forum non conveniens*. However, the act of deference does not end judicial participation; it merely confines it to features of the controversy other than the challenge directed at the validity of foreign governmental acts.

[17] This observation is supported by a recent study of nationalization experience in the period following World War II: WHITE, NATIONALISATION OF FOREIGN PROPERTY 231–43 (1961).

should not defer but rather should apply a substantive law with vigor. In effect, a requirement of social consensus is a condition precedent to the validity of any substantive rule of international law unless the rule is derived from a specific treaty obligation.[18] This encourages courts both to act in areas where the general disposition of the community supports the rule and to refrain from action in areas where a division in the community nullifies the social bases for common standards. Noneconomic human rights illustrate an area within which courts might contribute to the formulation and application of common standards, thereby making a positive contribution to the development of international law. Such a view of domestic judicial function requires courts to make the initial determination of whether or not a consensus of states supports the alleged legal standard, as well as to develop criteria identifying what constitutes a relevant consensus.[19] The proper performance of these tasks is certainly difficult, and it is to be expected that courts will not always reasonably and fairly determine the presence or the absence of a governing consensus. Nevertheless, this kind of role for domestic courts seems to take into proper account the nature of the judicial function, the encumbrance of national outlook, and the character of international society.

The second qualification is that judicial deference to executive authority—internal deference—must not be achieved by sacrificing judicial independence. The particular character of foreign relations should not influence a given judicial disposition. Thus, whether the United States is hostile or friendly to the state involved in the litigation should not be allowed to influence the judicial outcome. Internal deference should be based upon functional principles of

---

[18] However, a significant contrast between the outlook of a signatory and that of its successor should be taken into account in interpreting the meaning and validity of a treaty obligation. A treaty is governed by the general assumption that the development of effective international law depends upon finding ways to give formal expression to changes in power and policy relationships.

[19] What kind of support must be available to justify the inference of "a relevant consensus"? There is a need for a more systematic study of this aspect of the proposal. Voting patterns within the United Nations probably provide the best available evidence for the presence or absence of a consensus. Of course, votes are not recorded on every issue that a domestic court is called upon to decide. Furthermore, some plurality pattern must be used to define what constitutes a consensus; General Assembly voting is erratic and fails to distinguish between the views of tiny states and superpowers. Perhaps votes in the United Nations might be interpreted in the light of a formula for weighted voting.

allocation and not upon *ad hoc* subordinations to executive policy.[20] Therefore, judicial review of the validity of foreign expropriations of territorial property should not depend upon whether the executive seeks to harass or appease a particular state. The objective of deference is to make national courts operate as international institutions of restricted competence. Therefore, the nationality of the forum should have a minimum bearing upon the scope and the occasions of deference. Courts should be made responsive to principles of allocation but not to vagaries of foreign policy. The various inconsistent judicial responses to the status of claims made either on behalf of or against Castro's government in Cuba illustrate this need.[21] This pattern of litigation discloses a need for a more consistent approach in American practice. If the political element is allowed to be dominant, its priority induces disrespect for international law. National policy must be separated to the greatest extent possible from the application of international law in domestic courts. This is necessary to enhance the prestige of international law as a legal order. Domestic courts are an arena in which attitudes toward international law are disclosed and general impressions formed. If it

[20] If the objective of deference is to protect the unified control of the executive over foreign policy, then it is far more preferable that results come about by rules that are themselves not subject to political manipulation. For this reason, it is desirable to deny the discretion to both the executive and the judiciary to suspend international rules of deference. If deference rules are discretionary, then foreign policy tends to become relevant in judicial contexts. This tendency impairs judicial independence by inviting executive intervention and encourages courts to be nationalistic. The issue has been posed for American courts by holdings and dicta in a series of important cases. See Bernstein v. N.V. Nederlandsche-Amerikaanshe Stoomvaart-Maattschappij, 210 F. 2d 375 (2d Cir. 1954); United States v. Pink, 315 U.S. 203 (1942); see generally Chapters V and VI.

[21] Among the most important cases are Banco Nacional de Cuba v. Sabbatino, 193 F. Supp. 375 (S.D.N.Y. 1961), *aff'd*, 307 F. 2d 845 (2d Cir. 1962), *rev'd*—U.S. —(1964); Kane v. National Institute of Agrarian Reform, 18 Fla. Supp. 116 (1961); Pons v. Republic of Cuba, 294 F. 2d 925 (1961); Jorge v. Antonio Co., 19 Fla. Supp. 101 (1961); Rich v. Naviera Vacuba, S. A., 197 F. Supp. 710 (E.D. Va. 1961), *aff'd*, 295 F. 2d 24 (4th Cir. 1961); Dade Drydock Corp. v. The M/T Mar Caribe, 199 F. Supp. 871 (S.D. Tex. 1961); Ray v. Pan American Life Insurance Co., 19 Fla. Supp. 167 (1962); Rodriguez v. Pan American Life Co., 311 F. 2d 429 (5th Cir. 1962), *rev'd*, 84 Sup. Ct. 1130 (1964); Harris & Co. Advertising v. Republic of Cuba, 127 So. 2d 687 (Fla., 1961); a more complete listing can be found in the Solicitor General's Memorandum for the United States, No. 403, filed in the United States Supreme Court in Banco Nacional de Cuba v. Sabbatino, Appendix A, at 11–13 (1962).

becomes evident that international law is applied only when it is a convenient adjunct to foreign policy, then there is no persuasive reason for any state ever to subordinate its policy to the restraining claims of law.

Dominant nonrevolutionary states, in particular, have a responsibility to establish modes of behavior that are exemplary for the system of international relations. Domestic courts provide an excellent arena within which to exhibit either a scornful or a constructive attitude toward the relevance of international law to international behavior. For this reason, it is contended that the operation of courts should be governed by the structural characteristics of international society rather than by transient foreign policy considerations. Such an orientation requires a very determined and explicit commitment to judicial independence. This is not a facile attainment in a world burdened with intense ideological conflict and distrust, but neither is it easy to envision a permanent nuclear peace maintained by anything short of a gradual substitution of global loyalties for national loyalties. It seems, at least, that we could trust our own courts to apply international law.

This position can be put in topical terms. The domestic courts of the United States should be ready to apply substantive standards of international law when an effective consensus of states favors the implementation of the rule. Rules in valid international agreements, however, are applicable independent of the three propositions just stated.[22]

This presentation, although oversimplifying the conception of domestic courts that is developed in subsequent chapters, has tried to indicate the importance of the jurisdictional issue in a divided world community and to suggest the reasons for supporting maximum judicial independence of *ad hoc* executive intervention. The United States is the dominant law-oriented state. As a result, it possesses a special responsibility that can only be discharged by a self-conscious realization of its long-term interests in the develop-

---

[22] But even treaty rules should be construed in the light of a growing or a disappearing consensus; this is part of the pervasive requirement to assemble social support for law in order to have reasonable assurance of compliance. A formal argument about the character of legal obligations is a relevant factor, of course; but it must not be allowed to defeat the effort to make international law work by causing its rules to be effective. See also note 13 *supra*.

ment of a more stable world order.[23] The use of domestic courts provides a symbolic means for the promotion of these interests.

To suggest such a purpose is not to predict the future of world order, but merely to develop ideas that can be used if the total situation is favorable to the endeavor to create a stronger world legal order. Many other psychological, social, political, and economic factors must cooperate before a proposal such as mine can hope to have practical relevance.

[23] Drastic changes in the structure of international relations are not likely to be made as a result of acts of national volition performed beneath the sway of reason. Mankind lacks the imagination to subordinate immediate pressures and interests to more distant and fundamental principles. This failing may well be at the core of the tragic situation of the human species in its present state of evolution. *Cf.* RÖLING, INTERNATIONAL LAW IN AN EXPANDED WORLD, chs. X–XI (1960). Nevertheless, it is necessary to disregard this tragic awareness in the search for constructive alternatives. Within the realm of politics, reason must be encouraged to prevail. This book tries to develop a conception of domestic courts that accords with reason. Such an enterprise is not inconsistent with an acknowledgment of the inability—even the predictable inability—of reason to change political behavior. The odds against the acceptance of national guidance are increased by a refusal to give it.

Chapter II

Domestic Courts, the Modern State, and World Legal Order

A DISCUSSION of domestic courts presumes some understanding of the viability of the state system in the contemporary world. The significance of the fact that national courts are located within the domestic environment depends, in part, upon how their dual status as national institutions of contemporary states and as agents of an emerging world legal order is reconciled. Thus, a consideration of the position of the state in world affairs is essential to any appraisal of domestic courts.

1. *The Functional Obsolescence of the State System.* Part of the distinctiveness of the existing pattern of international relations is created by the persistent questioning of the adequacy of the nation-state as a fundamental mode of social organization. Of course, doubts about the adequacy of organizing units in world affairs are not new; for instance, such doubts arose when the state emerged to replace the feudal principality as the basic political unit of interaction in world affairs.

Today, doubts are caused by several factors. First, regional and global actors (international organizations) have emerged with an ever expanding competence in the regulation of the vital issues of global life. States are no longer the exclusive actors in the field of behavior delimited by such labels as "world politics" or "international relations."

Second, and of greater social significance, is the increasing inability of states to discharge by themselves the traditional functions of defense and welfare. The technology of war has developed so far that a violent conflict between dominant states threatens to be mutually destructive, if not jointly catastrophic. Thus, the state system is deprived of a reasonably safe or reliable way to resolve fundamental conflicts between its powerful states. At the same time,

14

the absence of a substitute for war is in itself dangerous. Granted, the international system has not been structured to keep peace over any extended period of time; the history of international relations contains many illustrations of war arising by a miscalculation of intentions and capabilities in a period of antagonism and tension. However, so long as war could be tolerated as an ultimate arbiter of international conflict, the state system seemed to provide an adequate if somewhat unpredictable political framework for human life in its global setting. But now that war is too destructive for resolution of conflict and that no substitute for war has emerged, the status of the state system is itself deeply compromised.

The third source of doubt arises from the growth of a global consciousness that has, through the organizational medium of the United Nations and through the improvement of communication and transportation facilities, led to an erosion of the boundaries of domestic autonomy, at least in those areas in which a common political outlook exists. This factor has seriously limited the significance of the traditional separation of matters of domestic jurisdiction and those of international concern. If the maintenance of peace *within* as well as between and among nations is acknowledged to be a subject suitable for supranational regulation on the grounds of maintaining international peace, then those matters that threaten internal peace are quickly drawn within the scope of supranational competence.[1]

Claims of extended competence have been illustrated by the responses of the United Nations Organization to events in the Congo, Angola, and the Republic of South Africa. In each instance, an internal conflict has been assumed subject to a resolution that fulfills the aspirations of a political consensus mobilized by foreign states within the United Nations.[2] Although this development responds to a new balance of forces in the world, it constitutes a central challenge to such organizing concepts as sovereignty and national independence. The effective capacity of nonnational actors to dictate the outcome of domestic social conflict seems radically

[1] This is the subject of a chapter of mine entitled *Janus Tormented: The International Law of Internal War*, in INTERNATIONAL POLITICS AND CIVIL STRIFE (Rosenau ed.) scheduled to appear in 1964.

[2] An attempt to examine these developments can be found in Falk & Mendlovitz, *Towards a Warless World: One Legal Formula to Achieve Transition*, 73 YALE L. J. 399 (1964).

inconsistent with the ideology of international relations as it has been organized by the state system.

2. *The Persisting Dominance of the State System in World Affairs.* Despite these tendencies to undermine the function and adequacy of the state system, there are certain countervailing trends that suggest the continuing dominance of the state in world affairs. First, the functional failures of the state in the contemporary world have not persuaded national leaders to transfer significant power to nonnational actors; thus, states retain a monopoly of the instruments of violence, even though there has been a diminution of formal discretion in selecting the occasions for recourse to national violence. The supranationalizing rule without a means of implementation is, at best, an ambiguous reduction of state power. Second, patterns of national allegiance seem to retain a dominant hold over political imagination, being abetted rather than curtailed by the existence of the "new states," zealous about the defense of their sovereign rights.

Third, the realization that nuclear warfare is mutually destructive has, in a variety of contexts, neutralized political inequalities. This gives to the national unit an unprecedented vitality, since big states are no longer in a position to impose their will upon small states.[3] Oddly enough, there is a closer approximation to the ideal of sovereign equality in the "bipolar world" than ever before.[4] One way to express this observation is to suggest that bipolarity with respect to nuclear warfare or strategic conflict has been accompanied by a new multipolarity with respect to nonstrategic conflict and relations. The neutralization of the power advantages of big states

[3] This general change is studied in CALVOCORESSI, WORLD ORDER AND NEW STATES (1962).

[4] The description of international relations as "bipolar" dramatizes the ideological and political conflict that is dominant in the world today, leading to the formation of alliance systems and supranational economic, cultural, and military units of more than national but less than global scope. However, bipolarity can also be a dangerous oversimplification. Unipolarity exists for anticolonial issues; multipolarity exists with respect to conflicts among secondary nations throughout the world. The settlement of the Kashmir dispute is scarcely influenced by the bipolarity that results from the cold war and from nuclear technology. As of 1964, however, both the Sino-Soviet dispute and the French rebellion against United States leadership of the West provide some evidence of an emerging multipolarity, even on the level of a strategic encounter between states with potential nuclear capability.

by prohibition, propaganda, world public opinion, and the fear of escalating minor conflicts gives to the tradition of territorial supremacy and territorial law a reality that it never possessed in pre-nuclear international politics. Powerful states are much less able to intervene in the affairs of weaker states to secure compliance with rules of international law, and especially with rules that are challenged by a consensus among weaker states.[5]

The growth of international organization paradoxically has helped to make the ideology of the state system more of a political reality in that it has provided the majority of states with a forum that rather effectively protects their autonomy. This observation seems especially relevant with respect to the treatment of property and economic interests. Much to the distress of the capital-exporting states, the interposition of national sovereignty as an obstacle to big power intervention is able to block the attempt of investor states to use force to coerce sufficient respect for alien property rights in order to uphold the traditional standards of state responsibility. In short, the will of the modern sovereign, no matter how weak it is in material terms, has become more important than either the traditional rules about acquired rights or the superior power of the complainant state.

Fourth, the ability to neutralize the inequalities of power gives greater significance to the repudiations by states of particular rules of international law, among which are those supporting the sanctity of alien property rights and investment. For if the basis of international obligation rests upon a manifestation of consent,[6] as the

[5] This general observation is inaccurate unless qualified. Rules of intervention have now attained unprecedented effectiveness with respect to the autonomy of a national government in matters of economic policy. No powerful state could intervene to protect the property of its aliens or to compel the weaker state to pay its debts. However, where there is a domestic struggle between rival ideological factions for political control of the state, then great power intervention is more frequent than in the past. The expansion of "empire" is now achieved by ideological rather than territorial annexation. Also, there is now an increased possibility of humanitarian intervention by multinational actors aroused by domestic abuses of fundamental human rights.

[6] An important study of the role of national consent in the formation of international obligation is found in Brierly's Hague Lectures of 1928 conveniently available in BRIERLY, THE BASIS OF OBLIGATION IN INTERNATIONAL LAW AND OTHER PAPERS 1–67 (Lauterpacht ed. 1958); Le Fondement du caractère obligatoire du droit international, 23 RECUEIL DES COURS 467, Hague Academy (1928).

traditional view of international law held, then the widespread assertion of dissent, especially by states that did not regard themselves
as participating in the formation of the original rules, weakens both
the formal status and the probable effectiveness of legal rules. This
challenge, when coupled with the unavailability of coercive self-
help to enforce the obligations of the weaker state, discloses a need
to base relations among states upon the realities of a *present* consensus. It is no longer sufficient to invoke a rule summarizing a consensus that antedated the independent existence of a complaining
state. In matters of economic and social organization, the state
enjoys a territorial supremacy that makes essential an adjustment
of its legal obligations to its sovereign disposition. This kind of
fragmentation of international legal standards takes place simply
because no overriding consensus either for or against a particular
set of substantive standards exists to mobilize effective support in
international organizations. This situation is in marked contrast to
the development of international standards in the field of human
rights where a political consensus often does exist. It points to a
sharpening distinction between the possibility of universal standards
and the necessity for relying upon sovereign discretion. The subject
matter of international relations does not fit neatly within one category of issues rather than another. However, such changes as the
altered structure of international relations brought about principally
by nuclear technology, the appearance of new states, and the growth
of international organization have resulted in a revision of our understanding of what is effectively within and what is virtually beyond
the reach of substantive rules of international law. This revision
reflects the combined effects of these contradictory pressures on
the state system causing states to be incapable of self-defense against
nuclear attack and yet unprecedentedly independent in the control
exercised over most aspects of domestic life.

These developments profoundly affect the effectiveness of the
old law, as well as the possibilities for new law, in international
relations. A norm cannot gain effectiveness in the contemporary world
because it serves the interests of a powerful state; the absence of
consensus among the most powerful states leads them to be unable
to use this power except, and even here to a diminishing extent,
against weaker states within their immediate sphere of influence.
This virtual neutralization of the big states gives effective reality

to the sovereignty of the weaker states. As a general proposition, this makes an active consent among the weaker states, or at least their consensus, a necessary precondition to the effectiveness of a contemporary rule of international law. Controversies about expropriation and confiscation of alien property are affected by this radical change in the position of the state in the international legal system.

The Impact of the State upon the Courts

In view of what has been said about the altered position of the state in the international system, is there any corresponding shift in the role and function of domestic courts? It is difficult to form a general response. We do not have enough information about the behavior of national courts that refer to external norms in controversies involving a challenge directed at internal policies. It would seem obvious, although significant, that there is no active concept of judicial independence in states with an autocratic or totalitarian system of domestic government. In such circumstances, the internal policies formulated by the center of governmental power are decisive in a judicial context; this assertion can be put in terms of reference familiar to students of American constitutional practice if it is observed that there is almost complete judicial deference to the executive department in those matters affecting foreign policy or alien rights.

It is almost inconceivable to imagine a conflict between the judiciary and the executive of a new state that arises in connection with the interpretation of a dispute involving the application of international law. Such solidarity at a national level produces political interpretations of international law whenever the controversy is perceived as one that engages the fundamental policy of the state. It is difficult to suppose, for instance, that a court in a communist state without a viable form of constitutional democracy would act to invalidate an expropriation of alien property on grounds of international law no matter how confiscatory and discriminatory a particular taking happened to be. This suggests the relevance of domestic politics to the character of judicial operations.

However, the fact of judicial dependence does not make international law irrelevant to the settlement of legal disputes. So long as the fundamental policy of the forum is not challenged by a litigant, there is no reason why a domestic court in a totalitarian or auto-cratic society cannot apply the rules of international law with fair-ness and uniformity. In 1964, even the Soviet Union and the Republic of China were invoking international law in defense of their conduct toward one another. Nevertheless, it seems reasonable to conclude that there is no judicial independence in antidemocratic societies and that this puts a significant limit upon the role that domestic courts can be expected to play in the international legal system.

How should this factor influence the behavior of courts in dem-ocratic societies with a strong tradition of judicial independence? In order to offset the monistic control of domestic institutions in certain foreign societies, should one advocate a doctrine of judicial deference to executive policy as a guide for courts in the United States or Western Europe? This question is treated later in the course of a general discussion of domestic courts.

Chapter III

International Jurisdiction: Horizontal and Vertical Conceptions of Legal Order

THE AGGREGATE of techniques used to delimit the contours of international legal competence is what is meant here by "international jurisdiction." [1] There are many relevant perspectives. One can discuss the delimitation of various types of international legal competence from the perspective of an individual, a nonindependent political entity (*e.g.*, Pennsylvania or Kuwait), an independent state, a private international entity (*e.g.*, an international trade association), or any one of the growing number of international organizations. This chapter, however, confines itself to the perspective of the independent state. It will first present a view of the general structure of international jurisdiction and then examine the particular techniques of delimitation as they appear from the perspective of the United States. The effort is one of analysis rather than of description. It is an attempt to discern the elements that constitute the distinctive character of international legal order by examining the extent of legal competence possessed by a state.

When jurisdiction is considered to be the delimitation of competence, it is helpful to think of it as the distribution of *authority* (as distinguished from power) among different legal institutions and separate political entities. It is a formalistic description of the legal order within any social system. There are two primary dimensions of order. There is vertical or hierarchical order among formally unequal centers of legal authority; there is horizontal or nonhierar-

[1] The writing of Professor Myres S. McDougal has exercised a great influence upon the development of my ideas on this subject. This will be evident to those familiar with his work. McDougal, *International Law, Power and Policy: A Conception,* 82 RECUEIL DES COURS 137 (1953). McDOUGAL & ASSOCIATES, STUDIES IN WORLD PUBLIC ORDER (1960). McDOUGAL & FELICIANO, LAW AND MINIMUM WORLD PUBLIC ORDER (1961). McDOUGAL & BURKE, THE PUBLIC ORDER OF THE OCEANS (1962). A fine presentation of the international aspects of delimiting jurisdiction in a significant manner is found in Katzenbach, *Conflicts on an Unruly Horse: Reciprocal Claims and Tolerances in Interstate and International Law,* 65 YALE L. J. 1087, especially at 1102–57 (1956). For a similar basic analysis, see REUTER, INTERNATIONAL INSTITUTIONS ch. 1 (1958).

chical order among equal centers of legal authority. For example, the relationship between the federal governments and the states is primarily vertical, whereas that between and among the states themselves is primarily horizontal.[2]

Compared to the domestic legal order, the international domain exhibits a low degree of centralization of authority. The international community lacks adequate institutions of impartial interpretation and enforcement to provide authoritative delimitations of state legal competence. To achieve international order, it is therefore necessary to rely upon a horizontal distribution of authority and power among independent states. This results in giving a central ordering role to various patterns of self-help and self-restraint. With the possible exceptions of the control of international violence and the avoidance of extreme unfairness to aliens, the maintenance of international order is primarily a horizontal endeavor. The persisting dominance of the notions of sovereignty and nationalism reveals that the outer limit of political identification today continues to be the independent state. This important sociological datum suggests that human aspiration continues to support the state as the center of primary authority. Therefore, it is quite likely that progress toward a more rational delimitation of jurisdiction will result from efforts to improve the horizontal methods of allocating legal competence rather than from efforts to centralize authority in such a way as to make possible the effective vertical institutions of order. From this viewpoint, one grows more cautious about investing a high percentage of one's enthusiasm in proposed expansions of the compulsory jurisdiction of the International Court of Justice or in attempts to narrow the scope of "domestic jurisdiction" in Article 2(7) of the United Nations Charter.[3]

Two tempting vertical models of analysis help to explain the failure to appreciate the distinctive horizontal character of the inter-

[2] The distinction between "horizontal" and "vertical" is a metaphor to describe the two basic distributions of power in a legal order. However, it is not a rigid distinction in which the presence of one form of legal order excludes the other. Thus, for example, when one state in the United States is compelled by a federal court to give effect to a judgment of another state by virtue of "the full faith and credit clause," there is introduced a vertical element in an essentially horizontal legal order (*i.e.*, the relations of the states *inter se*). See, *e.g.*, Magnolia Petroleum Co. v. Hunt, 320 U.S. 430, 439–40 (1943).

[3] U.N. Charter, art. 2, para. 7: "Nothing contained in the present Charter shall authorize the United Nations to intervene in matters which are essentially

national legal order. First, the current preoccupation with the maintenance of international peace, which does seem to require a vertical control of the national resort to force, is taken as the model for all problems of international concern.[4] Second, the more familiar vertical structure of the domestic legal order is taken as the model for the optimum international order. Mere *characteristics* of the domestic model are transformed into *prerequisites* for international order. The acceptance of either vertical model as a decisive test of the existence of legal order generates irrelevant cynicism about the stabilizing claims of international law. For example, Professor Corbett in his important book, *Law and Society in the Relations of States,* relies upon both vertical models of analysis to infer the following conclusion:

> The future of international law is one with the future of international organization. Concretely, this means that progress towards clarity and effectiveness of the international legal order will depend less upon the formulation and reformulation of general principles, or upon codification, than upon the arrangements for the supranational administration of specific common interests.[5]

Professor Corbett regards the only alternative to the development of effective vertical institutions to be the rather fruitless formulation of shared aspirations. Such an argument fails to take serious account of the horizontal possibilities to attain legal order.[6] This position also compels one to identify progress in the stabilization of international relations exclusively with centralizations of authority and power.[7]

---

within the domestic jurisdiction of any state or shall require the Members to submit such matters to settlement under the present Charter; but this principle shall not prejudice the application of enforcement measures under Chapter VII."

[4] My analysis assumes that it is possible and useful to separate the control of the resort to force from other major questions of international concern. I feel this to be especially true in regard to all private connections between nationals of different states.

[5] CORBETT, LAW AND SOCIETY IN THE RELATIONS OF STATES 12, 68–69 (1951).

[6] It should be noted that elsewhere in his book Professor Corbett does take a detailed account of the opportunities to improve international stability by strengthening horizontal structures of legal order. See *id.* at 259–300.

[7] The work of Professor Kelsen illustrates the other main direction taken by those who attempt to use an Austinian conception of law (*i.e.,* a vertical con-

A great merit of the approach of Professor McDougal is that he has described the horizontal forms of international order with extraordinary sophistication. He has demonstrated in a number of different contexts that the patterns of state behavior consisting of reciprocal patterns of assertion and deference produce a quality of stability that is often sufficient to warrant classification as law.[8]

One should not be reluctant to extend the conception of law to horizontal patterns of order. In the light of this predisposition, I have undertaken to describe the character of international jurisdiction.

THE BASIC HORIZONTAL EMPHASIS OF INTERNATIONAL LEGAL ORDER

The traditional formal requirements that govern the presentation of an international claim presuppose a basic deference to the state as the center of authority.[9] Recourse to an international decision-maker (*i.e.*, a vertical form of review) to determine the validity of a challenged exercise of jurisdiction is available only to the extent that the defendant State consents to such review.[10] Thus, the

---

ception) to describe the legal quality of the relations between states. Kelsen treats international relations *as though* they possess a pervasive vertical structure. This accounts for the abstract aura of unreality that is generated by his more theoretical treatment of international law. See KELSEN, PRINCIPLES OF INTERNATIONAL LAW (1952).

[8] *Cf.* references cited in note 1 *supra*.

[9] State responsibility for injuries to private interests is based upon the discretionary prosecution of the claim by a state on behalf of its injured national. International wrongs are traditionally conceived only in terms of state-to-state relations. Thus, there is no way for a national or a stateless person to proceed against a state. See, *e.g.*, *Research in International Law under the Auspices of the Harvard Law School, The Law of Responsibility of States for Damage Done in Their Territory to the Person or Property*, 23 AM. J. INT'L L., Supp., pt. 11, at 131–239 (1929). Article 1 of the Draft Convention reads: "A state is responsible, as the term is used in this convention, when it has a duty to make reparation to another state for the injury sustained by the latter state as a consequence of an injury to its national," *Research, supra*, at 140. A very persuasive attack upon the artificiality of the formal central position of the state in international law is found in JESSUP, A MODERN LAW OF NATIONS 15–42, 94–122 (1948).

[10] The World Court has strongly asserted that its jurisdiction depends upon a prior act of consent by the state. There is even an unwillingness to use an advisory opinion to weaken this requirement. See Request for Advisory Opinion Concerning the Status of Eastern Carelia, P.C.I.J., ser. B, No. 5 (1923); but see some qualification, especially as the situation is viewed by the dissenting judges in Interpretation of Peace Treaties, Advisory Opinion, [1950] I.C.J. Rep.

availability of a vertical settlement to an international dispute involving jurisdictional competence itself depends upon a prior horizontal decision. A state is never required by international law to resort to a supranational decision-maker, except perhaps if it is involved in disputes concerning the maintenance of peace or if it is party to a binding international agreement to submit the dispute.[11]

The Permanent Court of International Justice indicated in the *Lotus* case that, even after submission to an international decision-maker, the state claiming the legal competence to act possesses "a wide measure of discretion" to extend its control over men, resources, and events as it sees fit.[12] In fact, this discretion "is only limited by *prohibitive rules;* as regards other cases, every State remains free to adopt the principles which it regards as best and most suitable." The court continues: "All that can be required of a State is that it should not overstep the limits which international law places upon its jurisdiction; within these limits, its title to exercise jurisdiction rests in its sovereignty." [13] This authorizes a state to make any jurisdictional claim that is not explicitly prohibited by international law. This is far less of a restriction than would be the case if it were

---

65. That the competence of the court depends upon some acceptable form of consent on the part of a state with a legal stake in the controversy was affirmed in the Case of the Monetary Gold removed from Rome in 1943 (Preliminary Question), [1954] I.C.J. Rep. 19. For example, at 30 the court said: "To adjudicate upon the international responsibility of Albania without her consent would run counter to a well-established principle of international law embodied in the Court's Statute, namely, that the Court can only exercise jurisdiction over a State with its consent." The Statute in Article 36(2) does give states the option to give their consent in advance, on a reciprocal basis, to the jurisdiction of the court. To the extent that this option is acted upon, it does eliminate a degree of state discretion to resort to a supranational (or vertical) decision-maker. But many states have either not exercised the option or have attached broad reservations to their acceptance of the court's compulsory jurisdiction. For brief summary of practice under Article 36(2), *cf.* SOHN, BASIC DOCUMENTS OF THE UNITED NATIONS 204–18 (1956). *Cf.* generally STONE, LEGAL CONTROLS OF INTERNATIONAL CONFLICT, ch. V, at 107–43 (1954).

[11] The United Nations Charter does *require* states to settle disputes by peaceful means. U.N. CHARTER art. 2, para. 3 & 33–38.

[12] In this familiar case, a French ship collided with and sank a Turkish ship on the high seas not far from Turkey. Turkish nationals were killed as a result of the collision. Turkey instituted criminal proceedings against the French watch officer for his alleged contribution to the disaster. France asserted that the Turkish criminal prosecution violated international law. Case of the S.S. "Lotus," P.C.I.J., ser. A, No. 10 at 19 (1927).

[13] *Ibid.*

necessary to vindicate an exercise of challenged jurisdiction by establishing the existence of a permissive norm of international law that could serve as an authorization.

The continued accuracy of the *Lotus* view seems confirmed by the similarity of approach in the *Fisheries* case.[14] Here again, the conclusion of the court stated only that Norway's delimitation of its territorial sea by the method of straight base-lines was "not contrary to international law." [15] The court deferred to the decentralized delimitation of competence, even to the extent of allowing Norway to take account of "certain economic interests peculiar to a region" in selecting a base-line method.[16] This appears to be a particularly strong endorsement of the horizontal character of the international legal order because the core of the dispute—the proper legal classification of ocean water—was a matter of general international controversy.[17]

In a long dissenting opinion, Judge Sir Arnold McNair expressed the view that "the manipulation of the limits of territorial waters for the purpose of protecting economic and other social interests has no justification in law; moreover, the approbation of such a practice would have *a dangerous tendency in that it would encourage States to adopt a subjective appreciation of their rights instead of conforming to a common international standard.*" [18] The orientation of this criticism, it is believed, ignores the horizontal emphasis that dominates international relations. As will be indicated in some detail, this "subjective appreciation" that Judge McNair deplores is exactly what produces the major stability encountered internationally. If kept reasonable by mutual self-restraint, horizontal ordering is far

---

[14] Fisheries Case, [1951] I.C.J. Rep. 116.

[15] *Id.* at 143; and *cf.* at 139, court's conclusion that the United Kingdom "did not consider it [Norwegian delimitation] to be contrary to international law." For good discussions of the theoretical complexities that arise when precision is sought in stating the relations between contested state action and international law, see the discussion of the *non liquet* problem in STONE, *op. cit. supra* note 10, at 153–64 and Goldie, *Legal Pluralism and "No-Law" Sectors,* 32 AUSTL. L. J. 220 (1958).

[16] Fisheries Case, *supra* note 14, at 133.

[17] The controversy surrounds the standards applicable to the delimitation of internal waters, territorial sea, and the high seas. Some consensus was revealed at the recent Geneva Conventions on the Law of the Sea. For texts of the Conventions, see 52 AM. J. INT'L L. 836–62 (1958).

[18] Fisheries Case, *supra* note 14, at 169. (Emphasis added.)

from "a dangerous tendency"; rather, it is the necessary process of structuring a decentralized international society. The position of Judge McNair, recalling that of Professor Corbett, illustrates the consequence of using an exclusively vertical model of legal order to analyze international phenomena.

When is an assertion of competence by a state contrary to international law? This is the proper focus of inquiry from the vertical perspective. There is no case known to me in which an *international* decision-maker has determined that an assertion of national competence was prohibited by jurisdictional norms of international law.[19] Of course, there is some need for an effective means of determining the limits of national discretion. For example, the assertion by the United States of legal authority to use the high seas to test hydrogen bombs raises a serious question of exceeding limits.[20] However, the relevant observation is that where such an *incompatible overlap* is discerned, the most effective modes of adjustment appear to be strongly horizontal in character.[21]

OBSERVATION ON THE DELIMITATION OF LEGAL COMPETENCE BY THE UNITED STATES

If one views international law as the corpus of prohibitive norms applicable in an international tribunal (the traditional *Lotus* concept), there is almost no *legal* limitation upon the discretion of a State to extend its control over men, property, and events.[22] That

---

[19] However, the equivalent decision is made in the area of state responsibility whenever an international tribunal determines that a state has exceeded its competence in regard to the control of nationals of the claimant state. This also was the real consequence of the International Court of Justice determination that Mr. Nottebohm did not possess a strong enough "link" to allow Liechtenstein to confer nationality upon him for the purpose of asserting an international claim against Guatemala (a state to which Mr. Nottebohm had stronger links), Nottebohm Case (second phase), [1955] I.C.J. Rep. 4.

[20] *Compare with* the conclusions reached by Margolis, *The Hydrogen Bomb Experiments and International Law*, 64 YALE L. J. 629 (1955) and McDougal & Schlei, *Hydrogen Bomb Tests in Perspective: Lawful Measures for Security*, 64 YALE L. J. 648 (1955).

[21] See extended discussion in last section of this chapter.

[22] Such a conception of international law is incorporated in the typical definition, such as the one given by Judge Hackworth: "International law consists of a body of rules governing the relations between states." 1 HACKWORTH, DIGEST OF INTERNATIONAL LAW 1 (1940). This form of definition always assumes the *Lotus* background of discretion against which it projects its prohibitive rules.

is, a vertical conception of the nature of law makes law almost irrelevant to an inquiry into the methods used by a state to delimit its legal competence. There occurs a ritualistic deference to the prohibitive norms of international law in the form of a verbal demonstration of the conformity of State claims to international law. But it is not much more than ritual for two dominant reasons. First, the accepted prohibitive norms of international law are subordinated to general permissive principles of State jurisdiction which are capable of almost unrestricted extension.[23] Second, the domestic legal authority is usually able to give the authoritative *characterization* to the facts in order to bring the assertion of jurisdiction into harmony with the broad permissive jurisdictional principle that is invoked.[24] For example, it is acceptable to justify the classification of an event as territorial if a domestic impact ("a substantial effect") can be shown; how does one go about challenging the conclusion of the decision-maker that the event has produced a domestic impact? [25] A preliminary conclusion is that effective limitations upon decentralized exercises of competence are largely a consequence of horizontal

---

A similar vertical conception of international law explains why Professor Corbett finds that "the classification of international usages as law . . . involves wasteful self-deception and misdirection of energy." CORBETT, *op. cit. supra* note 5, at 11.

[23] The traditional approach to the formation of permissive principles available to delimit the legal competence of a state is illustrated by *Research in International Law Under the Auspices of the Harvard Law School, Jurisdiction With Respect to Crime*, 29 AM. J. INT'L L., Supp., pt. II, at 439 (1935) [hereinafter cited as *Harvard Research*]. The Draft Convention concerns only the criminal jurisdiction of a state, but, for general descriptive purposes, it illustrates the types of justification available to a state for all types of claims to exercise legal control. If anything, the procedural due process requirements, associated with the imposition of criminal responsibility, allow a state less discretion when it asserts criminal jurisdiction. For argument to this effect, see Haight, *International Law and Extraterritorial Application of the Antitrust Laws*, 63 YALE L. J. 639 (1954). *But see* Katzenbach, *supra* note 1, at 1140–47.

[24] States, by characterization, are able to extend the traditional reach of the jurisdictional principles, *e.g.*, United States v. Aluminum Co. of America, 148 F.2d 416, 439–48 (2d Cir. 1945) (territorial principle); Joyce v. Director of Public Prosecutions, [1946] A.C. 347 (nationality principle). These decisions are intended only to illustrate the *process* of characterization at work in rather extreme situations.

[25] The limitations of horizontal discretion to characterize in relation to the nationality principle of jurisdiction are reached in the Nottebohm Case (second phase), note 19 *supra*. Increased vertical control of state discretion to characterize facts would indeed be a significant development in international relations.

considerations. This makes it essential to examine the patterns of horizontal control. So far as horizontal control achieves a generally acceptable delimitation of competence, it attains the same desirable quality of order that one expects from vertical control. Thus, to be descriptive a definition of international law should be broad enough to include both dimensions of international order; it is deceptive to identify international law exclusively with vertical norms of prohibition.

In general, these comments will emphasize a judicial orientation, although the legal competence of the state should be understood in a far broader sense.[26] A long time ago, the United States expressed a territorial self-delimitation of legal competence. Chief Justice John Marshall, with customary vigor, related the ideas of jurisdiction, sovereignty, and competence to one another in expressing what he regarded to be the fundamental hypothesis of international order:

> The jurisdiction of the nation within its own territory is necessarily exclusive and absolute. It is susceptible of no limitation not imposed by itself. Any restriction upon it, deriving validity from an external source, would imply a diminution of sovereignty to the extent of the restriction, and an investment of that sovereignty to the same extent in that power which could impose such restriction.[27]

This remains an accurate account of the major allocation of competence, especially in regard to enforcement aspects of legal control. The conception of "sovereignty" serves in this context as a shorthand way to indicate the decentralization of legal authority in the

[26] The analysis offered here of legal competence appears to apply equally to any facet of legal control, whether viewed *institutionally* (legislation, administration, adjudication) or *processively* (investigation, prescription, enforcement). The distinction between the capacity to prescribe and to enforce "rules attaching legal consequences" offered in the RESTATEMENT, FOREIGN RELATIONS LAW § 1 (Tent. Draft No. 2, 1958) is useful to highlight considerations that are relevant to different kinds of claims to exercise legal control. A horizontal legal order must exhibit more self-restraint in enforcement than in prescriptive aspects of its legal process. See also *id.* § 2, comment *a* at 8–10 (Tent. Draft No. 2, 1958).

[27] The Schooner Exchange v. McFadden, 11 U.S. (7 Cranch) 116, 136 (1812). For the best discussion of the jurisdictional development and the problems in this and related areas, see Katzenbach, note 1 *supra*. See also Carlston, *Antitrust Law Abroad*, 49 Nw. U.L. REV. 569, 573–82 (1954).

world; it becomes deceptive as soon as it is treated as a revelation of the absence of international order.[28] For, on the contrary, Marshall's view introduces a very rigid allocation of competence into situations of potential conflict between states over legal claims: everything within the territory of a state is subject to its plenary legal control; everything outside is subject to no control. As long as events can be nicely separated and the concerns of a state are primarily local, such a system of allocation seems to maximize state autonomy and minimize the occurrence of conflict situations. The use of a spatial metaphor remains dominant in the leading current formulation of the scope of United States legal authority.[29]

However, as Marshall was ready to acknowledge and to apply in *Schooner Exchange,* the fundamental spatial allocation must be modified to accommodate many situations of interaction between states. Not all events can be meaningfully located in space, and reference to the place where most of the constituent acts are performed often is not the state with the best claim of legal competence.[30] The classic simplification of a wide series of problems is the man standing on the State A side of the border and fatally shooting a man in State B. There is no difficulty about either A or B initiating a criminal prosecution once either state acquires custody of the defendant, but many of the difficult jurisdictional controversies concern how far this analogy can be extended by a state in the position

[28] To derive from the fact of the decentralization of power and authority within the world the conclusion that no international legal order exists is to commit the fallacy of identifying law only with vertical structures of control, see notes 3 & 4 *supra.*

[29] See RESTATEMENT, FOREIGN RELATIONS LAW §§ 10–25 (Proposed Official Draft, 1962), 11–32. *But see* the approach taken in a predominantly domestic context by RESTATEMENT (SECOND), CONFLICT OF LAWS § 42 (Tent. Draft No. 3, 1956) [hereinafter RESTATEMENT (SECOND), CONFLICT OF LAWS].

[30] This has been well stated by Professor Katzenbach: "As the world community comes into being and grows *qua* community it becomes more difficult to allocate an exclusive competency to any one sovereign to prescribe with regard to acts or events which affect with varying intensity the values of the community as a whole. . . . Often more than one state has a legitimate interest in prescribing with regard to the same interstate facts, and the task of arbitrating differences of 'law', which may or may not be the formal embodiment of different policies, becomes more complex as it becomes intense." Katzenbach, *supra* note 1, at 1156–57. Although this was said of interstate relations, it is obvious from his article that Professor Katzenbach intends this to refer equally to international relations.

of B. A rigid territorial allocation of competence creates an immunity umbrella for all those able to act abroad to achieve their "illegal" domestic objectives.

The challenge confronting a horizontal system of legal order grows greater when the policies of A and B toward an event over which each seeks legal control are somehow incompatible (as opposed to the compatibility of the shooting illustration). This may result in unfairness to individuals, illustrated most simply perhaps by the multiplication of the tax burden upon an individual if the states concerned resort to different bases of tax liability. Another form of unfairness occurs when an individual is ordered to do act X by State A and ordered to refrain from doing X by State B.[31] Whenever such unfairness to a large number of individuals results, the system of legal order breaks down unless it can generate methods for eliminating this unfairness or at least reducing it substantially.[32]

Account must also be taken of the reverse pressure upon a state to expand its competence sufficiently to embrace a subject-matter that appears to require a legal control in order to protect important national interests.[33] This has induced an expansion of the territorial allocation of legal competence to authorize the assertion of control over events with only a remote spatial contact with the claimant state. It has also induced the formulation of supplementary prin-

[31] A vivid illustration of this possibility has been given by the recent attempts of the United States to require foreign acts in relation to the enforcement of the Sherman Act: United States v. Imperial Chemical Industries, 100 F. Supp. 504 (S.D.N.Y. 1951), decree, 105 F. Supp. 215 (S.D.N.Y. 1952); and British sequel: British Nylon Spinners, Ltd. v. Imperial Chemical Industries, Ltd., [1952] 2 ALL E.R. 780; British Nylon Spinners v. I.C.I., Ltd., [1954] 3 ALL E.R. 88.

[32] The dependence of any legal order upon effective ways to resolve contradictory claims of legal control has been well expressed in a discussion of federalism in the United States where it was said: "People repeatedly subjected, like Pavlov's dogs, to two or more inconsistent sets of directions, without means of resolving the inconsistencies, could not fail in the end to react as the dogs did. The society, collectively, would suffer a nervous breakdown." Hart, The Relations Between State and Federal Law, 54 COLUM. L. REV. 489 (1954).

[33] This nationalistic orientation is nothing more than a reflection of the primary location of power and authority on the state level. It should not discourage the hypothesis of a world community. In fact, a major need in a horizontal system of order is that calculations of national interest be made sensitive to the importance of international stability. This selfish desire for stability provides the most reliable motive for what purports to be international altruism, such as foreign aid programs.

ciples of legal competence each of which in special contexts appears to provide a more persuasive defense of a jurisdictional claim than X could be given by resort to the territorial principle.

Thus a state may base its claim upon the nationality principle (the actor was a national of the claimant state), upon the protective principle (the act threatened some vital national interest such as the security or the credit of the claimant state, *e.g.*, counterfeiting its currency), upon the passive personality principle (the victim of the act was a national of the claimant state), or upon the universality principle (the act is so contrary to international order that its mere commission is enough to give legal competence to any state that can obtain custody of the actor, *e.g.*, piracy).[34] Each principle is like a satellite with its own orbit that circles about a distinct area of subject matter. It is important that the state asserting jurisdiction invoke the most persuasive available rationale so that its assertion is made to appear as reasonable, and hence as acceptable, as possible. As will become more evident, horizontal order, with its emphasis upon reciprocity, depends heavily upon states' convincing one another that they are acting reasonably in regard to the delimitation of legal competence.

The United States has not always offered the most persuasive justification available for its recent controversial assertions of legal competence. This has been a consequence of its seeking to explain the modern scope of competence by exclusive resort to an extended conception of the territorial principle. For example, the efforts to vindicate the extension of antitrust regulation have concentrated upon locating a predominantly foreign event *within* the United States by indicating its *effect* upon the domestic economy; there is an effort to treat complex cartel arrangements as an analogy to the man standing in A and shooting into B.[35] Rather than to attempt to prove that

---

[34] For exposition and illustrative practice up to 1935, see *Harvard Research* art. 3, at 480–508 (territorial principle); art. 5, at 519–39 (nationality principle); arts. 7 & 8, at 543–63; arts. 9 & 10, at 563–92 (universality principle).

[35] For a survey of the leading cases, see U.S. ATTORNEY GENERAL'S NATIONAL COMMITTEE TO STUDY THE ANTITRUST LAWS REPORT at 66–91 (1955) [hereinafter ATTORNEY GENERAL'S REPORT]. The recent development in such a case as *Alcoa* is most clearly foreshadowed by the formulation in *Sisal Sales* that the United States may assert legal control over foreign acts and actors to prevent "forbidden results within the United States." United States v. Sisal Sales Corp., 274 U.S. 268, 276 (1927). See also Note, *Extraterritorial Application of the Anti-trust Laws,* 69 HARV. L. REV. 1452 (1956).

the event should be treated as if it took place inside United States
territory, it would seem more convincing to use the more flexible
approach expressed in Section 42(1) of the RESTATEMENT (SEC-
OND) CONFLICT OF LAWS:

> § 42. Definition of Jurisdiction.
>
> (1) A state may create or affect legal interests whenever
> its contacts with a person, thing or occurrence are sufficient to
> make such action reasonable. The power so to create or affect
> legal interest is "jurisdiction", as that term is used in the Re-
> statement of this Subject.[36]

This approach does not isolate a single factor and make its existence
or nonexistence crucial to the claim of jurisdiction. Instead, it takes
account of any element of the facts which is relevant to the total
reasonableness of the claim to exercise legal control. Such an approach seems to have been taken in a series of Lanham Act cases
dealing with misleading uses of American trademarks in foreign
markets.[37] There are thus two methods: (1) the use of alternate
jurisdictional principles, each of which isolates a motive for the
exercise of legal control and (2) a total appraisal of the reasonableness of a claim to exercise legal control. The ensuing discussion of
illustrative cases is intended to support a preference for the second
method, which is believed to produce more flexible results and to
allow a decision-maker to give more persuasive explanations of particular delimitations of legal competence.

Geographical isolation as a self-conscious fact would seem to

[36] See note 29 *supra*.

[37] In these cases, a conclusion for or against the assertion of legal control
has been derived from an explicit consideration of all seemingly relevant factors;
there was no attempt to dispose of the case simply by showing that the defendant was a national or that the event could be considered to have taken place
within territory. The courts showed an awareness of the need to be more sophisticated about delimitations of legal competence when dealing with subject matter
that was of legitimate concern to a second state. See especially the reasoning
used to support the dismissal of the foreign aspects of the complaint in Vanity
Fair Mills v. T. Eaton Co., Ltd., 234 F. 2d 633 (2d Cir.), *cert. denied*, 352 U.S.
871 (1956). See also Steele v. Bulova Watch Co., 344 U.S. 280 (1952); Ramirez
and Feraud Chili Co. v. Las Palmas Food Co., 146 F. Supp. 594 (S.D. Cal.
1956), *aff'd per curiam*, 245 F.2d 874 (9th Cir. 1957). *Cf.* interpretation of these
cases as emphasizing nationality "as a key to the extraterritorial application of
the statute [The Lanham Act]." RESTATEMENT, FOREIGN RELATIONS LAW, Explanatory Notes § 31, Reporter's Note on comment *c*, at 91 (Tent. Draft No.
2, 1958).

underlie the strong United States endorsement of the dominance of the territorial principle in the time of Marshall and Story. Its modern survival is at least partly a result of Mr. Justice Holmes' opinion in the *American Banana case,* which contains very forceful language.[38] Holmes strongly urges that claims to exercise legal control over allegedly wrongful conduct must be justified by strict *lex loci actus* standards. This position has shaped the United States approach to the delimitation of legal competence in the international sphere whenever the question presented concerns activity that has taken place, at least in part, within another state. The core of the approach is derived from the following well-known passage in the opinion:

> It is obvious, however stated, the plaintiff's case depends on several rather startling propositions. In the first place the acts causing the damage were done, so far as appears, outside the jurisdiction of the United States and within that of other states. It is surprising to hear it argued that they were governed by the act of Congress.
>
> No doubt in regions subject to no sovereign, like the high seas, or to no law that civilized countries recognize as adequate, such countries may treat some relation between their citizens as governed by their own law. But the general and almost universal rule is that the character of an act as lawful or unlawful must be determined wholly by the law of the country where the act is done.[39]

It would appear that *American Banana* requires a state to make a spatial delimitation of legal competence. The state where the primary action took place is given exclusive legal competence to exercise control; another state can either refrain from asserting legal control or it must apply the law of the state of occurrence. From such a viewpoint, it does indeed seem absurd to challenge the validity of

[38] This was a private treble action between two American corporations concerning acts performed in another state and based upon the foreign commerce clause of the Sherman Act. The Supreme Court affirmed a dismissal of the complaint, which had alleged, in essence, that the defendant, United Fruit Co., had instigated the government of Costa Rica to seize and destroy property of the plaintiff, American Banana Co. v. United Fruit Co., 213 U.S. 347 (1909).

[39] *Id.* at 355–56; see also at 357–58. This language is confined to "a concurring and clarifying comment" in a footnote of the ATTORNEY GENERAL'S REPORT 67 n. 8. The explanation in the text emphasizes deference based upon the act of state aspect of the case.

conduct performed by the territorial sovereign. Note, too, that *American Banana* did not regard as relevant, except perhaps to compel the defendants to participate in the trial, the fact that both participants were of American nationality. Why not? International law (vertically conceived) allows a state to exercise almost unlimited legal control over its nationals; no foreign state possesses even the procedural capacity to make a formal challenge. The decision expressed horizontal self-restraint (a restrictive interpretation of the reach of a United States statute); it did not purport to be a consequence of vertical requirements (that is, the application of a prohibitive norm of international law of the *Lotus* variety).[40] This is rather significant. The United States relied upon horizontal considerations to specify the limits of its competence even in a situation in which the court regarded the assertion of jurisdiction as dependent upon "several rather startling propositions." [41] It suggests how marginal is the impact of the vertical norms of international law.

It is possible to find language in the *American Banana case* to support a wider conception of state discretion to delimit its own legal authority. For example:

> They [states] go further, at times, and declare that they will punish any one, subject or not, who shall do certain things, if they catch him, as in the case of pirates on the high seas. *In cases immediately affecting national interests they may go further still* and may make, and if they get the chance, *execute similar threats as to acts done within another recognized jurisdiction.*[42]

Given the separation of the world into independent states, each bound to maximize the welfare of its own society, the concept of "national interest," as a valid basis for the assertion of legal control,

[40] The court decided on nonassertion of the claim to exercise legal control on the basis of the absence of statutory *intent* rather than the absence of statutory *power* to reach the subject matter of the claim.

[41] It is quite possible that the court would disallow the claim of legal control even if Congress had clearly expressed an intention to make it. But it is probable then that this would be done on the basis of the obligation of a state to accord deference to acts of state performed within the territory of the acting state, rather than on the ground that the jurisdictional claim made by the United States was contrary to international law. Problems of the internal separation of powers are also relevant to international law.

[42] *Op. cit. supra* note 38, at 356. (Emphasis added.)

establishes the same flexible method of delimitation as is found in Section 42(1) of the RESTATEMENT (SECOND) CONFLICT OF LAWS.[43] This does not mean to endorse claiming as much legal competence as a state's power makes it feasible to claim; it must be remembered that an important aspect of "national interest" is to maintain a desirable quality of international order, and that international order, because of its horizontal character, depends upon reciprocal self-restraint on a mutually satisfactory basis. But a justification for a disputed assertion of legal control by reference to the specific national interest at stake does get closer to the essence of the motive of the claimant state.

The United States has expanded its delimitation of legal authority to allow the assertion of legal control over economic arrangements centered in other states. Such practice is notable especially in the area of antitrust regulation. It has occasioned protest. The United States is accused of efforts to export its domestic legislation to regulate the economic affairs of other states possessing incompatible attitudes towards the proper regulation of business activities.[44] It is not possible to examine these cases here. The basis of legal competence has been explained to be *the substantial domestic impact* of the regulated conduct; it has produced "forbidden results" within the United States (raising domestic prices, reducing the volume of exports or imports, or decreasing the competitive atmosphere of business practices).[45] An illustrative explanation is found in the important *Alcoa* opinion delivered by Judge Learned Hand:

[43] See also, RESTATEMENT (SECOND) CONFLICT OF LAWS § 42, comment *a*, at 3–7.

[44] *National Security and Foreign Policy in the Application of American Antitrust Laws to Commerce with Foreign Nations*, REPORT OF THE SPECIAL COMMITTEE ON ANTI-TRUST LAWS AND FOREIGN TRADE, ASSOC. OF THE BAR OF THE CITY OF N.Y. (1957); Haight, *supra* note 23; Whitney, *Anti-Trust Law and Foreign Commerce*, 11 RECORD OF N.Y.C.B.A. 134 (1956); Burns, *Report on Foreign Trade Conference Abroad*, 1 ANTITRUST BULL. 303 (1955). For defense of the United States' claim of legal competence, see Timberg, *Extraterritorial Jurisdiction under the Sherman Act*, 11 RECORD OF N.Y.C.B.A. 101 (1956); Timberg, *Antitrust and Foreign Trade*, 48 NW. U. L. REV. 411 (1953); Edwards, *Regulation of Monopolistic Cartelization*, 14 OHIO ST. L. J. 252 (1953).

[45] The most important cases are discussed and cited in sources discussed in note 35 *supra*. See also Holophane v. United States, 352 U.S. 903 (1956). The most nearly complete discussion pro and contra this type of assertion of legal control is found in the decision and dissenting opinions in United States v. Timken Roller Bearing Co., 341 U.S. 593 (1951).

> It is settled law—as "Limited" [foreign corporate defendant] itself agrees—that any state may impose liabilities, even upon persons not within its allegiance, for conduct outside its borders that has consequences within its borders which the state reprehends; and these liabilities other states will ordinarily recognize.[46]

This broad delimitation is not to be read without a consideration of the accompanying cautionary language, which exhibits all the horizontal motives that induce the state to use self-restraint.

> Almost any limitation of the supply of goods in Europe, for example, or in South America, may have repercussions in the United States if there is trade between the two. Yet when one considers the international complications likely to arise from an effort in this country to treat such agreements as unlawful, it is safe to assume that Congress did not intend the Act to cover them.[47]

One observes that here, as in *American Banana*, the source of the limitation upon the scope of legal authority derives from a judicial construction of legislative intent and not from the vertical authority of prohibitive norms of international law. What these cases fail to do is to justify the assertion of competence by a determination that it is more reasonable to assert than to refrain. This would require justification in terms of the dominant horizontal criterion of reciprocity. Considerations of the impact of reciprocity upon patterns of state assertion and deference receive no explicit mention in the decisions. The failure to do this is an implicit refusal to regard horizontal structures of order as really law. This neglects an opportunity to use these structures to achieve mutually acceptable self-delimitations of legal competence. But suppose a state articulates a standard of reciprocity unacceptable to other states? Then, at least the basis of incompatibility becomes explicit, making evident the need to resort to more formalized horizontal structures of legal order, by way of negotiation or international agreement.

The most spectacular "international complications" produced

[46] United States v. Aluminum Co. of America, 148 F.2d 416, 443 (2d Cir. 1946).
[47] *Ibid.*

by the challenged assertions of United States legal control have
concerned the remedial portions of judgments.[48] For example, in
the I.C.I. decree, I.C.I. (a British corporation) was ordered to
reconvey certain patents to Du Pont (an American competitor);
this order contradicted an I.C.I. contractual obligation to British
Nylon Spinners (an exclusive British licensee). In a British court,
Nylon Spinners received a preliminary injunction restraining I.C.I.
from reconveying the patents in conformity with the American decree.[49] Far from contradicting the existence of horizontal order, this
is an expression of it. The United States decision, after explaining
why it did not regard British Nylon Spinners as an "innocent party,"
acknowledged that a British court, as was the case, might nevertheless restrain enforcement. Furthermore, there was a so-called "saving
clause" declaring that the American decree was not meant to penalize I.C.I. for complying with foreign (presumably British) law. Such
a clause is all that can be expected in a horizontal order in those
situations in which incompatible claims of legal control overlap.
The American court expressed its view of the reasonable extent of
legal control from the perspective of the United States and explicitly recognized that a subsequent inconsistent assertion of legal
control by another state may require some modification.[50] Each state

---

[48] For citations of relevant cases, see note 31 *supra;* for a discussion of the
"international complications" encountered in efforts to obtain documentary evidence located abroad, see Emmerglick, *Antitrust Jurisdiction and the Production
of Documents Located Abroad,* 11 RECORD OF N.Y.C.B.A. 122 (1956); *cf.* also
Société Internationale pour Participations Industrielles et Commerciales, S.A. v.
Rogers, 357 U.S. 197 (1958).

[49] British Nylon Spinners, Ltd. v. Imperial Chemical Industries, Ltd., [1952]
2 ALL E. R. 780 (C.A.).

[50] "We do not hesitate therefore to decree that the British nylon patents may
not be asserted by I.C.I. to prevent the importation of nylon polymer and of
nylon yarn into Great Britain. What credit may be given to such an injunctive
provision by the courts of Great Britain in a suit brought by B.N.S. to restrain
such importations we do not venture to predict. We feel that the possibility that
the English courts in an equity suit will not give effect to such a provision in our
decree should not deter us from including it." United States v. Imperial Chemical
Industries, Ltd., 105 F. Supp. 215, 231 (S.D.N.Y. 1952). Thus, the assertion is
made with explicit awareness that its finality is subject to a counterassertion of legal
competence by the second state (here Great Britain). See discussion *supra,* at 228–
30. A concurring British judge recognizing this potential deference finds this to be
the basis for avoiding a conflict of orders to I.C.I., British Nylon Spinners, Ltd. v.
Imperial Chemical Industries, Ltd., *supra* note 49, at 784. This allows reconciliation

must seek to delimit the extent of its legal control by good faith and by a reasonable specification of its authority; balance is eventually restored by automatic factors of feasibility. Thus, here the immediacy of British control over the subject matter of dispute gave it what became the paramount claim. One could reasonably criticize the United States only if it acted subsequent to the British decisions to punish I.C.I. for noncompliance; but this kind of reassertion is precisely what the saving clause waives. If the equilibrium produced by such successive assertions of legal control does not produce a mutually satisfactory result, it becomes desirable to seek to negotiate an improved allocation of competence.

These few observations on the process of self-delimitation of international legal authority by United States courts have tried to suggest the nature of the task. The pressures favoring the extension of state legal control must not lead the decision-maker to ignore the unavoidable impact of horizontal structures of legal order, e.g., reciprocity, feasibility. The very character of horizontal order makes a voluntary acceptance of a claim by other states significant; in a dominantly vertical system of order, centralized power can operate as a temporary substitute for acceptance. Thus, it is necessary to make self-delimitation appear as reasonable as possible to induce reciprocal reasonableness and perhaps to induce cooperation, e.g., enforcement of judgments, collection of evidence. Differing policies in an interdependent legal atmosphere lead to an inevitable overlap of incompatible assertions of legal authority, but horizontal techniques are available to reduce the friction. It seems appropriate now to look directly at the horizontal structure of international relations in order to describe its main elements.

SOME ASPECTS OF A HORIZONTAL IDEA OF INTERNATIONAL LEGAL ORDER

1. *Self-Imposed Restraint.* As was indicated in connection with the *Lotus case,* the prohibitive impact of international law upon the discretion of a state to delimit its legal competence is marginal.

---

of overlapping claims to exercise legal control. See note 34 *supra. Cf.* explicit non-assertion of competence over acts outside of United States territory in consent decree cases. *E.g.,* United States v. Amsterdamsche Chininefabriek, C.C.H., Fed. Trade Reg. Serv. 4186 (S.D.N.Y. 1928).

Effective limitations are derived from what might usefully be described as the *permissive* impact of international law; this is another way to formulate the influence of horizontal systems of order upon the exercise of state discretion. The existence of this influence is most basically illustrated by the phenomenon of state self-restraint exhibited by all parts of the domestic legal system.

Legislative self-restraint exists whenever the legislature declines to use all of its potential competence to assert legal control over people, property, and events.[51] It may be illustrated by the general failure of the United States (and other states) to extend the applicability of its statutes to most acts of nationals that are performed in other states. Rare use is made of the competence conferred upon a state by the nationality principle.[52] This generally spares Americans abroad from the burden of conforming to a legal standard in addition to the one established by the territorial state. It also saves the United States from making inconvenient assertions of legal control in which the tribunal would find itself often quite remote from the evidence, the context of occurrence, and witnesses. Hence, complete deference, without even the option of a secondary assertion of legal competence, is accorded to the territorial state. This encourages a reciprocal deference and simplifies the legal superstructure of the private lives of those who cross borders.

Executive self-restraint is more difficult to discern because it consists mainly of invisible action. It involves countless decisions not to assert legal control in situations where an assertion would not constitute a reasonable claim by the state, given more compelling bases for other states to favor nonassertion. This happens automatically, since a state must be selective in the assertion of regulatory claims as a result of its inability to pursue more than a small percentage of potential violators. One factor that induces the decision not to assert legal control is the existence of the prospect of its assertion by another state with a primary interest. That is, the claims most likely to produce international friction because they compete with legal authority of another state are those claims that

[51] Perhaps the most fundamental self-restraint imposed upon assertions of legal competence by the United States emanates from the Constitution in the form of "due process" considerations.

[52] For illustrative cases and discussion, see RESTATEMENT, FOREIGN RELATIONS LAW OF THE UNITED STATES, Topic 2 (Tent. Draft No. 2, 1958). RESTATEMENT (SECOND), CONFLICT OF LAWS, § 43f.(1) (c), comment *f*, at 28–30.

a state is often most willing to give up. Of course, when subject matter is important to national interest, the very fact of a competing inconsistent claim may lead a state to press its claims of legal control harder so as to shape the event in the manner that it favors. Coordination of law enforcement with other policies of government, such as promoting international stability for trade and investment purposes, induces an account to be taken of factors that favor non-assertion of legal control.[53]

Judicial self-restraint expresses itself in a variety of ways. First, as in *American Banana*, it tends to presume a territorial application for legislation and to make extraterritorial extension depend upon the establishment of *exceptional* conditions justifying it.[54] Second, self-restraint relies upon conflict of laws principles to reduce the discretion of the state that is normally conferred upon it by international law. This includes almost unlimited deference to foreign acts of state. In general, interference with the decentralized administration of justice in another state occurs only when there is a strong basis for the claim. Third, the United States to some extent limits unreasonable claims of all kinds by making the administration of all its justice subject to the criterion of "due process." [55]

Perhaps all that can and should be achieved by means of self-restraint at the level of the unilateral assertion of legal control is

[53] See a discussion of policy coordination in relation to the application of anti-trust laws to foreign activity, ATTORNEY GENERAL'S REPORT 92–98; *but see The American Antitrust Laws and American Business Abroad,* AMERICAN CHAMBER OF COMMERCE IN LONDON (1955).

[54] But state discretion to characterize foreign activity as "territorial" makes this a less significant restriction than it might appear. The United States, for example, combines a conspiracy theory with an idea of domestic impact to reach predominantly foreign events. See, *e.g.,* United States v. Nord Deutscher Lloyd, 223 U.S. 512, 517–18 (1912); United States v. American Tobacco Co., 221 U.S. 106, 172, 184 (1911); United States v. Sisal Sales Corp., 274 U.S. 268, 276 (1927). It is, in general, the *scholarly commentary* and not the *formal justification* of the jurisdictional claim that describes the assertion of legal competence as "extraterritorial." *E.g.,* Note, *Application of the Anti-Trust Laws to Extra-Territorial Conspiracies,* 49 YALE L. J. 1312 (1940). And see the literature cited note 43 *supra.* For unusual reference to "extraterritorial application" in a decision of an American court, see Vanity Fair Mills v. T. Eaton Co., 234 F.2d 633, 641–43 (2d Cir. 1946). But the extraterritorial legal control is limited to situations where alternative validation by the nationality principle is possible, *id.,* at 643.

[55] The leading case is International Shoe Co. v. Washington, 326 U.S. 310 (1945); see also Home Insurance Co. v. Dick, 281 U.S. 397 (1930).

that the claimant state possess a reasonable basis for the claim, such reasonableness including a degree of deference to inconsistent interests of other states. There are frequent occasions, especially in regard to property interests, where there is an incompatible overlap of equally reasonable claims; for example, the relation of the capital-exporting state to the capital-importing state in regard to the proper degree of protection to be given to property rights may come into hopeless conflict. When there exists an overlap of inconsistent and yet mutually reasonable claims, there is a need to attempt settlement by recourse to more formalized modes of horizontal relationship, *e.g.*, international agreement, compromise. The role then of self-restraint is to balance the pressure to assert legal authority in order to maximize the interests of the state against whatever makes it unreasonable to do so. The evaluation of the content of reasonableness includes the importance of preserving a desirable quality of horizontal order; whatever is disruptive by arousing opposition of other states must be justified by dominant domestic needs.

2. *Restraint Imposed by Circumstances* (feasibility of the claim). Here it can be assumed that there exists a strong *volitional* basis for the state to extend its legal control. However, modesty in the form of nonassertion or reduced assertion is prompted by an insufficiency of power: the claimant state is prevented by the circumstances of the situation from achieving the objectives of full assertion. This insufficiency of power often itself merely expresses the decentralized character of the international order in which each state is a final authority. It is more a matter of "the given" within which processes of international jurisdiction must operate than is it a reflection of the weakness of the claimant state.[56] "The given" includes self-delimitation based upon considerations of volitional self-restraint, reciprocity, convenience, and fairness; it can be described as the objective structure of horizontal order that imposes fixed conditions upon the exercise of any particular jurisdiction claim.[57]

---

[56] Power is but one of many relevant variables in the horizontal structure of international order. It is believed that the exaggeration of its role in international relations leads to underestimating the possibilities for an international legal order that is not based upon power. Among many illustrations of an overemphasis on power are MORGENTHAU, POLITICS AMONG NATIONS: THE STRUGGLE FOR POWER AND PEACE (1948); SCHWARZENBERGER, POWER POLITICS: A STUDY OF INTERNATIONAL SOCIETY (2d ed. 1951).

[57] It includes prior interactions of assertion and counterassertion of legal competence; *e.g.*, an American court, framing a decree for facts similar to those

For example, suppose X, a national of State C, commits a serious crime in State A and escapes to State B; assume A has a strong motive to prosecute X. In the absence of relevant agreement between A and B, there is no way to prosecute X so long as he stays in B. The basic territorial allocation of competence applies, virtually without exception, to the exercise of police powers; only the consent of B would authorize the arrest of X by A in the territory of B. The assertion of competence by A to prosecute X while absent would raise domestic due process difficulties related to basic conceptions of fairness (a form of volitional self-restraint), and it would give to C a basis of seeking vertical protection of X ("denial of justice"). State A would also be reluctant to claim against X because of the estoppel implications in the event that a state in the future sought to make a similar claim against a national of A. Even if A did convict X it might not be able to impose a sanction for the same reasons that it was unable to arrest X; no *power* can be exercised in foreign territory.[58] The same reasoning applies in a variety of situations in which evidence, witnesses, or defendants are located in a foreign state which is unwilling or unable to facilitate the assertion of the claim by the state seeking to impose some form of legal control. Certain unpopular United States efforts to prosecute foreign corporate defendants under the antitrust laws have induced foreign states to use their own domestic competence as a self-conscious shield against what was regarded as an aggressive sword of jurisdictional assertion by the United States.[59]

An important distinction between two situations exists: in the first, State A (claimant) and B are in agreement as to the desirability of exercising legal control expressing a common attitude toward the event and, in the second, B dislikes the legal control that A seeks to impose. In the first situation, the decentralization of the world

present in the I.C.I. Case, would probably *somehow* take account of the British response to the I.C.I. decree. *But see* United States v. Holophane Co., Inc., 119 F. Supp. 114 (S.D. Ohio 1954), *aff'd*, 352 U.S. 903 (1956).

[58] See distinction in RESTATEMENT, FOREIGN RELATIONS LAW §§ 6–7 (Proposed Official Draft, 1962), between the capacity of a state under international law "to prescribe" and "to enforce" its law; see also *id.* § 2, Illustration 1., at 26. However, if X has property located within the United States, a sanction is available. See Blackmer v. United States, 284 U.S. 421 (1937).

[59] The clearest illustration is provided by the I.C.I. litigation. *But see also In re* Investigation of World Arrangements with Relation . . . Petroleum, 13 F.R.D. 280 (D.D.C. 1952); *In re* Grand Jury Subpoena Duces Tecum Addressed to Canadian International Paper Co., 72 F. Supp. 1013 (S.D.N.Y. 1947).

is an *artificial* barrier to the extent of state competence; this can be reduced by international agreements, which usually recognize the shared purposes and are based upon the principle of reciprocity. An obvious illustration is an extradition treaty which, in essence, allows A to extend its competence in a way that will reach X in the above example, giving B the like opportunity to reach a fugitive from its justice who is located in A and thereby implementing the common purpose to control crime. Agreement between A and B could overcome barriers to competence whenever A and B share a common policy to reach X. If B agrees with what X did, it has more interest in preventing A from acting than it does in securing a reciprocal claim against one who acted as did X. Where there is a clash of policies between A and B, as in the sphere of economic regulation, an agreement based on a reciprocal exchange of identical tolerances is not a fruitful approach to the reduction of friction.[60]

Horizontal order then is conditioned upon the *grasp* of the claimant state, as well as upon its *reach.* The United States may assert competence to control the anticompetitive business operations of a foreign corporation not doing business in the United States; it may even get such a defendant properly before its court and obtain a valid conviction on the "substantial effect" theory that includes a decree ordering the defendant to do all the acts needed to establish competitive conditions.[61] But how is the mandate of the decree to be translated into actual enforcement? [62] The rhetorical nature of this question becomes more evident if the states oppose the control claimed by the United States.[63]

Considerations of feasibility at every stage of assertion of legal authority automatically condition the delimitation of jurisdictional competence. Their tendency is to reduce the overlap of inconsistent claims to control, since the claim lacking feasibility must eventually give way. They do, however, exhibit a deficiency of the horizontal order since they tend to allocate competence by certain rigid cri-

[60] However, reciprocity based upon mutual compromise might remove overlap, *e.g.*, if A refrains from certain claims of legal control and, in exchange, B defers to others.

[61] *Cf.* cases cited note 54 *supra.*

[62] *E.g.*, DeBeers Consolidated Mines, Ltd. v. United States, 325 U.S. 212 (1945).

[63] See RESTATEMENT, CONFLICT OF LAWS § 94 (1934). *Cf.* broader view RESTATEMENT (SECOND), CONFLICT OF LAWS § 94 (Tent. Draft No. 4, 1957).

teria—physical presence and control—which may overlook important needs of a state or even the international community.[64] However, the very rigidity of the spatial allocation of *power*—and this is the essence of restraint-by-circumstance—does tend to protect decentralized autonomy. This aspect of horizontal order arises because of the comparative flexibility of the allocation of *power*.[65]

3. *Reciprocity.* The possibilities for order in a horizontal system strongly depend upon how well mechanisms of reciprocity are used. Considerations of reciprocity may influence a state to either expand or contract its delimitation of competence to exercise legal control. First, State A refrains from the assertion of a claim X and defers to the competing interest of State B in order to encourage B (and possibly other states as well) to refrain from making a claim similar to X when A has a competing interest in its nonassertion. Second, State A asserts a claim Y despite the inconsistent interest of State B because B has in the past asserted a claim similar to Y, thereby ignoring the competing interest of A. These illustrations are simplifications, since reciprocity may be the most effective device to restructure any failure in relations between states. For example, B refuses to accord recognition to a new government in A because A has abused the property interests of nationals of B; the resultant deterioration between A and B occurred because B failed to exercise what A regarded to be reasonable self-restraint in its delimitation of competence. However, the mutual interest in stability creates a reciprocal movement toward the restoration of normal relations; eventually, it is probable that B will recognize A and that A, in exchange, will do something about the property interests of B.[66] By analogy to such a compromise, it can be seen that all doctrines of deference in international law rest upon a foundation of reciprocity; that is, it is mutually more advantageous to defer on a reciprocal basis than it is to assert legal control. The best known and purest

[64] Suppose, for example, a state allows its territory to be used as a distribution center for narcotics traffic.

[65] Once again, it is evident that competing state policies relating to enforcement of claims to exercise legal control raise special problems because of the absence of vertical institutions in the world.

[66] *Cf.* eventual resolution of United States policy of nonrecognition of the Soviet government by the Litvinov Assignment. See United States v. Pink, 315 U.S. 203 (1942). And see Latvian State Cargo & Passenger S.S. Line v. McGrath, 188 F.2d 1000 (D.C. Cir. 1951).

illustrations are the doctrines of act of state and sovereign immunity. Each state defers to the primary competence of the other in exchange for the expectation of reciprocity.[67]

Reciprocity is closely related to the horizontal conceptions of self-restraint and estoppel. Reciprocity by nonassertion is simply an exercise of self-restraint, whereas reciprocity by assertion is a response to what is regarded as a prior failure to exercise self-restraint by the state with the competing interest. The relation of reciprocity to estoppel is merely that it is difficult for an asserting state to challenge a similar assertion by another state in the future. Considerations induced by either direction of reciprocity encourage states to delimit their jurisdictional competence in accord with standards of reasonableness. If an assertion is, in effect, a retaliation, then it makes negotiation of a compromise more compelling for both states. Reciprocal patterns can preserve a desirable legal order so long as states feel that there is more to gain from international stability than from international instability. Whatever can strengthen this desire for stability is hence a useful instrument for the preservation of world order; thus, the very danger from nuclear weapons is a stabilizing factor if seen under the aspect of reciprocity.[68]

Reciprocity is not always useful as an ordering mechanism. There must be present in the specific relationship of states an interchange that makes each have something rather similar to gain by restraint.[69] Dependent states used to be subject to Great Power intervention if they did not abide by the economic standards established to protect the interests of the investor states.[70] Today the situation is almost reversed. Expropriating states have almost nothing to lose by confiscating property within their borders, since they lack investment abroad. Unless there is factual reciprocity, then the mere logic of normative reciprocity becomes misleading. On the other

[67] McDougal, *International Law, Power, and Policy: A Conception*, 82 RECUEIL DES COURS 137 (1953).

[68] That is, incentives exist to delimit competence in a way that reduces friction between states. Pressure also is generated to overcome the fragile stability of mutual restraint, and thus the prospect for adequate vertical institutions improves.

[69] See Abi-Saab, *The Newly Independent States and the Rules of International Law*, 8 How. L. R. 95 (1962).

[70] This analysis is sharply and persuasively made in CALVOCORESSI, WORLD ORDER AND NEW STATES 11–33 (1962).

hand, the factual reciprocity need not consist of symmetrical interests; even though an expropriating state lacks investment abroad, it might better serve its interests by refraining from confiscating alien capital, either because it lacks the skills needed to exploit domestic industry profitably or because it would benefit more by attracting additional foreign capital than by acquiring what is present there today.

4. *Fundamental Fairness.* An appraisal of any legal order must depend finally upon its fairness to those made subject to its competence. Considerations of fundamental fairness should be made relevant to every aspect of the delimitation of state legal authority. Fairness is perhaps the basic component of the aim of horizontal order to achieve a delimitation that embraces only reasonable claims. Thus, the Second Restatement of the Law of Conflicts is quite correct to regard fairness as a basic component of reasonableness. Fairness here refers especially to the *procedure* used to institute, conduct, and enforce a judicial or administrative proceeding against any non-national interest. By analogy, it also refers to claims of legal control made by the legislature. Fairness is a perspective useful to give shape to patterns of reciprocal assertion and nonassertion of legal authority, since states seeking to receive fair treatment for their interests must be willing to accord it in exchange. Limits of feasibility reduce automatically the possibility of unfair assertions in many situations.[71]

Fairness is a motive as well as a goal. It operates to discourage the assertion of unreasonable claims of legal authority. Thus, as an ideal providing a guiding criterion to decentralized decision-makers, the concept of fairness is itself a structure of horizontal order. It gives shape to the regime of reciprocity. If it can be made explicit on this basis, it can be a potent force in securing a rational self-delimitation of competence beyond the minimum rationality imposed by the vertical instituitons of the international order.[72]

---

[71] Such factors as expense, inconvenience, lack of interest, and difficulty of enforcement discourage states from many unreasonable claims of legal competence.

[72] That is, the residual legal competence possessed by a state, given the *Lotus* approach, is not enough protection against unfair claims of legal control. There is, in addition, the law of state responsibility to protect aliens against limited forms of extreme abuse by a state, but more extensive international protection is required.

What produces unfairness? It is difficult to be specific. Thus, an important recent decision of the Supreme Court has said in an analogous domestic interstate situation that the process of asserting legal control must satisfy basic conceptions of "fair play and substantial justice." [73] It is a conception of procedural due process that must give the defending interests an adequate notice and a full opportunity to present their position, including access to documentary and human evidence. The formal initiation of the proceeding should not ordinarily be premised upon an arbitrary event. Enforcement should not ordinarily require an action in another state that is contrary to the public policy of that state, and certainly it should be exceptional to expose the defendant to potential legal liability by requiring it to act contrary to its legal obligations in another state.

5. *International Agreement.* The relations of states may, of course, become the subject of an international agreement. This is a more formal means of introducing order into an essentially horizontal legal system. When the agreeing states mutually desire to extend the regime of reciprocity to subject matter previously subject to overlapping claims of legal competence (such as to tax, to demand military service, to regulate business operations), formalized exchanges of self-restraint tend to reduce the hardship of multiple burdens that would otherwise be placed upon nationals of one state who have contact with other states.

Agreements are also useful to specify the respective scope of primary interest in relation to subject matter that will be of simultaneous concern to more than one state, *e.g.*, criminal jurisdiction over the servicemen of one state stationed in another state.[74] The creation of an allocation mechanism in advance, especially if a conflict tends to arouse strong nationalistic sentiments, introduces a de-

---

[73] International Shoe Co. v. Washington, 326 U.S. 310 (1945). *Compare with* United States v. Scophony Corp. of America, 333 U.S. 795 (1948); Home Insurance Co. v. Dick, 281 U.S. 397 (1930); Young v. Masci, 289 U.S. 253 (1953) for some aspects of due process in situations relevant to the existence of horizontal legal order.

[74] See Agreement Between the Parties to the North Atlantic Treaty Regarding the Status of Their Forces, art. XVII, 4 U.S.T. & O.I.A. 1792, T.I.A.S. No. 2846 (effective August 23, 1953). See Wilson, Secretary of Defense v. William S. Girard, U.S. Army Specialist, 31C, 354 U.S. 524 (1957) dealing with a provision in the treaty between Japan and the United States that was the same as Article XVII of the NATO agreement. Agreement With Japan, 4 U.S.T. & O.I.A. 1846, T.I.A.S. No. 2848 (effective October 29, 1953).

gree of stability that could not be achieved by a mere reliance upon more spontaneous forms of horizontal order. Without a treaty in advance, domestic pressure probably would have prevented the United States from yielding Girard to Japanese criminal authorities.

A refusal by the United States to release Girard for Japanese prosecution might have caused a serious deterioration of Japanese-American relations, perhaps even creating pressure compelling the withdrawal of the armed forces of the United States from Japan. It should be noted that rules are helpful guides for the conduct of foreign policy at the executive level, especially when, as here, there is a need to prepare the American public to accept the essential territoriality of law enforcement. This kind of acceptance, however, is based upon principles of allocation agreed upon in advance to reflect the political interests of the States. It should not be confused with the arguments, considered in later chapters, that the executive should be free to withdraw cases from domestic courts on an *ad hoc* basis to avoid the international complications that may result from the adjudication.

Areas of strong common policy, especially against the commission of certain crimes, may be implemented by reciprocal grants of special competence. The extension of personal criminal jurisdiction to foreign territory by extradition treaties is an obvious illustration, as are multilateral conventions for the control of narcotics traffic and white slave trade. A quite different illustration is the common policy of conserving fisheries and other resources of the high seas.

In other areas the mere process of seeking agreement is valuable. It often sharpens the real area of dispute, making partial agreement possible elsewhere and perhaps encouraging a compromise of the dispute itself. The recent Geneva Conventions on the Law of the Sea are illustrative.

Where the agreement allocating competence provides for the resolution of dispute by its reference to an international decision-maker, a vertical component is introduced into an essentially horizontal form of order. However, in the past such provisions have been restricted by "vital national interest" or "domestic jurisdiction" exceptions. This reaffirms the basic horizontal character of the arrangement, since the state retains wide discretion to resolve what it regards as "important" disputes by continued resort to horizontal methods of adjustment.

6. *Delimitation of Legal Competence as a Defense.* What may

State B do to resist what it regards to be an unreasonable claim of legal authority by State A? The question itself points to the horizontal emphasis of international order. Even where vertical channels of recourse to an international decision-making do exist, it is still necessary to seek a horizontal diplomatic settlement first. The effectiveness of a vertical decision (e.g., International Court of Justice judgment) depends on the willingness of the claimant state to accept an adverse decision, since there is as yet virtually no vertical enforcement.

The most primitive horizontal method of defense is resort by B to force or threat of force. This is an important aspect of international relations, since it tends to allow the strong states to determine the limits of legal authority on the part of the weak states. So far as the strong state delimits its own competence on a similar basis to what it requires from the weaker state, it makes the attitude of the stronger state decisive as to the content of reasonable competence. That is, the contours of horizontal order may reflect to a large extent the outcome of power struggles between states. There are numerous ways to exercise legal control so as to make it a form of peaceful self-help. Instructive illustrations may be taken from the role of protest and threats of reprisal, from various kinds of refusals to allow enforcement, from obstructive acts of state that interfere with the exercise of legal control in the state asserting the unreasonable claim, and from any kind of effective counter-assertion that makes legal control less feasible for the asserting state.[75]

CONCLUSION

There has been no intention here to disparage the efforts to improve the vertical institutions available to delimit state authority. My polemical thesis has been only that those international lawyers who try to explain all legal order on the basis of a vertical model of law are deceived about the character of international relations. A description of the horizontal structures of legal order seems to

---

[75] See, *e.g.*, the restrictions upon the freedom of Soviet officials to travel in the United States imposed in retaliation for earlier Soviet travel restrictions on American officials in the Soviet Union, *Travel Restrictions for Soviet Officials in the U.S.*, 26 DEP'T STATE BULL. 451 (1952). See generally, MOORE, REPORT ON EXTRATERRITORIAL CRIME AND THE CUTTING CASE (1887); Katzenbach, *supra* note 1, at 1147–57.

provide the best account of the stability that exists in the relations of states to one another.

The essence of horizontal order is that rational self-delimitation should take maximum account of the existence of other states and give effect to a mutually satisfactory standard of reciprocity. What is tentatively advocated is a pervasive conflict-of-laws approach to the self-delimitation by a state of its legal authority in regard to all matters of international concern, whether this concern be the control of alien property or the recognition of a new foreign government. In essence I am suggesting the self-conscious extension of the methods of private international law to the area of public international law.

Finally, it appears necessary to abandon reliance upon rules (traditional principles of international jurisdiction) to perform the task of self-delimitation. The complexity of much of the modern phenomena subject to legal control is now so great that it is not enough to identify a single element—whether it be the locus of occurrence, the locus of wrongdoing, the locus of injury, or the nationality of victim and actor. Rather, it is better to make a total appraisal to determine whether it is reasonable to assert state legal control. Because of the decentralization of legal authority, it is important that the delimitation of legal authority be expressed in a persuasive form so that it induces other states to accept it willingly and to cooperate with its implementation. As a result of incompatible policies toward matters that concern more than a single state, some friction is unavoidable. It can be reduced by the use of the more formal horizontal techniques, e.g., explicit compromise by international agreement. A part of the task is to learn to use the resources of horizontal order that are available to states.

A theory of jurisdiction is, of course, necessary for the development of an understanding of the role of domestic courts in the international legal order. Unless the allocation of legal authority can be achieved with minimum friction, there is no realistic prospect of liberating domestic courts from national control. States must have reasonable expectations that considerations of functional deference and fair play are being taken into account by most foreign courts most of the time before they can accept a commitment of self-denial for themselves.

Reciprocity, as we have argued, is the structuring principle of jurisdictional analysis. A demonstration of reciprocity combines matters of legal history with those of policy science, for the effective limits of reciprocity are determined by the manner in which each national actor combines a sense of precedent with a sense of expectation. Self-interest and the interests of others in jurisdictional stability must be appraised in relation to particular rules and with regard to the over-all character of international life.

Later chapters will examine the appropriate degree of deference to foreign social policy in a variety of substantive contexts. There is an interesting connection between the deference to behavior that is classified as "foreign" within the jurisdictional context and the deference to acts just because they are performed by a foreign government (act of state). It would be useful to analyze the extent to which normal rules of conflict of laws should be adapted to take into account the official character of the foreign actor.

Chapter IV

The Relevance of Contending Systems of Public Order to the Delimitation of Legal Competence

JURISDICTION is one of those basic Alice-in-Wonderland legal abstractions used in so many different ways that it is constantly in danger of losing all of its content. Jurisdiction designates the process by which the limits of legal competence are specified, that is, how far a decision-maker may go in asserting a claim to exercise legal control over men, things, and events. In addition, jurisdiction is concerned with identifying who has the final authority to specify the outer limits of legal competence. This is particularly important when two or more decision-makers assert inconsistent claims of legal control over the same subject matter. Jurisdictional concepts assume special international importance because adequate supranational techniques are not available to resolve conflicts between independent states. Resort to international tribunals remains largely marginal to major areas of international dispute; in addition, the international decision-maker, when called upon, as in *Lotus* or *Norwegian Fisheries,* views the specification of the limits of legal competence as a matter properly to be kept mainly within the discretion of the asserting state. This does not suggest that no control over the limits of legal authority exists beyond the extent of national aspiration and power. It only means that generally these limits must be sought somewhere other than in a higher impartial decision-maker, as is done in the domestic legal order.

International law, in contrast to domestic law, is much like a Victorian lady and must depend upon an excess of self-restraint to achieve virtue. States do encourage the development of patterns of deference. They feel that generally national values are better served by a reciprocal forbearance than by a reciprocal assertion of legal authority.[1] The logic and morality of reciprocity is what explains the success of doctrines of deference such as acts of state or sovereign immunity. It is this same logic and morality that control the delimi-

---

[1] A fuller exposition of this position is found in Chapter III.

tations of legal authority in private international law or in conflict-of-laws situations. Here is the center of an inquiry into the function of jurisdiction in the international realm.

The traditional approach works on the basis of minimums and thus neglects these considerations.[2] The most comprehensive minimum is expressed by the territorial principle. Can the event be regarded as taking place within the territory of the claimant state? If the answer is yes, then the jurisdictional inquiry is at an end. This is the substance of the *Lotus* doctrine. The most celebrated formulation and documentation of this approach is found in the Harvard Research Draft Convention on Jurisdiction with Respect to Crime. It is traditional to talk of various principles of jurisdiction: the territorial principle, the nationality principle, the passive personality principle, the protective principle, and the universality principle. Each of these principles isolates a strong regulatory impulse that explains why a state might seek to assert its legal control. But this is too artificial a method to cope with modern complexity. It fails to take account of the relevance of interaction, interdependence, and reciprocity. This is especially serious for the international legal order, because it relies heavily upon self-delimitation and possesses only very marginal techniques to reconcile inconsistent national claims of legal competence. Thus, there exists an obvious need to enlarge the framework of inquiry beyond the Harvard Research formulation. For this reason, one is grateful for the fluid approach to jurisdiction taken by the *Second Restatement of the Conflict of Laws* as illustrated by the basic definition of jurisdiction offered in Section 42(1):

> A state may create or affect legal interests whenever its contacts with a person, thing or occurrence are sufficient to make such action reasonable. The power to create or affect legal interests is "jurisdiction" as that term is used in the Restatement of this subject.[3]

This formulation obviously gives little guidance; it merely confers discretion. But the very abandonment of the older Harvard Research approach tends automatically to expand the horizon of rele-

[2] See an enlightening discussion of jurisdiction in JESSUP, TRANSNATIONAL LAW 35–71 (1956).

[3] RESTATEMENT (SECOND), CONFLICT OF LAWS § 42(1) (Tent. Draft No. 3, 1956).

vance. How does a decision-maker formulate delimitations of legal competence when his standard is this broad? I will not attempt to discuss this general question,[4] since my inquiry is limited to the extent to which the existence of diverse and contending systems of public order should form a routine part of an inquiry into the reasonableness of a jurisdictional claim. Even this relatively narrow inquiry should, of course, be carefully particularized. The initial task is to clarify the decision-making perspective. What kind of decision-maker is expected to specify the proper limits of legal authority? For example, a judge of the World Court has a quite different role than does a delegate to the General Assembly of the United Nations. Similarly, the judicial decision-maker in the domestic system takes an approach different from that of a foreign office decision-maker. Of secondary importance is a categorization of the issue. It is one thing to discuss the claims of a state to conduct hydrogen bomb tests on the high seas and quite another to discuss the failure of a state to accord decent treatment to an alien. In each case, we are dealing with a jurisdictional question since the issue involves the proper outer limits of legal authority; but the quality and quantity of relevance of a public order conflict seem significantly different in the two situations. The legal right to test nuclear weapons is much more a part of the present struggle between contending public order systems than is the legal right to molest a Soviet tourist. One must also distinguish among description, appraisal, and recommendation. It is quite different to describe the influence of contending public order systems upon various delimitations of legal authority, to evaluate this influence, and to recommend its change.

What is a public order system? Professors McDougal and Lasswell define it to be:

> the basic features of the social process in a community—including both the identity and preferred distribution pattern of basic goal values, and implementing institutions—that are accorded protection by the legal process.[5]

---

[4] But for a most interesting series of suggestions as to the proper content of reasonableness in a jurisdictional situation, see McDougal & Burke, *Crisis in the Law of the Sea: Community Perspectives Versus National Egoism*, 67 YALE L. J. 539, 570–73 (1958).

[5] McDougal & Lasswell, *The Identification and Appraisal of Diverse Systems of Public Order*, 53 AM. J. INT'L L. 1, 10 (1959).

This raises two questions: what are the important differences between public order systems, and how are these differences relevant to allocations of legal competence? The most obvious contemporary difference arises from the degree of coercion used internally to control the discretion of individuals. Today, for example, the central political conflict is between the relatively democratic public order systems in Western Europe and in the United States and the relatively totalitarian public order systems of the Soviet Union and China. Each exhibits a certain desire to universalize its internal system of public order.[6] This aspiration produces a struggle to determine which way of life shall prevail. Law is one of many instruments of use in this conflict. Classic Communist theory has always asserted this struggle to be inevitable and total. Only recently have modifications been made that assert even the possibility of a temporary equilibrium in the relations between these two contending systems of public order. Nevertheless, when one's way of life is at stake, it is well to become aware of the available ways to defend against attack. One such way is law; therefore, it may be important to delimit legal competence with an awareness of the relevance of the underlying contention of public order systems.

Perhaps this relevance can be made clearer by an illustration taken from recent history. World War II was a war between contending systems of public order, in which it became obvious to all that a way of life was very much at stake. One important German asset was the centralization in Germany of many important worldwide cartels. The sophisticated manipulation by Nazi officials of the activities of these cartels had the consequence of depriving the enemies of Germany, especially the United States, of critical inventions, research, and materials in a time of national crisis. This conclusion has been abundantly documented.[7] Thus, in retrospect, the pre-World War II failure by the United States to assert its maximum legal authority to break up or at least weaken the cartels was a serious shortcoming of national defense. Even if legal authority had been used only to achieve a minimum objective—ending the partici-

---

[6] Brodie describes this struggle as taking place between an expanding system (Soviet) and a *status quo* system (United States). *The Anatomy of Deterrence,* 11 WORLD POLITICS 173 (1959).

[7] See, *e.g.,* A CARTEL POLICY FOR THE UNITED NATIONS 1–69 (Edwards ed. 1945).

pation of American firms in German-controlled cartels—it would have at least compelled an independent United States economic development in these sectors prior to the commencement of war. As it happened, some major United States companies failed to cooperate fully in the war effort, since their leadership was divided in allegiance, and still other companies were hampered in their operations by their earlier reliance upon a cartel.

The failure to use law as an anticartel weapon was as much a deficiency of national defense as was either the corresponding refusal to build enough bombers or the lack of adequate defenses against attack at Pearl Harbor. Post-World War II antitrust regulation may suggest to some observers that the lesson has been learned too well. If this is true, it may only indicate a failure to distinguish between the response to a *contending* public order system, such as that of Nazi Germany, and to *diverse* public order systems, such as those of Western Europe, which allow more cooperation among competitors than we do. Thus, the recent antitrust cases seek to impose the American policy upon largely compatible public order systems in a way that may unnecessarily strain the structure of reciprocity which has been said to underlie any mutually satisfactory delimitation of international legal competence. But perhaps such an appraisal of this aspect of the reasonableness of the jurisdictional claim is not part of the *judicial,* as distinguished from the executive or legislative, province. However, it is hard to avoid the relevance of such an appraisal at least at the stage when a court is called upon to provide a remedy. Here again, though, the prayer for relief prepared by government attorneys could be taken to imply a prior executive decision in favor of asserting legal authority in the disputed manner. This is a matter of internal distribution of function which will be discussed shortly.

Clearly, it is always important to understand the connections between legal controversy and public order conflict. Once again, it is necessary to gain focus. There are many gradations of conflict short of contending for the universal acceptance of one's public order system. Each gradation has its appropriate bearing upon the delimitation of legal competence. Consider, for example, the relations between capital-importing and capital-exporting states. There may be many incompatible interests, but the underlying premise of the relationship ordinarily includes a considerable respect for the autonomy of the internal public order systems. Accordingly, jurisdictional endeavors should tend to be moderative. There should ordinarily be a compromise between incompatible expectations so as to promote an optimum quality of stability. Jurisdiction here operates as a balancing process and not as an instrument of war, as it might have been if it had been used as an anticartel weapon. An interesting illustration of this is provided by the relations between the United States and Latin America. Despite a history of strong influence, the United States has not often undermined the basic autonomy of the Latin American public order systems. The inherent conflict of interests between an investor state and an underdeveloped state has often been formulatd as a dispute over the proper limits of legal competence. The United States has defended its position by seeking to emphasize the importance and validity of state responsibility for injuries to aliens and for rights to accord diplomatic protection. Latin American jurists, with considerable ingenuity, have countered with various formulations of principles of nonintervention that, in recent multilateral agreements, have been increasingly accepted by the United States. The concept of nonintervention is essentially jurisdictional in character, since it is concerned with the allocation of legal competence between the territorial state and the intervening state.

In contrast, the Soviet intervention in Hungary and the United States intervention in Guatemala were both, again to varying degrees, evidently premised upon the desirability of imposing a particular system of public order in an apparent disregard of existing internal sentiment. Perhaps there is a profound new development disclosed by these incidents. If an independent state attempts to establish a public order system that poses a threat to the security of a different concept of public order that prevails in the region, then it loses some of its traditional claim to autonomy. That is, it may be a condition of current international equilibrium that the world community consists of contending regional systems of public order that are, in turn, themselves each composed of homogeneous public order systems.[8] This produces a kind of fragmented world federalism in which states join more or less together in regional groupings.

---

[8] For an excellent discussion of the philosophical basis of the relationship between internal public order systems and international stability, see LOEWEN-STEIN, POLITICAL RECONSTRUCTION (1946).

Only thus can one reconcile the explicit prohibitions against intervention in inter-American treaties with the Caracas Resolution of the Tenth Inter-American Conference of 1954, which seems to authorize any degree of interference necessary to prevent the emergence in the Western Hemisphere of a Communist-oriented public order system.

Within a region, incompatible legal claims that do not pose a threat to the fundamental way of life of any of the states present a different kind of problem. For instance, although the conflict in the Atlantic community, centering upon the application of the United States antitrust laws to foreign acts and actors, involves an important difference in attitude toward the proper degree of state regulation of large-scale business activity, it does not seriously threaten the integrity of the affected public order systems. There is a general respect for the diversity of approach, despite some accusations that the United States is seeking to export its competitive standards to other states not eager to accept them. The central difficulty really seems to stem from the nature of the situation itself. It is the interdependence of the subject matter, rather than the public order conflict, that makes it almost impossible to allocate jurisdictional competence in a mutually acceptable way. That is, it is quite impossible to regulate the internal economy in the desired way without reaching out to control the events that have an important impact upon it. An agreement in Switzerland among foreign producers to place a quota upon exports of a certain product to the United States has the obvious consequence of restricting the supply of the commodity in the American market and thereby producing a noncompetitive price; this is especially true if the leading American producers participate in the arrangement and agree, tacitly or explicitly in exchange, to restrict their exports to foreign markets. It is not possible to achieve competitive standards in the United States without imposing them elsewhere, but it is also not possible to tolerate the control of competition in Switzerland without also tolerating the introduction of noncompetitive elements into other economies. This creates a serious jurisdictional problem. There are contradictory preferences—regulation and *laissez faire* in a context of interdependence. Does this require one set of public order preferences to prevail and the other to give way? Or is it possible to achieve an adjustment that preserves the essential quality of each by compromising the areas of incompatible overlap? Can such a compromise be achieved by a traditional reliance upon the conflict-of-laws approach, or is it necessary to formalize an adjustment either by a negotiated agreement between relevant states or by the establishment of a supranational agency of control?

What does seem to emerge, then, is a basic distinction between adjustable and irreconcilable conflicts in the two major order systems. It is only the irreconcilable conflict that seriously threatens the public order system to which one owes allegiance. Here, a sophisticated defense of one's way of life may require an extension of legal control on a partisan basis. The adjustable conflict, on the other hand, calls for a compromise of the incompatibility in a mutually satisfactory way.

A method must be developed to enable this distinction to be taken into account. One aspect of this method concerns the internal distribution of functions. In this regard, the celebrated *Pink* case is most interesting.[9] It establishes, in the context of the then recent recognition of the Soviet Union, that the relations between public order systems may take precedence over what would otherwise be the ordinary legal disposition and, furthermore, that judicial decision-makers should give deference to the policy of the executive decision-maker where matters of recognition are concerned. Recent cases, as one might have predicted, have extended the method of *Pink* to the nonrecognition situation in which the existence of a struggle with another public order system is given external prominence.[10] Thus, the proper limits of legal competence (which is jur-

---

[9] United States v. Pink, 315 U.S. 203 (1942). This case was initiated by the United States government to recover assets allegedly conveyed to it by the Litvinov Assignment. The validity of this claim depended upon a prior judgment that these assets could be reached by a Soviet confiscatory decree.

The Litvinov Assignment represented a bilateral effort to satisfy claimants in the United States who had been victims of Soviet economic policies and thereby to assure domestic backing for the simultaneous decision to accord diplomatic recognition (after sixteen years of nonrecognition) to the Soviet government. The majority of the Supreme Court felt that the executive policy underlying recognition and entering into the Litvinov Assignment must be given precedence in a judicial context over the normal rule of conflict of laws denying validity to foreign acts that confiscate property located in the forum state. This process of subordinating the normal judicial outcome to the vagaries of executive policy (as judicially construed) makes this case of capital importance for the argument of this book.

[10] See, *e.g.*, Latvian State Cargo & Passenger S.S. Line v. McGrath, 188 F.2d 1000 (D.C. Cir. 1951), and cases cited at 1004 n. 13.

isdiction in my sense), at least in the area of recognition and non-recognition, are made to reflect current executive thinking as to the relevance of diverse systems of public order. The various phases of the *Bernstein* case might be read to introduce the same method of deference into the acts of state context.[11] There is a strong basis to oppose this *Pink* method of introducing legal effect into private litigation in order to take account of a conflict between public order systems. It often arbitrarily makes victims of individuals and their property. Why should a good-faith foreign purchaser of goods from Communist China be made to bear the burden of the United States policy of nonrecognition? In other words, the security of private expectations may often be a far more important consideration than any gain won by treating a routine legal controversy as an arena of conflict between contending systems of public order. A sufficient mutual benefit may be derived from stabilizing interactions between contending systems so as to justify excluding the fact of contention from most legal contexts. This seems to be true of Soviet-American commercial relations in which decision-makers on each side now appear to make an effort to be fair to the claims of "the enemy" public order system.[12]

This underscores the importance of identifying in each particular situation the connection, if any, between the legal delimitation of authority by the decision-maker and the underlying contention between public order systems. Perhaps, from an internal perspective, the *Pink* method provides part of a comprehensive answer. That is, the contention of public order systems is as relevant as the

---

[11] Bernstein v. Van Heyghen Frères Société Anonyme, 163 F.2d 246 (2d Cir.), *cert.* 332 U.S. 772 (1947); Bernstein v. N.V. Nederlandsche-Amerikaansche Stoomvaart-Maatschappij, *denied,* 173 F.2d 71 (2d Cir. 1949); Bernstein v. N.V. Nederlandsche-Amerikaansche Stoomvaart-Maatschappij, 210 F.2d 375 (2d Cir. 1954). For in the course of the Bernstein litigation, the judiciary acted to suspend the normal operation of the act of state doctrine only after it had received formal executive permission. It is the contention of this book that the judiciary should rely upon its own criteria to suspend the act of state doctrine and that these criteria should be based upon the character of the subject matter. In particular, a central distinction should be introduced to separate those matters upon which a universal consensus exists from those upon which major national systems have incompatible viewpoints. This distinction is developed in detail in Chapter V.

[12] For a very able and balanced presentation of the Soviet perspective, emphasizing the fairness accorded to non-Soviet claims, see Pisar, *Soviet Conflict of Laws in International Commercial Transactions,* 70 HARV. L. REV. 593 (1957).

executive explicitly sees fit, but not more so. Thus, one does not often burden the judicial decision-maker with the duty of evaluating the impact of a decision upon the contending public order system.

However, the *Pink* method *shifts* rather than *answers* the basic question. It confers upon the executive decision-maker the primary responsibility for determining the jurisdictional relevance of contending public order systems. Judicial decision-makers ignore the underlying contention until they are instructed to do otherwise. An interesting, well-known illustration of such a procedure is in the Tate letter, which indirectly recommends that courts adopt a restrictive theory of sovereign immunity.[13] This action no doubt reflected to some extent the felt need to have equality of legal regulation in relations between public order systems possessing different degrees of state participation in economic activity.

My conclusions are highly tentative. One thing is obvious: jurisdictional situations are not necessarily neutral arenas unaffected by the struggle between contending systems of public order. It is also clear that no general answer exists about the degree to which decision-makers should take account of the contending systems when delimiting legal competence. The specific answer depends to some extent upon the exact quality of relations at the moment between the legal systems. In this regard, one can contrast the relative stability that now seems to characterize Soviet-American legal interactions with the much greater instability of Chinese Communist-American interactions. Although the same underlying struggle of contending systems exists, the delimitation of legal competence in relation to China is made to reflect the contention to a far greater degree by giving maximum effect to the executive policy underlying nonrecognition of the Communist regime. Thus even between similarly contending systems, a basic choice exists. Shall the contention be overlooked, or shall it be reflected in various legal contexts? The answer is not simple because of the pervasive implications of reciprocity. Travel restrictions for American diplomats in the Soviet Union lead to travel restrictions for Soviet diplomats in the United States. Contrariwise, fairness to American commercial interests in

---

[13] The Tate Letter was published as *Changed Policy Concerning the Granting of Sovereign Immunity to Foreign Governments,* 26 DEP'T STATE BULL. 984 (1952); the general subject of restrictive immunity is discussed throughout Chapter VII.

the Soviet Union leads to fairness to Soviet commercial interests in the United States.

What seems crucial beyond dispute is the need to become *aware* of the precise impact of contending systems upon alternative delimitations of legal authority. This is imperative so that one may be in a position, should it become necessary, to defend one's public order system against threats to its survival, as was the case in regard to the almost unmolested Nazi control of many cartels. The presence of contending systems of public order in today's world community requires us to entreat the goddess of jurisdiction to remove her blindfold.[14]

[14] This point is made most persuasively in connection with a discussion of the law of war. See McDougal & Feliciano, *International Coercion and World Public Order: The General Principles of the Law of War*, 67 YALE L. J. 771, 822 n. 160 (1958).

Chapter V

Toward a Theory of the Participation of Domestic Courts in the World Legal Order: A Critique of *Banco Nacional de Cuba v. Sabbatino*

How should a domestic court in the United States treat transfers of property that arise from the expropriation decrees of foreign nations? Is an American court obliged to give respect to the governmental acts of Castro's Cuba if they violate either our public policy or the applicable substantive norms of international law? Such questions arise directly from the programs of socialization undertaken by radical governments throughout the world. The Cuban confiscations of American property, in an atmosphere inflamed by the Cold War, vividly present these questions to American courts. The problems justify a consideration of Judge Dimock's District Court opinion in *Banco Nacional de Cuba v. Sabbatino*.[1]

Chapter VI will consider the further development of the *Sabbatino* case in the case in the Court of Appeals. The *Sabbatino* litigation is examined in detail because its various phases deal crucially with the issues surrounding the optimum participation of domestic courts in the international legal order. It provides a concrete set of legal developments that serve as a setting for an argument in favor of a theory. With this consideration in mind, the substantive controversy is of subordinate interest, as is the fact that the litigation has not yet been finalized by a decision of the United States Supreme Court. If it is remembered that the litigation is a scaffolding for a theory, then the eventual outcome of the litigation is not very important. However, it will be most interesting to discover the extent to which the Supreme Court discloses a sensitivity to the issues raised in this and in the succeeding chapter.

This chapter explores the role of domestic courts in the political environment within which international law exists today. The primary objective is to develop a series of ideas that form the basis for

[1] 193 F. Supp. 375 (S.D.N.Y. 1961) [hereinafter referred to as *Sabbatino*]; the subsequent development of the case is considered in Chapter VI.

64

a theory about the proper response of a domestic court to a litigation involving a legal policy that has been officially adopted by a foreign state. A domestic court, it is contended, should respond to the distinctive demands of a decentralized legal system when it applies international law.[2] For an American court today, these demands are conditioned by the dominating factors of the Cold War, nuclear weapons, and socialism. Thus it is necessary to depict the over-all political atmosphere that accompanies the effort of a domestic court to discharge its functions in a given case, such as *Sabbatino*. This accounts for the extensiveness of the ensuing introductory discussion.

Let us begin by observing that the decentralized quality of international law places a special burden upon all legal institutions at the national level. Domestic courts are agents of a developing international legal order, as well as servants of various national interests; this double role helps to overcome the institutional deficiencies on a supranational level.[3] It is readily appreciated that domestic courts have a responsibility to improve the quality of international legal stability when reference is made to the transactions across boundaries within the Western bloc. But, suppose the transaction in-

[2] The "decentralized" character of the international order refers to the concentration of power and authority, and *hence* responsibility, on the national level. The peculiar quality of the current pattern of decentralization is created by the focus of world power in the Soviet Union and the United States; this latter concentration is commonly referred to as "bipolarity." In contrast, the domestic order is relatively "centralized"; that is, legal norms are applied by effective central institutions upon the units subject to the norms. International law, as a horizontal decentralized order, depends largely upon the self-restraint of the units or upon one unit applying norms to the behavior of other units in the system. States remain the dominant unit in the international order, although other increasingly important units include the United Nations, regional organizations, private associations, and individuals. The notion of horizontality, then, is a crude first approximation of the structural quality of contemporary international law. See Chapter III.

[3] The most evident shortcomings of supranational judicial review are: (1) the denial of access to individual litigants, since generally only states may participate; (2) the small scope of compulsory jurisdiction; (3) the weakness of enforcement procedures—as there is no supranational equivalent to the sheriff or marshal (see Schachter, *The Enforcement of International Judicial and Arbitral Decisions*, 54 AM. J. INT'L L. 1 (1960) for a survey of existing techniques); and (4) the slowness and uncertainty of the supranational remedy where it is available; a state has discretion to refuse to pursue relief on behalf of its nationals.

volves a conflict of values between the two social orders contending for dominance in the Cold War. How, then, does a domestic court strike a balance between international legal order and national interest? In the background of the Cold War is the threat of nuclear war. This gives us every incentive to find tension-dissolving techniques at the margins of the political conflict. Also in the background is the worldwide tendency of the newly independent states to foster rapid economic development by acquiring coordinated control of internal capital resources. This generates a strong pressure for the governments of those countries where aliens own extensive property to expropriate property and to defer compensation as long as possible. External political alignment depends at least partly upon support for such programs of radical change. This reverts once more to the Cold War, of which a major aspect is competition for influence in the newly developing states. Finally, the role of domestic courts relates to the increasing participation in world affairs of nations with diverse normative traditions. It is generally acknowledged that international law—as a dynamic system—suffers from its historical attachment to European culture. If law is to bring increasing stability to international relations, then it must progressively liberate itself from its somewhat provincial past. This requires a respect for diversity more than an agreement upon universal standards.[4] It suggests the significance of self-restraining allocations of jurisdictional competence on a national level and returns us to the supranational responsibilities of domestic courts.

We turn now to examine the influence of the Cold War upon the international legal system. This influence relates to an adequate analysis of *Sabbatino* and accounts for the derived generalities about the participation of domestic courts in the struggle to improve the quality of international law.

----

[4] No genuine legal foundation for a universal order presently exists. See McDougal & Lasswell, *The Identification and Appraisal of Diverse Systems of Public Order,* in STUDIES IN WORLD PUBLIC ORDER 3–10 (McDougal ed. 1960); Falk & Mendlovitz, *Some Criticisms of C. Wilfred Jenks' Approach to International Law,* 14 RUTGERS L. REV. 1, 4–16 (1959); see also the suggestive study by BOZEMAN, POLITICS AND CULTURE IN INTERNATIONAL HISTORY (1960).

NUCLEAR WEAPONS, THE COLD WAR, AND SOCIALISM

The nuclear stalemate conditions the growth of international law. The contending blocs in the Cold War continue to be wary of taking big steps to reduce the stakes in the power struggle for world domination. This hesitation appears to be rational. At present, the Soviet Union and the United States each possess sufficient counterstrike capacity to make recourse to direct aggression unlikely. Even a fulfilled surprise attack would probably lead to the devastation of the attacking nation. At the same time, the implementation of major arms reduction schemes, especially during transitional periods, creates the possibility of successfully using nuclear weapons to compel surrender without incurring a substantial risk of retaliation. Responsible statesmen seem reluctant to exchange the dreadful stability of nuclear deterrence for the fearful instability of a progressively denuclearized world. Arms reduction, then, does not appear feasible so long as tension and mistrust prevail.

Actually, the military hazard is even graver than the threats of nuclear devastation suggest, if a worse extreme is imaginable; for even the control of nuclear weapons would leave us with an unhinderable capacity to wage radiological, bacteriological, and chemical warfare. Such a condition especially evokes fright if one recalls the frequency with which history has been made by the irrational hostility of self-destructive men.[5] It would seem that nothing short of evolutionary change that heavily favors altruistic sentiment could rescue us from this position of continuing peril.[6]

In the meantime, mankind survives beneath this live volcano. Eruption is unpredictable and dependent upon factors that evade rational control by the nuclear nations, for war by accident, by catalytic agency, or by escalation is a significant possiblity in the years ahead. With the spread of nuclear capacities to secondary

[5] See the remarkable letter by SIGMUND FREUD on the relations between human personality and war, reprinted in WHY WAR? A CORRESPONDENCE BETWEEN ALBERT EINSTEIN AND SIGMUND FREUD 8 (Gilbert transl. 1939); for an anthropological account see ARDREY, AFRICAN GENESIS (1961).

[6] Some authors do see some prospect for a basic revision in human disposition and, consequently, in social institutions and international relations: AUROBINDO, THE IDEAL OF HUMAN UNITY (1950); DOBZHANSKY, THE BIOLOGICAL BASIS OF HUMAN FREEDOM (1956); KAHLER, THE TOWER AND THE ABYSS (1957); TEILHARD, THE PHENOMENON OF MAN (Wall transl. 1959).

nations and with the development of improved detection and delivery systems, a nuclear war becomes a definite probability, even a
virtual certainty, unless other basic variables in the international
situation shift to a support of peace. At present, human civilization
seems entrapped between the intersecting lines of technological advance in the science of Hot War and the intensity of political rivalry
in the Cold War.

Attitudes of resignation and signs of extremism are evident on
the popular level, but the prevailing public mood is one of vague
concern except in periods of national crisis. Policy planners treat the
fragile nuclear balance as a fixed coordinate in international relations. Their energy centers upon an ever enlarging explication of the
strategic permutations likely to arise within the existing framework.[7]
Meanwhile, we seem content to allow the military context to become
the ultimate human context. Such quietism is absurdly unrespon-
sive to the challenge.

The Cold War assumes an almost hopelessly rigid posture. Nevertheless, it is imperative to seek ways to overcome the present political situation. We must not neglect the few existing opportunities
for denuclearizing the Cold War. Such achievement presupposes the
emergence of minimum trust in international relations.[8] Yet the
presence of trust is a mystery; trust cannot be induced by mechanical means. Respect must precede trust. Manifestations of mutual
respect by rivals in the Cold War could help express a serious decision to achieve reliable techniques to protect mankind against the
ravages of war. International law presents nations with institutions,
processes, and norms that permit respect to be manifested in rela-

---

[7] There are significant exceptions: CLARK & SOHN, WORLD PEACE THROUGH
WORLD LAW (2d rev. ed. 1960); FROMM, MAY MAN PREVAIL? (1961); JASPERS,
THE FUTURE OF MANKIND (Ashton transl. 1961); RAMSEY, WAR AND CHRIS-
TIAN CONSCIENCE (1961); RAPOPORT, FIGHTS, GAMES AND DEBATES (1960);
Hughes, *The Strategy of Deterrence*, 31 COMMENTARY 185–92 (1961); and
see readings contained in LEGAL AND POLITICAL PROBLEMS OF WORLD ORDER
(Mendlovitz ed., Temp. ed. 1962).

[8] There are formidable obstacles. Among the realistic studies of the growth
of political order in the international domain, see NIEBUHR, THE STRUCTURE
OF NATIONS AND EMPIRES (1959); DEUTCH, POLITICAL COMMUNITY AT THE
INTERNATIONAL LEVEL (1954); THE WORLD COMMUNITY (Q. Wright ed. 1948);
SCHIFFER, THE LEGAL COMMUNITY OF MANKIND (1954); CARLSTON, LAW
AND STRUCTURES OF SOCIAL ACTION 85–189 (1956); WEST, CONSCIENCE AND
SOCIETY (1945).

tively depoliticized atmospheres. As such, it is a valuable, although surprisingly unexplored, instrument available to those eager to rescue the world from the nuclear trap.

This is not a ground for optimism. The Socialist bloc is most reluctant to rely on supranational institutions for Cold War accommodations. In addition, the Soviet Union uses international law in an opportunistic fashion.[9] However, the Soviet attitude toward international law has grown less explicitly hostile,[10] and there are broad areas of effective legal coordination between the rival blocs in the Cold War.[11] Thus, given the urgent need for greater international stability and given the absence of acceptable alternatives, it seems essential that the United States manifest maximum respect for the restraining claims of international law.

In fact, however, the recent American foreign policy displays a trend away from using law as a creative force in the struggle to establish trust. Intervention in Cuba, the U-2 incident, and the retention of the Connally Amendment are spectacular manifestations of this reluctance to confine national interest to the limits set by international law.[12] Such a pattern of action contrasts with the pleas of

[9] This point hardly requires documentation for an American audience. For succinct characterization, see LIPSON, OUTER SPACE AND INTERNATIONAL LAW, Rand Paper, P-1434, pp. 12–17, (1958); Triska and Slusser, *Treaties and Other Sources of Order in International Relations: The Soviet View*, 52 AM. J. INT'L L. 699 (1958). Perhaps these statements overclarify Soviet opportunism.

[10] See, *e.g.*, Tunkin, *Co-Existence and International Law*, 95 RECUEIL DES COURS, 5 (1958).

[11] For excellent evaluations of Soviet efforts to establish legal stability in international commercial transactions, see Pisar, *Soviet Conflict of Law in International Transactions*, 70 HARV. L. REV. 593 (1957); Pisar, *The Communist System of Foreign-Trade Adjudication*, 72 HARV. L. REV. (1959). These Pisar studies suggest the capacity of the Soviet Union to use legal technique to achieve ordered relations with other states. National advantages are sought, but not to an extent that interferes with the overriding desire to establish a quality of legal order that satisfies the minimum expectations of other states. It is evident that the Russians have the flexibility to overcome their doctrinaire suspicion of international law when it suits their interest to do so. One should remain wary of facile or cynical accounts of the Soviet attitude toward the international legal system. This is true despite a continuing Soviet willingness to manipulate legal abstractions like "sovereignty" and "self-determination" in a highly political manner.

[12] Wright, *Intervention and Cuba in 1961*, 55 ASIL PROCEEDINGS 2 (1961) (and see the excellent series of articles by Professor Wright cited in footnote 1); Falk, *American Intervention in Cuba and the Rule of Law*, 22 OHIO ST. L. J. 546 (1961); Falk, *Space Espionage and World Order: A Consideration of the*

our statesmen to substitute the rule of law for the rule of force. These pleas are based upon a perception that the choice is between decentralized recourses to force and mutual adherence to legal standards as implemented by progressively stronger centralized sanctions.[13] This is not merely a rhetorical invocation of an aspirational ideal; however difficult it may be to translate the validity of the perception into the operational planning of the Cold War. The guidance of international lawyers seems necessary for the formation of national policy, since survival and national interest may depend upon restraint as often as coercive action. This truth applies especially to the liberal democracies that base foreign policy upon popular support. The need to justify international conduct to domestic critics leads to ineffective lawbreaking by Western nations. Consider the Suez campaign or the American sponsorship of the Cuban exiles in April, 1961. Even a Machiavellian perspective suggests that the United States should view seriously the applicable legal norms when it acts in international affairs. Such prudence should extend also to the assertion of unilateral claims that provoke protest from other nations acting individually or in the United Nations.[14]

The decentralized character of the international legal system requires that powerful states restrain their conduct to reasonable limits, even when no prohibitive legal rule exists. This is one of the most shocking aspects of the 1961 Soviet nuclear test series that included atmospheric blasts of thirty and fifty-seven megatons.[15] The

---

Samos-Midas Program, in ESSAYS ON ESPIONAGE AND INTERNATIONAL LAW 45–82 (Stanger ed. 1962); see also Lewy, *Superior Orders, Nuclear Warfare, and the Dictates of Conscience,* 55 AM. POL. SCI. REV. 3 (1961).

[13] Such an either/or formulation is a crude approximation of the choice that faces mankind today. For representative pleas by United States leaders, see *Special Committee on World Peace through Law,* COMPILATION OF QUOTATIONS, A.B.A. (1960); Nixon, *World Peace through World Law,* address given to the Academy of Political Science on April 13, 1959, reprinted in NUCLEAR WEAPONS, MISSILES, AND FUTURE WAR: PROBLEM FOR THE SIXTIES 217 (McClelland ed. 1960).

[14] Such an observation seems to have illustrative bearing upon the claims of nuclear powers to test and use their weapons in the face of overwhelming opposition, as expressed by resolutions in the United Nations. See, *e.g.,* N.Y. Times, Nov. 15, 1961, p. 1.

[15] For a nontechnical appraisal of the contamination of the atmosphere that resulted from the 1961 Soviet test series, see Deakin, *Poison in the Air,* NEW REPUBLIC, Nov. 6, 1961, p. 10; see also *Fallout from Iodine–131,* SSRS NEWSLETTER, No. 111, Nov. 1961. For an evaluation of the legality of nuclear weapons

Soviet unilateral claim invites a reciprocal United States unilateral claim; this is the basic mode of international legal order. Even without this authorization, however, the United States should not act without due regard for the overwhelming appeal from the United Nations to forgo further atmospheric testing.[16] If we are committed to the growth of international order through the development of the United Nations, then we must also respect its action when it conflicts with American foreign policy. Otherwise, the opportunism of our own commitment to international law undermines the attempt to increase the relevance of law to contemporary world affairs.[17]

This chapter brings these considerations to bear upon a fairly technical problem: how should domestic courts approach legal issues that arise from the Cold War? The answer argues for a partial separation of the Cold War from international law for the purpose of improving the institutional resources of the international legal system. Specifically, domestic courts are urged to work out formal rules that will accord respect to rival social systems that act within their own sphere of competence. In this struggle today, domestic courts have the distinctive role of creating trust through manifestations of respect,[18] for they enjoy an independence of the executive and legislative branches of government, especially in a democratic government. This separation encourages a resolution of conflict in a relatively depoliticized setting. It enhances the ordering and justice-fulfilling contribution of courts to solutions of domestic conflicts.[19] Unfortunately, judicial deference to national policy in international

---

that places emphasis upon the analogy to poison gas, see SINGH, NUCLEAR WEAPONS AND INTERNATIONAL LAW (1959).

[16] The Soviet testing legitimates an equivalent testing by the United States vis-à-vis the Soviet Union. But fallout constitutes a universal hazard. Therefore, *all* nations have reasonable grounds to resist *any* particular claim to test nuclear weapons. Fallout is an ultimate illustration of contemporary interdependence. Wide adherence to the Limited Test Ban Treaty formally expresses the concern of the nonnuclear states.

[17] Bertrand Russell offers an incisive condemnation of both the United States and the Soviet Union on this ground: Russell, *Thoughts on the 50-Megaton Bomb,* NEW STATESMAN, Nov. 3, 1961, p. 638.

[18] For a preliminary statement of a general approach, see Falk, *Jurisdiction, Immunities, and Act of State: Suggestions for a Modified Approach* 1–20, in ESSAYS ON INTERNATIONAL JURISDICTION (Falk ed. 1961).

[19] It is useful to compare, in this respect, the unanimous decision of the United States Supreme Court in the segregation cases with the incapacity of Congress to act.

affairs has tended to impair the objectivity of legal decisions in the area of international law.[20] It is important to demonstrate that domestic courts must act as agents of the international order, as well as constituent institutions of the national order.[21] The welfare of the world community and the promotion of national interest are both relevant to the optimum discharge of this function by domestic courts.

Such apparently marginal legal activity pertains to the role of law in our thermonuclear age,[22] for domestic courts can demonstrate that a basis for trust really does exist by settling legal controversies in a manner that protects the autonomy of opposed social and political systems.[23] Briefly, the position is this: in general, municipal courts should avoid interference in the domestic affairs of other states when the subject matter of disputes illustrates a legitimate diversity of values on the part of two national societies. In contrast, if the diversity can be said to be illegitimate, as when it exhibits an abuse of universal human rights,[24] then domestic courts fulfill their role by refusing to further the policy of the foreign legal system. In instances of illegitimate diversity, where a genuine universal sentiment exists, then the domestic courts properly act as agents of international order only if they give maximum effect to such universality.

It is postulated here that the existence of capitalist and socialist national societies is an instance of legitimate diversity in the world

---

[20] KAPLAN & KATZENBACH conclude that "rather than playing important creative roles in determining common international standards, national courts have more and more become apologists for national policies determined by political aims of government." THE POLITICAL FOUNDATIONS OF INTERNATIONAL LAW 270 (1961).

[21] SCELLE, PRÉCIS DE DROIT DES GENS I, 43, and II, 10, 21, 51 (1932–34) develops this fully with his notion of *dédoublement fonctionnel*. See also Scelle, *Règles générales du droit de la paix,* 46 RECUEIL DES COURS, 327–703 (1933).

[22] For a perceptive study of the growth of international law by reference to marginal conduct, see CORBETT, LAW AND SOCIETY IN THE RELATIONS OF STATES (1951).

[23] But there are limits: see Fuller, *Adjudication and the Rule of Law,* 54 ASIL PROCEEDINGS 1 (1960). *Cf.* generally LARSON, WHEN NATIONS DISAGREE (1961).

[24] But there is, of course, widespread disagreement with my characterization of the differences between current rival social systems as "legitimate." See, *e.g.,* Dietze, *The Disregard for Property in International Law,* 56 Nw. U. L. REV. 87 (1961).

community. Domestic courts, accordingly, should approach any legal controversy emerging out of this diversity with tolerance and respect, developing principles of self-restraint and justifying interferences with foreign economic policy by reference to variables such as extraterritoriality rather than to differences implicit in the contrasting status of property in the two societies.

The Eichmann trial provides an instance in which a domestic court appropriately reaches out to nullify the governmental policy of a foreign state arising from an illegitimate diversity of official policy.[25] The illegitimacy of the German extermination of the Jews was formally acknowledged on a supranational level. The Principles of the Nuremberg Judgment received unanimous endorsement, and various United Nations votes revealed a universal sentiment to bring Axis war criminals to justice.[26] Although a domestic court in Israel was not the ideal forum for the Eichmann trial, it seems clear that such a domestic court acts on behalf of the world community, as well as in the interests of the national social order.[27] The supranational

[25] For legal discussion of the technical problems in the Eichmann trial, see Cardozo, *When Extradition Fails, Is Abduction the Solution?*, 55 AM. J. INT'L L. 127 (1961); Silving, *In re Eichmann: A Dilemma of Law and Morality*, 55 AM. J. INT'L L. 307 (1961); Baade, *The Eichmann Trial: Some Legal Aspects*, 1961 DUKE L. J. 400.

[26] *Cf. Principles of International Law Recognized in the Charter of the Nürnberg Tribunal and in the Judgment of the Tribunal* as formulated by the International Law Commission, 1950, U.N. GEN. ASS. OFF. REC. V, Supp. 12 (A/1316), pp. 11–14; *Draft Code of Offenses Against the Peace and Security of Mankind*, U.N. GEN. ASS. OFF. REC. IX, Supp. 9 (A/2693), pp. 11–12.

[27] There are reasons to criticize the Eichmann trial: a hostile atmosphere that required a bullet-proof cage to protect the defendant and a limited access to defense witnesses are conditions that fall short of the normal situation for a fair trial; the failure of Israel to give the United Nations a *first* chance (of perhaps six months) to organize a trial before an *ad hoc* supranational tribunal; and the untested assumption that a grant of wide publicity of Nazi atrocities will deter rather than stimulate repetition. However, despite such genuine reservations, Israel's assertion of universal standards in the Eichmann trial seems to contribute to the growth of decentralized responsibility for the application of centralized (or supranational) norms. Technically, of course, Israel's claims against Eichmann rested upon national legislation empowering prosecution and judgment. But national norms depend for validation on their participation in the international legal order. In this respect, at least, Kelsen is helpful when he analyzes the link between a domestic legal order and the international legal order. KELSEN, PRINCIPLES OF INTERNATIONAL LAW 207–99 (1952). For an extralegal assessment of the Eichmann trial, see Bundy, *On Misunderstanding Eichmann*, 98 ENCOUNTER 132 (1961).

role of a domestic court would be clearer in the Eichmann case if any nation other than Israel (or Germany) had been the scene of the trial. Nevertheless, Eichmann and expropriation are useful paradigmatic instances of apt responses for domestic courts acting as agents of a developing international legal system.

It should also be noted that domestic courts have a different functional relation to world order than do supranational courts.[28] The location of domestic courts within the national system makes it desirable to curtail their consideration of the hostile substantive policy of another unit in areas of legitimate diversity. In order to guard against provincialism, domestic courts should be deprived of competence over such a case by the use of quasi-jurisdictional doctrines like act of state.[29] In a supranational forum, such as the International Court of Justice, competence to accord substantive review exists. However, national diversity should lead such a forum to avoid an obsolescent application of international standards that expresses an older, but now nonexistent, consensus. In other words, the vertical development of international law depends on the maximum accommodation of the diverse politics of national and regional units. An international court would be in a position to forge compromise standards in areas of legitimate diversity. For example, a state might be given considerable discretion to expropriate property for social reforms if it did so without discrimination. The scope of legitimate diversity would be confined to the taking of property on the nondiscriminatory basis of furthering a socioeconomic program. Failure to restrict the taking of property to this scope would make the taking illegitimate and violative of substantive norms of international law. A

---

[28] This observation depends somewhat on the composition of a supranational tribunal. For example, the contrast between a mixed arbitral commission and a domestic court is less great, in this respect, than between a domestic court and the International Court of Justice. But even in the ICJ, the rule allowing a litigant to appoint a national judge (if there is not one already sitting in the court) indicates a pervasive relevance of nationality to international adjudication. For a rough comparison of functional roles on domestic and supranational levels, see tables in this chapter.

[29] Jurisdiction is here used to refer to "competence" in its broadest sense; that is, it concerns any delimitation of the forum's authority to govern controversy by its legal policy. An inevitable ambiguity exists, since one way to govern a controversy is by a refusal to apply the usual substantive standards. This is what happens when the act of state doctrine is found relevant. But the basis of this "application" is a concept of the proper limits for forum inquiry, and it is this aspect that we identify as "jurisdictional."

supranational forum would then award appropriate judicial relief to the aggrieved litigant.[30]

The preference for formal deference on the decentralized level is likely to provoke misinterpretation. Many lawyers allege that it is a progressive tendency to encourage substantive review by domestic courts because this tends to increase the application of international norms. Rules of deference—such as act of state—are seen as regressive, for they tend to prevent the use of international substantive norms to settle legal disputes. This is the claim of the American Law Institute Tentative Draft Restatement of Foreign Relations Law.[31] The difficulty with this plausible position is that it overlooks the confusion of substantive norms in the economic area that exists as a result of the widespread emergence of socialism.[32] Domestic courts are not equipped emotionally or technically to cope with this confusion, and tend to invoke norms that correspond with the national preference. *Sabbatino* is itself an illustration of institutionalized bias. Rules of deference are a formal way to confess the untrustworthy quality of a judicial application of substantive norms of international law in areas of legitimate diversity. These comments apply, of course, to the inverse situation vis-à-vis the economic subject matter that confronts domestic courts in socialist states. It is desirable that they self-delimit their competence along similar lines.

[30] There are problems here of judicial technique. A supranational tribunal would usually have a preferable relation to the litigation, especially if its decision-makers included exponents of the rival economic systems. Also, the specialized emphasis of a supranational tribunal upon international litigation would equip it with great technical skill and international judicial experience. Such considerations contribute to increased prospects for rational outcomes on the supranational level.

[31] In order to simplify reference to the District Court opinion, I am retaining references to the Tentative Draft Restatement (except as specifically noted otherwise) rather than converting them into the Proposed Official Draft that became available on May 3, 1962. The Proposed Official Draft retains the language of the Tentative Draft, adding a long paragraph on the relevance of the *Sabbatino* opinion by Judge Dimock in RESTATEMENT, FOREIGN RELATIONS, Explanatory Notes § 43, Reporters' Note § 3, at 142–43 (Proposed Official Draft, 1962). This new note in the RESTATEMENT is especially important because of its comments on the *Ricaud* case; *cf.* analysis here, pp. 129–31.

[32] In this connection, see the unconvincing demonstration of the wide cultural support for traditional property norms in Domke, *Foreign Nationalization*, 55 AM. J. INT'L L. 585 (1961); a more persuasive analytical and functional defense is given by Carlston, *Nationalization: An Analytical Approach*, 54 Nw. U. L. REV. 405, 419–33 (1959).

But suppose, as is probable, that domestic courts in socialist nations consistently apply provincial notions of substantive international law? Should the absence of reciprocity lead to a consequent restatement of the recommended scope of deference in a capitalist domestic court? It would not seem so, although further experiences and analyses are needed for a fully rational decision. States must take some losses in the process of building the foundations for a modern international legal order; temporary setbacks to American economic interests must be balanced against the struggle to bring more stability to world affairs. Second, the use of domestic courts to protect American investor interests is, in any event, a sporadic and ineffective weapon and provides little more than emotional comfort to the American investment community; [33] other more beneficial means exist to improve the quality of investment protection.

This general orientation serves to introduce a study of a recent decision by an American domestic court that was, in essence, a judicial response to hostile expropriation laws. My ensuing criticism of this decision emphasizes its insensitivity to the role of a domestic court in the international legal system. Incidental attention is given to internal failures of judicial craftsmanship manifest in the disposition of the dispute. This is not, however, an attack upon the substantive outcome that could have been acceptable if it had been reached by alternate rationales.

A domestic court located in the United States faces certain distinctive problems when it approaches the subject matter of international law.[34] First, a rather indefinite constitutional and traditional allocation of function and responsibility exists between the executive and the judiciary with respect to foreign affairs. It is necessary, therefore, to look closely at the degree to which executive preference should control the outcome of different kinds of legal controversies that come before our domestic courts. For instance, what influence should an executive policy of nonrecognition have upon a litigation that emphasizes competing claims of two governments to property? Second, the reference to domestic courts in the United States includes both the federal systems and the fifty state judicial systems. It is assumed that identical criteria control the proper judi-

---

[33] Cf. Reeves, *Act of State Doctrine and the Rule of Law*, 54 AM. J. INT'L L. 141 (1960).

[34] See the brilliant analysis of these problems in McDougal, *supra* note 4, at 157–236.

cial approach to the impartial application of international law in both types of courts. Third, there are the relevant, but unconsidered, problems that surround the degree to which federal authority is available to override provincial state applications of international law. This is a significant authority, since state courts tend to be more insular in their perception of relevant responsibilities, relying more readily upon local substantive policy as governing every legal controversy. A cosmopolitan identity must develop, however, if United States courts are to accord respect to the operating principles of socialist societies. In this connection, the development of federal review is very important. These distinctive United States problems, shared somewhat with other federal states, should not be confused with the basic appeal to the domestic courts of all nations to perceive that their duties include fidelity to international law. This fidelity must take direct account of the international system as being horizontal and decentralized.[35]

EXPOSITION

In *Banco Nacional de Cuba v. Sabbatino* the financial agent of the Cuban government commenced an action to recover money for a sugar shipment. The plaintiff Banco Nacional de Cuba (the state-owned bank) claimed ownership of the sugar by virtue of Cuban expropriation. The claim was brought against two defendants: the American purchaser of the sugar (Farr Whitlock) and the New York receiver of the prenationalization Cuban owner of the sugar (Compañía Azucarera Vertientes-Camaguey—C.A.V.).[36] The receiver was appointed by the New York State Supreme Court to look after the New York assets of CAV. Farr Whitlock complied with a court order to turn over the proceeds of the sale to a New York trust company. The Banco Nacional was trying either to get the money paid into court or to recover independently from Farr Whitlock. In February and July, 1960, Farr Whitlock contracted with CAV for the purchase of sugar.[37] The contracts called for the delivery of sugar "at specified prices free alongside steamers." Farr Whitlock agreed

[35] See Chapter III.

[36] The formal vendor of the sugar was a wholly owned subsidiary of CAV, but the opinion treats CAV as the vendor.

[37] Judge Dimock's version of the facts is taken as authoritative for purposes of describing the case.

to supply cargo vessels at a designated Cuban port. Payment by Farr Whitlock was to take place in New York "upon presentation of the necessary shipping documents." On August 6, 1960, a resolution nationalizing CAV was signed by the Cuban President and Prime Minister. This implemented a general nationalization law that was directed against "Cuban enterprises in which United States' physical and corporate persons held a majority interest." [38] Judge Dimock said that the law described itself as "a necessary defensive measure against the recent aggressive acts of the Congress and President of the United States . . . reducing the participation of Cuban sugars in the American sugar market." Farr Whitlock on August 11, 1960, five days after nationalization, signed contracts with the Cuban governmental successor that incorporated the terms of the original contract of sale with CAV. These contracts were made by Farr Whitlock "in order to obtain the necessary consent of the Cuban government to have the loaded vessel depart." [39] The vessel was sent to Casablanca to deliver the sugar to a customer of Farr Whitlock. In New York City, the plaintiff's agent delivered the shipping documents (sight draft and bill of lading) to Farr Whitlock. These documents were accepted by Farr Whitlock, which had received the purchase money of $175,250.69 from its customer. Advised that the CAV receiver claimed the proceeds, Farr Whitlock refused to pay plaintiff's agent and instead turned over the proceeds to the Kings County Trust Company pursuant to a state court order. The money was "to be held by it, subject to the further order of the court and not to be withdrawn except on such order." [40]

The Banco Nacional charged conversion of the bills of lading and of the proceeds of the sugar sale and sought recovery from either Farr Whitlock or the receiver. The plaintiff also asserted the unconstitutionality of the New York state law authorizing receivership and sought relief by injunction and declaratory judgment. Farr Whitlock, in the event that it was liable to pay plaintiff, sought "recovery over from the receiver."

After rejecting several jurisdictional motions not relevant here,

[38] For the text of the nationalization law, see Law 851, OFFICIAL GAZETTE OF CUBA, July 7, 1960; most of the text of the implementing decree is printed in footnote 14 of *Sabbatino, supra* note 1, at 382.

[39] All quotations in text since reference to footnote 36 are from *Sabbatino, supra* note 1, at 376.

[40] *Id.* at 377.

Judge Dimock turned to consider the Banco Nacional's motion for summary judgment against the two defendants. Judge Dimock first disposed of a claim that title to the sugar had already passed to Farr Whitlock when the nationalization decree took effect. In accord with "the law merchant common to civilized countries," the court held that Farr Whitlock could not acquire title to the sugar until payment was made in New York.[41] CAV owned the sugar at the time of nationalization. If the decree was effective, it entitled Banco Nacional to assert a right to the proceeds on behalf of the Cuban Government.

A second defense claim asserted that the nationalization did not affect the sugar, since it was located outside Cuban territory and was awaiting loading at the time that the decree took effect. Judge Dimock ruled, however, that the sugar was loaded onto the vessel in "a well-defined archipelago . . . four to six miles off the Cuban port of Santa Maria" but properly "part of Cuban territory."[42] Therefore, the sugar was within Cuban territory at the time of the decree, and the defense claim that the nationalization decree should be refused an extraterritorial effect was irrelevant. Judge Dimock included a dictum, however, that accepted the idea that, had the sugar been located abroad, then the decree, regardless of its intent, could not be given any effect.[43]

The narrow attacks upon the decree thus failed. It was impossible to exempt the sugar from the decree by showing that title passed

---

[41] *Id.* at 378.

[42] *Id.* at 379.

[43] In passing, it might be observed that a foreign claim to give extraterritorial effect is not, as such, void. Rather, domestic courts feel constrained to disregard an extraterritorial claim that, in addition, violates forum policy. See, *e.g.*, RESTATEMENT, FOREIGN RELATIONS LAW OF THE UNITED STATES § 28(e) (1) (Tent. Draft No. 4, 1960) [hereinafter cited as RESTATEMENT, FOREIGN RELATIONS]; *compare* Vladikabkazsky Ry. v. New York Trust Co., 263 N.Y. 369, 189 N.E. 456 (1934) (extraterritorial decree found violative of forum policy and refused effect), *with* Anderson v. N.V. Transandine Handelmaatschappij, 289 N.Y. 9, 43 N.E. 2d 502 (1942) (extraterritorial decree found consistent with forum policy and given effect). Judge Dimock fails to make this distinction, observing merely that he "could not give effect to the decree if it purported to affect property interests . . . located outside of Cuba at the time the decree took effect." *Sabbatino, supra* note 1, at 379. This is a point of judicial craftsmanship, since later it is true that Judge Dimock finds the decree confiscatory, and presumably violative, of public policy. However, his formulation does contribute a misleading dictum.

to Farr Whitlock prior to the date on which CAV was nationalized
or to use the special rule allowing a domestic court to refuse an
extraterritorial application of an objectionable foreign law. Therefore, the court was forced to evaluate the attack upon the nationalization decree itself. Banco Nacional was said to have no case because
the nationalization decree was unenforceable in a United States
court. The court took up three possible grounds of invalidity. First,
the failure to publish the decree in the *Official Gazette of Cuba,* as
Cuban law required, was alleged as a basis for refusing enforcement.
Judge Dimock, relying on extensive authority, held that this allegation, even if true, was not relevant to his decision to enforce the decree.[44] A foreign law cannot be attacked in an American court on
the ground that it does not comply with formal requisites of validity in its state of origin. Second, the court should refuse enforcement of a foreign law upon its compatibility with the public policy
of the forum. Thus, the nationalization decree would be enforce-
able even if formally defective under Cuban Law or violative of
United States public policy. And third, the refusal to enforce should
result from the substantive invalidity of the Cuban nationalization
decree under applicable norms of international law. The affirmative
response to this allegation is what gives significance to Judge Dimock's decision.

   As a preliminary, it was necessary to determine whether the act
of state doctrine foreclosed inquiry into the validity of the Cuban
decree under international law. Judge Dimock concluded that regardless of whether it is decided that the act of state rule is merely
a matter of self-restraint imposed by American conflict of laws or is
a mandatory rule of international law, there is no requirement that
an American court must give effect to a foreign act of state that violates international law. The act of state doctrine is available only to
assure respect for *foreign territorial acts of state that violate our
public policy without violating international law.*[45] United States
courts are supposedly kept from reviewing foreign acts by recourse

---

[44] *But see* Zander, *The Act of State Doctrine,* 53 AM. J. INT'L L. 826, 845–46
(1959).
[45] That is, act of state shields from review any foreign governmental acts that
conform to substantive norms of international law, but nevertheless violate domestic public policy. It is hard to think of such an instance; Judge Dimock's
opinion refrains from giving an illustration.

to provincial notions of policy, but they retain capacity (and responsibility) [46] to limit a foreign sovereign to the universal standards set by international law.

Judge Dimock also observed that courts in the United States refuse to judge the validity of a foreign act of state so as to avoid embarrassment to the executive branch "in its conduct of foreign relations." Here, however, the executive "delivered a note to the Cuban government declaring the very nationalization law which plaintiff seeks to enforce to be in violation of international law." [47] The opinion contains no statement of the doctrinal or policy basis for judicial deference. Even more surprising, it offers no rationale for the peculiar use of an external note of diplomatic protest for the purpose of discerning the appropriate internal behavior of a domestic court. Why should a domestic court pay any attention whatsoever to a note that passes between states on a diplomatic level? Such a communication seems clearly different from an executive communication to the judiciary written with the objective of influencing the outcome of the particular legal controversy. In fact, the executive did not convey a direct evaluation of the Cuban nationalization measures to the court; evidently, there was neither a request for nor an exercise of executive participation.

Having thus disposed of the inhibitions that might otherwise prevent judicial review, Judge Dimock went on to give affirmative reasons for review in this particular case. The posture of the litigation made the Cuban government the party seeking to invoke the American court to implement its decree. The decision suggests that "it would be almost incomprehensible" for an American court to enforce the decree and extend "to the forum the operation of this international wrong." Here, the court is obviously impressed by the fact that the initiating litigant rested its claim on the nationalization decree and that no intervening sale to a third party of the nationalized property had been made. This makes the Cuban government the beneficiary of any award.[48]

[46] See RESTATEMENT, FOREIGN RELATIONS, Explanatory Notes § 28d, comment *e* and Reporter's Note at 19–22 (Tent. Draft No. 4, 1960).

[47] *Sabbatino, supra* note 1, at 381.

[48] It is relevant to the equities of the dispute that Farr Whitlock renegotiated the contract of sale with the agent for the Cuban government on August 11, 1960, five days after the expropriation took effect. The opinion explains this as an effort of Farr Whitlock "to obtain the necessary consent of the Cuban

More significantly, the decision stresses the obligation of domestic
courts to enforce international law. This results "not only by virtue
of this country's status and membership in the community of nations
but also because international law is a part of the law of the United
States." [49] An American court is evidently obliged to review the validity of the Cuban decree as part of its general duty to apply international law in domestic litigation. Judge Dimock defends this by
saying that "the effective method to promote adherence to the standards imposed by international law is to enforce these standards in
municipal courts, particularly in view of the poverty and inadequacy
of international remedies." Despite the earlier confession that "no
court in this country had passed on the question," the decision, gain-
ing confidence from the momentum of its own analysis, found "the
conclusion . . . inescapable that the decree in the present action is
subject to examination in the light of the principles of international
law." [50]

With this safely established, Judge Dimock at last turned to appraise the substantive validity of the Cuban nationalization decree.
He noted that it was enacted as an explicit retaliation against the
United States decision to reduce Cuban participation in the American sugar market. The reduction of the Cuban quota was officially
explained in the United States as a measure taken to safeguard
American sources of sugar supply rather than to penalize Cuba.[51]
But, as Judge Dimock observes, "the legislative history . . . leaves
no doubt that the basic reason for the legislation was to impose sanctions on a Government which Congress believed to be unfriendly and
to place in the Executive a bargaining tool to obtain a change in the
relations of the Cuban State toward this country." [52] After describing the hostile political background, the decision jumps back to the
status of the decree, referring to the executive determination that

---

government to have the loaded vessel depart" (*id.* at 376), but there are no
grounds given to support this inference. Why should Farr Whitlock care which
claimant receives the proceeds?

[49] *Id.* at 381–82, citing The Paquete Habana, 175 U.S. 677 (1900), and
U.S. CONST., art. 1, § 8, cl. 10.

[50] Both quotations are from *Sabbatino, supra* note 1, at 382.

[51] For texts, see 43 DEP'T OF STATE BULL. 171 (1960); prior relevant protests
against Cuban nationalization measures are in 42 *id.* 158 (1960); 43 *id.* 141
(1960).

[52] *Sabbatino, supra* note 1, at 383–84.

the decree was violative of international law. However, the executive conclusion reenforces an independent judicial determination of invalidity: "The facts and law of the case, irrespective of that determination of the Executive, require the same conclusion by the Judicial [*sic*] with regard to the decree." [53] Thus, it would be incorrect to attribute the result in *Sabbatino* to judicial abdication in the face of executive policy.

Several grounds were relied upon to invalidate the expropriation decree. First, CAV's property was taken to retaliate for the cut in the sugar quota rather than to accomplish a legitimate public purpose. In other words, nationalization of property conforms to international law only if the property is taken in order to fulfill a public purpose of the expropriating government. Judge Dimock noted that "this fact alone is sufficient to render the taking violative of international law." [54] Second, the decree violated international law as it discriminated against United States nationals.[55] The discrimination was called arbitrary since it did not relate to the wrongful conduct of the United States property owners but only reflected the intergovernmental Cuban-American rivalry. In effect, the opinion says that international law forbids governmental retaliations directed against the nationals of another government.

A final ground of invalidity rested upon the failure of the decree to provide adequate compensation for the nationalized property. The opinion reviews the compensation provision in the law pursuant to which the decree was rendered, concluding that the terms of interest and amortization are below the minimum international legal requirement.[56] Thus, this domestic court in the United States, following the apparent lead of the *Rose Mary* case,[57] reviewed the international adequacy of a compensation provision contained in a foreign nationalization law.

The opinion ends by asserting that "since the Cuban expropria-

---

[53] *Id.* at 384.

[54] *Id.* at 385.

[55] The opinion pierces the Cuban corporate veil of CAV far too easily. This result might be reached, but it should at least explain the reasons that justify looking beyond the nationality of the corporation to the nationality of the dominant stockholders.

[56] See *Sabbatino, supra* note 1, at 385, for details.

[57] Anglo-Iranian Oil Co. v. Jaffrate, (The Rose Mary), [1953] 1 WEEKLY L. R. 246; 1953 INT'L L. REP. 316.

tion measure is a patent violation of international law, this court will not enforce it." [58] It adds that CAV owned the sugar involved in the litigation. Therefore, Banco Nacional's motion for summary judgment was denied, and instead a summary dismissal of the complaint was ordered.

In summary, *Banco Nacional de Cuba v. Sabbatino* holds that a domestic court in the United States is entitled, and is perhaps required, to ascertain whether foreign acts of state violate international law and, if so, must deny effect to such an act. On this basis, the court held that the Cuban nationalization decree, applicable to the sugar involved in the litigation before the court, violated international law in three respects: it did not seek to obtain the property for a legitimate public purpose; it singled out American-owned property in a discriminatory fashion; and it failed to provide adequate compensation for the expropriated owners. The specific inquiry, following the general mandate to review foreign acts of state, led the court to refuse to enforce the Cuban nationalization decree in a United States domestic court. It is important to observe that Judge Dimock limited his holding to a refusal to enforce the Cuban decree and did not expressly hold the decree itself to be void.[59]

CRITICAL COMMENTARY

It is difficult to tell from the facts whether there exists a fully acceptable way for a domestic court to resist the kind of claim made by the Banco Nacional. But it is also clear that it is not necessary to deny the claim in order to assure that Castro (or, more generally, an unfriendly government) does not gain possession of the assets. The executive has independent ways to protect its foreign policy interests.[60] However, the facts do suggest that Judge Dimock might

---

[58] Sabbatino, *supra* note 1, at 387.

[59] The decision asserts, however, that the decree violates international law; if this is correct then it is formally void everywhere, although, of course, it may not be possible to test this assertion in Cuba or in a supranational tribunal.

[60] For instance, the disposition of the *Sabbatino* assets would not depend solely upon the outcome of the litigation. For, subsequent to the District Court decision, the Treasury Department issued the Cuban Assets Control Regulations to freeze Cuban assets in the United States and to prevent their transfer to Cuba. 28 Fed. Reg. 6974–85 (July 9, 1963). Thus, even a decision in favor of Banco Nacional would not lead it to acquire control over the assets. The Solicitor General's amicus brief in the *Sabbatino* case, submitted when the case reached the United States Supreme Court, emphasized that the executive department

have reached the same result by certain judicial techniques that less obviously transgressed the role of domestic courts as an agent of the international legal order.[61] For instance, the opinion might have relied upon the *retaliatory and discriminatory* features of the Cuban decree in order to apply the well known conflicts rule that courts of one jurisdiction will not enforce foreign penal or fiscal laws.[62] The characterization of the Cuban law as "penal" might have been reached alternatively by a demonstration of its *confiscatory* nature.[63] The holding could have been further restricted to the situation in which the expropriating foreign government itself invokes the aid of domestic courts.

Another possibility existed: the case could have been disposed of as a technical matter of burden of proof.[64] If a foreign government (or its financial agent) seeks to invoke the aid of our judicial system, it must demonstrate the validity of its nationalization measures. That is, the act of state doctrine protects areas of legitimate diversity from interference by domestic courts, but it does not require domestic courts to cooperate in the enforcement of foreign governmental policy that it views as inconsistent with international law. There is a difference between the refusal to accord validity under this approach and the determination of invalidity made by Judge

---

had a number of ways to protect the United States position other than by judicial action of the kind taken by Judge Dimock. See Brief for the United States as Amicus Curiae, pp. 32–34, Banco Nacional de Cuba v. Sabbatino 376 U.S.—(1964), reprinted in 2 INTERNATIONAL LEGAL MATERIALS 1019–20 (1963).

[61] Judge Waterman's opinion in the Court of Appeals is to be preferred just because it chose a narrower basis to reach Judge Dimock's outcome.

[62] DICEY, CONFLICT OF LAWS 667 (Morris ed., 7th ed. 1958); WOLFF, PRIVATE INTERNATIONAL LAW 525 (2d ed. 1950).

[63] See the provocative essay by Hjerner, *The General Approach to Foreign Confiscations*, in 2 SCANDINAVIAN STUDIES IN LAW 177–218 (1958); EHRENZWEIG, 1 CONFLICT OF LAWS 168–71 (1959) (very full documentation given in footnotes); ADRIAANSE, CONFISCATION IN PRIVATE INTERNATIONAL LAW (1956).

[64] This approach, however, has difficulties. If the plaintiff must show the validity of his claim by reference to substantive norms of international law, he will be in trouble where no clear substantive rule exists, as in the property area. Such a technique also would place overemphasis on traditional norms. Part of the trouble here is that it is so difficult to achieve a change in governing substantive norms. See discussion of this problem by Christol, *Remedies for Individuals Under World Law*, 56 Nw. U. L. REV. 65, 65–68 (1961); see generally SMITH, CRISIS IN THE LAW OF NATIONS (1947); STONE, LEGAL CONTROLS OF INTERNATIONAL CONFLICT 402–13 (1954) (in the context of the revision of neutrality norms in the light of technological changes in methods of waging war).

Dimock. This discussion should bear in mind the dubious current status of that portion of international law designed to protect the private property rights of aliens.[65] The main point here is one of craftsmanship: a domestic court called upon to pass judgment on the validity of foreign governmental action in an area of legitimate diversity (such as protection of foreign investment) should accord validity, or, that failing, should use the most technical basis for avoiding the hostile foreign claim. *Sabbatino* unnecessarily invalidated the Cuban expropriation claim, despite the existence of these technical grounds for reaching the same outcome.

The expansiveness of the decision, however, explains why it has a lasting interest for students of the role of domestic courts in the development of international law. It encourages a critical discussion of the broader claim of invalidity in *Sabbatino*. Four issues seem paramount: (1) the degree to which the hostile state of Cuban-American political relations should influence the outcome of commercial litigation in a United States domestic court; (2) the appropriateness of the conclusion that a United States domestic court may, and perhaps must, determine the validity of foreign nationalization measures under international law; (3) the aptness of an independent review by a domestic court in the United States of the adequacy of compensation provided by foreign expropriation laws; and (4) the conditions imposed by international law upon a nation that seeks to expropriate property owned by aliens. This last issue acknowledges the uncertain status of private property in the contemporary world. I propose to discuss these issues mainly as they bear upon the optimum role of domestic courts. This relies upon the specific legal controversy in *Sabbatino* only to provide a concrete setting for abstract speculation.

1. *Judicial Deference to Executive Policy.* In the background of the Banco Nacional's claim is the relevance of executive policy in foreign relations to the judicial discharge of function. The Banco Nacional pressed its claim on behalf of the Castro government in an atmosphere inflamed by Cold War considerations that had contributed to the steady deterioration of Cuban-American relations.

---

[65] For an illustrative response from nationals of noninvestor nations see Abi-Saab, *The Newly Independent States and the Scope of Domestic Jurisdiction*, 54 ASIL PROCEEDINGS 84 (1960); Godoy, *International Law and the New Political Movements in Latin America, id.* at 96.

At the time of this legal controversy, the executive department—acting through the Central Intelligence Agency—had authorized and was sponsoring the April 1961 invasion of Cuba by Castro exiles. A second set of hostile responses by our executive followed the confiscation by Castro of foreign investments owned in large quantities by American nationals. How, if at all, should an American court take account of these developments? Here we have one dimension of the over-all inquiry into the proper role of a domestic court when it is acting as an agent of the international legal order.

Professor Katzenbach gives an unusually perceptive account of the rationale of judicial deference in the course of his extended inquiry into interstate and international conflict of laws.[66] He contrasts the precedence of "legal" factors in interstate relations with the dominance of "political" factors in international relations. The international "context of divided power" encourages domestic courts "to seek political guidance in the resolution of political problems." Katzenbach regards this as a healthy tendency that is "inhibited by concepts and theory borrowed from a domestic setting." [67] Such borrowing is not desirable, according to Katzenbach, since it overlooks the fact that "objectivity of judgment and judicial independence are vital domestic principles that have a more limited scope in the jungle of international affairs." [68] The proper occasion of judicial deference is illustrated by the *Rose Mary* decision,[69] which involved title to oil that had been confiscated from British interests by the Mossadegh government in Iran. Katzenbach observes that:

> The English government had unequivocally expressed and widely circulated its views—what the court [in Aden] called its "public policy"—with regard to the "illegality" of the Iranian nationalization decree; as an incident of diplomatic pressure, it was clearly desirable from the government's point of view to limit the salability of Iranian oil in the world market. *That the English court could have responsibly ignored this policy is inconceivable.*[70]

[66] Katzenbach, *Conflicts on an Unruly Horse: Reciprocal Claims and Tolerances in Interstate and International Law*, 65 YALE L. J. 1087 (1956).

[67] What makes a problem "political"? Its treatment as such. There is an evident circularity here. All quotations are from Katzenbach, *id*. at 1155.

[68] Katzenbach, *id*. at 1155.

[69] *Supra* note 57.

[70] Katzenbach, *supra* note 66, at 1155. (Emphasis added.)

The British judge in Aden did defer to executive policy and void the nationalization decree, whereas an Italian and a Japanese court both refused to invalidate the effect of the same decree in essentially similar circumstances.[71] Professor Katzenbach explains the disparity between the judgments in Aden and in Venice with this comment: "The Italian judge . . . [in contrast to the Aden judge] had no such clear political guidance; the position of Italy, both with regard to the governments involved and the substantive issue, was too equivocal to warrant a similar decision." [72] This observation suggests the extent to which the legal outcome in a domestic court should be tailored to suit the needs of executive policy. It relegates the role of domestic courts as agents of a nascent international legal order to the marginal circumstance where the political considerations bearing on the controversy are ambiguous or nonexistent. It nationalizes, as well as politicizes, the function of domestic courts in relation to international litigation.[73] This is the attitude that seems to underlie the initiative of the American court in *Sabbatino*. Judge Dimock was asked to pass upon Cuban nationalization in a political atmosphere of executive protest that closely resembled the situation of Judge Campbell in Aden when he was confronted by an attack upon the Iranian nationalization decree.

The issue is posed in simple form: to what extent should a domestic court suspend its normal application of international law in order to avoid conflict with relevant executive policy? A more specific reference to the facts of this litigation is whether normal judicial deference to foreign economic legislation should give way to executive policy. Judge Dimock would resent this phrasing of the basic issue. He would most probably point out that *Sabbatino* limited judicial deference to the modest finding that the *normal* application of international law would not embarrass the executive, and thus judicial deference involves only a condition precedent to the appli-

---

[71] Anglo-Iranian Oil Co. v. S.U.P.O.R. Co., [1955] INT'L L. REP. 19 (1953) (Ct. of Venice); Anglo-Iranian Oil Co. v. S.U.P.O.R. Co., [1955] INT'L L. REP. 23 (1954) (Civil Ct. Rome); Anglo-Iranian Oil Co. v. Idemitu Kosan Kabushiki Kaisha, [1953] INT'L L. REP. 305, 312 (Dist. Ct. Tokyo, *aff'd* by High Court Tokyo).

[72] Katzenbach, *supra* note 66, at 1155.

[73] That is, it gives the preferred national outcome, and it involves judicial deference to political considerations. See generally JAFFE, JUDICIAL ASPECTS OF INTERNATIONAL RELATIONS (1933).

cation of international law, and no more. My interpretation of Judge Dimock's opinion, however, leads me to contend that a quite novel inquiry was undertaken in an atmosphere in which the executive appeared to have a strong desire for judicial support.[74]

Judge Dimock observed that among the reasons given for the failure of a court to review the validity of a foreign act of state under international law was the fact that courts have not wanted to "embarrass the Executive in its conduct of foreign relations." [75] It was observed, citing the *Bernstein* case,[76] that prior judicial refusals to inquire disclose nothing more than this intention to avoid embarrassment for the executive. In relation to the proceeds of Farr Whitlock's purchase, however, this basis for judicial self-restraint was absent, since the executive—through the Department of State—sent protest notes to the Cuban government complaining that the nationalization decrees violated international law. How could the executive be embarrassed by a judicial determination that merely sustained a formal complaint made by the State Department? [77] This posing of the question falsely assumes that the judicial and executive functions are identical with regard to the review of foreign acts of state under international law.

Several lines of criticism are suggested by the rationale of *Sabbatino* on this issue. First, there does not seem to be any logical or precedential support for the inference of the court. Notes of protest on an intergovernmental level are quite distinct from the desirability of internal adjudication. There was evidently no attempt by the litigants or the court to obtain a direct authorization from the executive for the proposed inquiry into the validity of this Cuban expropriation law.

The *Bernstein* precedent has a peculiar bearing upon the approach used by Judge Dimock.[78] In *Bernstein,* the court declined to review

---

[74] The novelty arises from the judicial claim to examine the validity under *substantive norms* of international law of *tangible* property located *within the territory* of the expropriating government that has been accorded diplomatic *recognition* by the United States.

[75] *Sabbatino, supra* note 1, at 381.

[76] Bernstein v. Van Heyghen Frères, 163 F.2d 246 (2d Cir.), *cert. denied,* 332 U.S. 772 (1947).

[77] See text at note 75 *supra.*

[78] Most commentators agree that Judge Dimock was creating "new" law rather than construing "old" law in *Sabbatino.* Therefore, the explanations of precedents seek to offer evidence that there is nothing in earlier cases that for-

the validity of official acts of the Nazi government in a controversy that arose after World War II. The controversy concerned the effectiveness of confiscations based on race in order to transfer title to property. Executive hostility toward the Nazi government and its confiscatory laws was made clear by the postwar denazification program. Despite this, a federal court of appeals refused to undertake inquiry. Later, the executive issued a statement of policy entitled "Jurisdiction of United States Court Re Suits for Identifiable Property Involved in Nazi Forced Transfers," [79] which encouraged inquiry and invalidation of the confiscatory Nazi legislation.[80] It seems important to realize that the *Bernstein* court did not feel free to review the validity of the Nazi official acts until the general posture of executive hostility was expressed in a mandate to the courts. For other reasons,[81] the *Bernstein* approach to judicial deference is not here endorsed. *Bernstein* does not support *Sabbatino's* delimitation of the proper scope of judicial restraint and inquiry with regard to foreign official acts.[82]

The brunt of this point is that an external intergovernmental note of protest sent to the Cuban government is not equivalent to an internal mandate specifically directed at American domestic courts. This distinction assumes the wisdom of judicial deference, criticizing only its application in *Sabbatino*. The criticism is not merely a matter of fidelity to precedent. There are significant policy reasons for requiring an explicit mandate. The external protest may

---

bids the result that Judge Dimock reaches. In other words, precedents are not invoked to show that the doctrine of *Sabbatino* is expressed by the earlier cases. I am grateful to Professor Lillich for making this important point clear to me. See Lillich, *A Pyrrhic Victory at Foley Square: The Second Circuit and Sabbatino,* 8 VILL. L. REV. 155 (1963). However, as Judge Dimock is unclear on this issue, the text will criticize the doctrine as an extension of *Bernstein* and as a new rule that stands or falls on its own merits.

[79] STATE DEPARTMENT RELEASE No. 296, April 27, 1949.

[80] This policy was applied in Bernstein v. N. V. Nederlandsche-Amerikaansche Stoomvaart-Mattschappij, 210 F.2d 375 (2d Cir. 1954).

[81] The result in the first *Bernstein* case was an improper failure of a domestic court to apply *universal* substantive norms. This view becomes clearer, it is hoped, in the course of subsequent discussion. The main point now is that it was not necessary to solve the problem by awaiting an Executive Mandate.

[82] Note, however, that this support is not necessary if Judge Dimock is merely concerned to show that the *Bernstein* precedent does not forbid adherence to the RESTATEMENT's approach to the act of state doctrine. The decision itself is unclear on the issue of whether it is following precedent in a new situation or developing a new doctrine to cope with the *Sabbatino* facts.

seek various specific objectives that are either unrelated or antagonistic to internal review: appeasement of expropriated domestic investors, initiation of negotiations to achieve a settlement, and exhaustion of diplomatic remedies preparatory to the pursuit of relief in an external forum such as the International Court of Justice. Such objectives may account for an external protest without expressing an executive policy to use domestic courts to examine the foreign acts of state. An express mandate from the State Department should be required as a minimum condition precedent to a departure from the usual standard of respect given to a foreign act of state so long as peace prevails between the nations.

The language of the opinion in *Sabbatino* suggests that courts are restrained from passing on the validity of foreign acts of state by affirmative executive policy. Thus, here, the absence of any executive policy of deference to Cuba allows a court to undertake inquiry without fear of embarrassing those responsible for foreign relations. It is submitted that this is a very misleading formulation of the rule, at least as it has been applied in earlier cases. Before *Sabbatino*, it would seem that foreign acts of state received respect in American domestic courts even when executive hostility existed, unless an added variable like nonrecognition[83] or extraterritoriality[84] was present. Certainly, embarrassment to the executive would not have resulted from an inquiry into the validity under international law of the contested foreign governmental act in the cases that led to the emergence of the act of state doctrine.[85] The inquiry of *Sabbatino* did not seem to follow from the preexisting balance between respect for foreign acts of state and deference to executive policy in foreign affairs.

Three points of criticism have been made thus far: first, *Sabbatino* misused the *Bernstein* precedent by construing it so as to allow intergovernmental hostility to influence the scope of inquiry under-

[83] For an interesting selection of leading cases, see KATZ & BREWSTER, INTERNATIONAL TRANSACTIONS AND RELATIONS, CASES AND MATERIALS 782–816 (1960).

[84] *E.g.*, Vladikavkazsky Ry. v. New York Trust Co., 263 N.Y. 369, 189 N.E. 456 (1934); *but see* United States v. Pink, 315 U.S. 203 (1942) for the link between recognition and extraterritorial validation.

[85] In any event, Sir Wilfrid Greene is quite persuasive when he says: "I do not myself find the fear of embarrassment of the Executive a very attractive base upon which to build a rule of English law." The Nailsea Meadow v. Bantham S.S. Co. Ltd., 55 T.L.R. 503, 504 (1939) quoted by JESSUP, THE USE OF INTERNATIONAL LAW 84 (1959).

taken by a United States domestic court; second, the disregard of
foreign governmental acts in domestic courts had previously depended upon either an express mandate from the State Department
or a variable such as nonrecognition or extraterritoriality; third,
it was misleading to suggest that inquiry is all right if it does not
embarrass the executive; the maximum reading of prior cases indicates that inquiry is permissible only when the executive directs
it.

How should we measure the judicial duty to defer to executive
policy when litigation concerns foreign relations? Thus far, criticism
of *Sabbatino* has dealt with its use of prior judicial practice to answer this question. Now the critical focus shifts to the wisdom of
judicial deference, supposing even an explicit communication by
the executive of his policy to the court.[86] Admittedly, this inquiry
abandons the realm of *lex lata* to visit the shadowy domain *de lege
ferenda*. We are dealing with an issue of the distribution of powers
between the judiciary and the executive. It is traditional to assume
that the nation should speak with one voice in the area of foreign
affairs. Such an attitude assumes that there is a univocal meaning
of "national interest" applicable in every political and legal situation. This overlooks the "national interest" that inheres in the growth
of international law. For instance, the American policy may benefit
more from a depoliticized approach to adjudication than from the
promotion of a narrow executive policy to harass Communist China
or Castro Cuba.[87] Is it efficacious to allow the vagaries of international relations to control the outcome of legal controversies in
domestic courts? [88] Whenever adjudication takes place in an external forum, we presuppose that the intergovernmental relations
of the disputing states are irrelevant to the outcome of the controversy. Why should not a commitment to the rule of law induce the
same approach in a domestic court?

[86] To recall, in *Sabbatino* the content of executive policy is inferred by the
court rather than disclosed by an executive mandate.

[87] See Fisher, *Fighting Fire with Fire* (unpublished paper on the Cuban intervention); Falk, *American Intervention in Cuba and the Rule of Law*, 22 OHIO
ST. L. J. 546 (1961); JESSUP, *op. cit. supra* note 85, at 86, 151, *et passim.*

[88] *Sabbatino* explicitly allows the executive view of foreign affairs to act as a
potential check upon the scope of normal review. That is, executive policy may
lead a court not to apply international law. The question in the text shifts the
focus from judicial method to the outcome of substantive controversies.

Opposition to the Connally Amendment and advocacy of compulsory jurisdiction in the World Court have, as an evident internal correlate, the use of domestic courts as independent agents of judicial review. The impartial application of international law by domestic courts would tend to promote uniformity of outcome, overcoming tendencies toward "national" outcomes. Such uniformity would itself improve the quality of international justice, since it would no longer allow a factor as unrelated to the merits of the controversy as the national locus of the forum to control the determination of legal rights and duties.[89] This would also help to enhance the prestige of international law to the point where peoples of diverse ideological and cultural background can come to trust the objectivity of its processes. Discarding the advantages of national bias would give an increasing relative value to stability, thereby diminishing the rational grounds for refusing to vest external forums with compulsory jurisdiction. Thus, the horizontal fulfillment of the requirements of the international legal system establishes the condition for vertical growth. Such a use of domestic courts is one way to loosen the bonds of nationalism that inhibit the supranational development of a legal order.

The opposing view, which tends to absorb the domestic courts into the national unit, refuses to institutionalize a supranational role for these courts. This is especially true since Cold War pressures exist to put all national resources into the fray. By this regressive view, judicial determinations should accept the leadership of those responsible for foreign affairs.[90] The net result, of course, is to give political considerations precedence over normal legal evaluation. This is itself a deprecation of the commitment to international law. The prestige of international law in domestic courts is undermined if its application depends upon a prior political authorization. It is one thing to agree with Louis Halle that "everyone knows that, when its survival turns on an issue, any nation must do what is

[89] The courts of the expropriating state would be free to review the governmental acts of expropriation by the application of substantive standards. Perhaps it is better to view my position as advancing a theory of *venue* for international litigation in domestic courts, for it is mainly a matter of finding the proper forum in which to test two sets of legal issues: (1) legitimate diversity: strict *venue* rules; (2) universal standards: no *venue* requirements.

[90] For an imprudently generalized statement of the link between foreign affairs and judicial method, see Chapter IV.

essential to its self-preservation, even if this involves violations of moral principles and specific legal obligations." [91] It is quite another matter to extend the suspension of law and morality beyond the realm of survival to encompass any contact with a hostile nation. Such judicial deference adopts the outlook of the *Pink* case [92] toward executive-judicial relations. In *Pink* the majority held that the executive policy of establishing friendly relations with the Soviet Union controlled the interpretation of an international agreement to settle outstanding claims between the two nations.[93] This agreement, then, was absorbed into the federal supremacy clause of the United States Constitution in order to overcome a refusal by a New York state court to give effect to a Soviet nationalization decree. Translating *Pink* into the rhetoric of *Sabbatino,* one would say that the Supreme Court refused to allow a domestic court to invalidate a foreign act of state, *even an extra-territorial act,* if such an invalidation would tend to embarrass the conduct of foreign relations by the executive.[94]

In contrast, the rupture of diplomatic relations, the use of economic sanctions against Cuba, and the specific protest against the Cuban nationalization measures tended to indicate that a judicial invalidation of the decree would endorse prevailing executive policy and certainly would not, in any event, embarrass the executive. In other words, there was no apparent executive reason to restrain the application of normal international legal standards in this case. It would have seemed easy to assent to this, although its effect would have been to distort the role of domestic courts. In addition, it was a misconstruction of the executive will, as the amicus brief of the government in the final stage of *Sabbatino* has decisively demonstrated. For whatever else remains unclear, there is no further excuse for a court to suppose that it is carrying out the wishes of the executive when it assumes that expressions of executive hostility toward a given foreign act of state should lead a domestic court to feel itself free to suspend deference.

Alongside this question of the propriety of deference is a more

---

[91] Halle, *Lessons of the Cuban Blunder,* NEW REPUBLIC, June 5, 1961, pp. 13, 15.

[92] United States v. Pink, *supra* note 84.

[93] But beware of *Pink, supra* note 84. See inversion of *Pink* in cases involving the legal rights of communist claimants. *E.g.,* Latvian State Cargo & Passenger S. S. Line v. McGrath, 188 F.2d 1000 (D.C. Cir. 1951).

[94] The *Pink* case involved a federal determination that a New York state court implement executive policy accompanying the recognition of the Soviet Union in 1933. This is a special problem.

fundamental question: "What does it mean for a domestic court to apply international law to a foreign nationalization decree?" Two responses are plausible. Either the rule of deference implicit in the act of state doctrine is itself an application of international law, or it remains additionally necessary to review the decree under international law despite its quality as a foreign act of state, if the court is *genuinely* to apply international law. Judge Dimock's choice of the latter view will be considered in the section devoted to the act of state doctrine.

If it were possible to separate the issue of judicial deference from the act of state doctrine, then *Sabbatino* would seem to represent a narrowing of deference,[95] since a domestic court evidently operates under the broad constitutional mandate to apply international law as often as it is relevant, exempting only those special instances, such as *Pink,* where the executive interest in friendly relations overcomes the judicial duty. This interpretation is strained, however, in view of *Sabbatino's* claim to reconcile its review of Cuban nationalization with prior cases. The only differentiating factor then becomes the intergovernmental hostility between Cuba and the United States.

Sabbatino thus seems to state a confusing approach to the relation between executive and judiciary in matters of foreign relations, an approach that neither agrees with precedents nor enunciates an acceptable new direction of policy. It is important to work for judicial independence so that domestic courts can act as objective agents of the international legal system. The *Pink* case is inapposite, since it concerns itself primarily with the consequences of a federal interpretation of an international agreement that contradicted state judicial action; this is a problem of federal supremacy. An insistence upon judicial unity in a federal system is quite different from a rule of judicial deference to executive policy.[96] The only precedents bearing on the scope of judicial deference arise in recognition cases.[97]

[95] It did not express an acceptance of the *Pink* tendency to make domestic courts conduits for the fulfillment of executive policy. Judge Dimock's view of executive participation allows only for an initial veto of the normal judicial application of international law.

[96] See *supra* note 94.

[97] And see validation of confiscatory expropriation of tangible property situated, at the time, within the territory of an unrecognized government. M. Salimoff & Co. v. Standard Oil Co. of New York, 262 N.Y. 220, 186 N.E. 679 (1933).

The approach recommended here emphasizes the irrelevance of executive policy toward a foreign state for the adjudication of a legal claim in a domestic court of the United States. The judicial function and the desiderata of international legal order[98] join to commend the reenforcement of the ideals of judicial independence in the context of litigation involving the application of international law. It is contended here that the court in *Sabbatino* undertook an expanded review of foreign economic legislation that cannot be defended by reference to precedent or justifiable policy and that the width of the review was disguised by a confusing claim made by the court that it was applying international law. *Sabbatino* gives internal judicial implementation to political pressures. This is in the spirit of the *Rose Mary* decision; as such, *Sabbatino* politicizes and nationalizes the judicial function in international litigation, thereby accepting Professor Katzenbach's dubious advice to disengage the international conflicts problems from the objectivity of a decision appropriate to "the domestic setting."

We are led now to examine why Judge Dimock's disarming claim that he was merely applying international law disguises a major extension of the judicial power of a domestic court in the United States to review foreign economic legislation.

2. *How Does a Domestic Court "Apply" International Law?* The response to this question is central to an understanding of *Sabbatino*. Judge Dimock asserts that precedent and authority require a domestic court "to respect and enforce international law not only by virtue of this country's status and membership in the community of nations but also because international law is part of the law of the United States." [99] In one sense, this is truly unimpeachable. This imperative was used, however, to support the dubious conclusion that the Cuban nationalization measures were subject to review by the District Court. There is inadequate basis in policy and precedent to suggest the existence of a duty to apply international law by subjecting a Cuban nationalization decree to judicial review.

There is more than one way for a domestic court to fulfill its duty to apply international law. It is important to specify that the alien's claim here is that a foreign state has taken his property in

[98] That is, existing supranational tribunals are weak and very restricted.
[99] *Sabbatino, supra* note 1, at 381–82.

violation of international law.[100] The duty to apply substantive standards of international law exists in the nation that is charged with a violation of international law. This situation has led to the growth of standards and procedures of state responsibility on the part of the defendant nation. However, such responsibility emerges as a consequence of a failure in the defendant nation to govern its treatment of aliens in accord with international law. This responsibility presupposes an exhaustion of local remedies by the alien and, quite possibly, a failure of diplomatic remedies by the alien's nation. It gives rise to a state-to-state claim in an external forum pursued on behalf of the alien. Such a procedure is *formally* available in the present instance, it would seem, to assert the claims of American nationals against the Cuban government.[101] This traditional method of settlement is impaired when a foreign municipal court attempts to give relief by passing judgment on the contested official act of the government.[102]

This basic pattern for the settlement of international claims seems to account for the acceptance of the act of state doctrine. One standard effect of the act of state doctrine is that it requires an alien to obtain direct relief by exclusive recourse to judicial remedies at the situs. If such recourse fails, then the alien is entitled to seek diplomatic protection. If diplomatic remedies fail, then it is permissible to ask for supranational judicial review. This sequence is complemented by rules of exhaustion of local and diplomatic remedies. The point is that international law, as it has traditionally developed, seems to have quite consciously excluded domestic courts from this realm of international controversy.[103] This pattern of deference to foreign acts of state, then, is truly a deference

[100] The claim is used here as a shield against *Sabbatino;* that is, title did not pass to the Cuban state if the expropriation violated international law.

[101] However, it is hardly worth the expense of resorting to Cuban courts under present circumstances.

[102] Several negotiations have arrived at lump sum settlements with socialist nations since the end of World War II. *E.g.,* United States–Poland Claims Agreement, July 16, 1960 [1960] 11 U.S.T. & O.I.A. 1954, T.I.A.S. No. 4545. See Rode, *The American-Polish Claims Agreement of 1960,* 55 Am. J. Int'l L. 452 (1961).

[103] "[I]f English Courts are to be required to examine the compatibility of foreign law with international law, a new burden is thrust upon them for which they are not particularly well equipped." Lipstein, *Comment in Re Helbert Wagg,* [1956] Camb. L. J. 138, 140. This observation proves too much if extended to instances where international law supplies universal norms.

to the modes of accommodation described roughly by the label "state responsibility."

There is virtually uncontradicted domestic authority for this proposition. In *Shapleigh v. Mier,* the Supreme Court observed that "the question is not here whether the proceeding was so conducted as to be a wrong to our nationals under the doctrines of international law, though valid under the law of the *situs* of the land. For wrongs of that order the remedy to be followed is along the channels of diplomacy." [104] The decision recalled an earlier dictum, descriptive of the growth of international law in this area: "[A] citizen of one nation wronged by the conduct of another nation, must seek redress through his own government." [105] This whole approach was very clearly sustained in the context of economic acts of state by the leading case of *Ricaud v. American Metal Co.,* which ended its refusal to undertake a review of the validity of a Mexican seizure of American property by observing that "whatever rights such an American citizen may have can be asserted only through the courts of Mexico or through the political departments of our Government." [106] It seems inexplicable that Judge Dimock did not feel obliged to take account of this unambiguous higher judicial authority in his effort to find out what is meant by the duty of a domestic court to apply international law.

Here as elsewhere, the first opinion in the *Sabbatino* litigation bears the heavy imprint of Tentative Draft No. 4 of the American Law Institute's Restatement of the Foreign Relations Law of the United States.[107] The Restatement, in turn, adopts a viewpoint that submits to the criticism of the act of state doctrine that has come from commentators in investor countries.[108] Part of the policy basis

---

[104] 299 U.S. 468, 471 (1937); *but see* Sulyok v. Penzintezeti Kozpont Budapest, 279 App. Div. 528, 111 N.Y.S. 2d 75 (1st Dep't), *modified per curiam,* 304 N.Y. 704, 107 N.E.2d 604 (1952), where "public policy" was used to create a special rule. In *Sabbatino,* Judge Dimock expressly holds forum public policy irrelevant to the proper scope of deference to foreign governmental acts.

[105] United States v. Diekelman, 92 U.S. 520, 524 (1876).

[106] Ricaud v. American Metal Co., 246 U.S. 304, 310 (1918).

[107] See especially RESTATEMENT, FOREIGN RELATIONS, Explanatory Notes § 28(d)(1)(2), comments *a–e* at 14–20, Reporter's Note at 20–22 (Tent. Draft No. 4, 1960).

[108] There is voluminous literature. Influential citations are given in *Sabbatino, supra* note 1, at 380, n.7. In addition to the RESTATEMENT analysis, intelligent arguments for an activist use of domestic courts are found in Carlston, *Nationalization: An Analytical Approach,* 54 Nw. U. L. REV. 405 (1959); Mann, *The Sacrosanctity of Foreign Act of State,* 54 L. Q. REV. 42, 155 (1943); Zander, *The*

urged for the approach adopted in *Sabbatino* is "the present inadequate state of remedies available to a private citizen who has been adversely affected by action taken in violation of international law." [109] This may provide the motive for a reduction in the scope of the act of state doctrine, but it does not justify the novel scope given to the duty to apply international law.

Confusion arises here from a failure to distinguish a norm of conflict of laws from a substantive norm of customary international law. Judge Dimock accepted the mandate to apply international law as requiring a review of the validity of the Cuban nationalization legislation. Prior American practice had held that *a domestic court applied international law when it refused to pass judgment.* Such a refusal buttressed the primacy of the territorial jurisdiction that is the touchstone of the traditional system of international law.[110] One need only recall the language of Mr. Justice Holmes in the *American Banana* case:

> [T]he general and almost universal rule is that the character of an act as lawful or unlawful must be determined wholly by the law of the country where the act is done. . . .[111]
>
> The fundamental reason [for not invalidating a foreign act of state] is that it is a contradiction in terms to say that within its jurisdiction it is unlawful to persuade a sovereign power to bring about a result that it declares by its conduct to be desira-

---

Act of State Doctrine, 53 AM. J. INT'L L. 635 (1959); Kunz, The Mexican Expropriations, 17 N.Y.U. L. REV. 327, 327–51 (1940).

[109] RESTATEMENT, FOREIGN RELATIONS, § 28e (Tent. Draft No. 4, 1960); and see *Sabbatino, supra* note 1, at 382; the basic position was originally outlined in the influential report made by the Committee on International Law of the Association of the Bar of the City of New York: *A Reconsideration of the Act of State Doctrine in United States Courts* (May 1959); in passing, one notes the contrasting solicitude for economic diversity expressed by spokesmen for the organized bar in the field of economic regulation. Here, deference to diversity liberates American business operations abroad from domestic competitive standards. *Cf., e.g.,* Haight, *International Law and Extraterritorial Application of the Antitrust Laws,* 63 YALE L. J. 639 (1954); *National Security and Foreign Policy in the Application of American Antitrust Laws to Commerce with Foreign Nations,* REPORT OF THE SPECIAL COMMITTEE ON ANTITRUST LAWS AND FOREIGN TRADE, ASSOC. OF THE BAR OF THE CITY OF N.Y. (1957).

[110] A brilliant exposition is found in HERZ, INTERNATIONAL POLITICS IN AN ATOMIC AGE (1959); see also KAPLAN & KATZENBACH, THE POLITICAL FOUNDATIONS OF INTERNATIONAL LAW 19, 135–72 (1961).

[111] American Banana Co. v. United Fruit Co., 213 U.S. 347, 356 (1909).

ble and proper. . . . The very meaning of sovereignty is that
the decree of the sovereign makes law.[112]

Continental jurisprudence achieves a somewhat equivalent [113] deference more directly by the notion of *lex situs*.[114]

Of course, it could be said that this notion of deference gives
way in the face of foreign legislation or executive acts that violate
international law. This, in effect, is the attitude in *Rose Mary* and
in *Sabbatino*. However, such a notion of the conflicts rule is not in
accord with the sweeping tradition of deference built up in earlier
cases. Attempts have been made to distinguish the cases other than
Ricaud [115] by saying that they concerned litigation in which the
victims of the contested legislation were nationals of the foreign
state and thus were not eligible for relief under international law.
This narrowing of precedent was criticized by a British court in
relation to the attempt to avoid the force of *Luther v. Sagor* [116] in
the *Rose Mary* case on the ground that the pre-nationalization
owner was a national of the nationalizing state: "[A]ll three judgments in *Luther v. Sagor* laid down the principle in perfectly general
terms and it was in no way limited, at any rate in express terms,
to a recognition of the validity of such legislation in relation only
to nationals of the confiscating State." [117] The generality of the
Underhill precedent is even more persuasive.[118]

Sabbatino acted as if the duty of domestic court to apply international law *automatically* meant that it should examine whether
the Cuban nationalization measure was valid under international
law. An argument can, of course, be made in favor of such an ex-

---

[112] *Id.* at 358.

[113] But continental jurisprudence relies upon a limiting, but infrequently invoked, public policy exception. A nonprovincial interpretation of public policy
could achieve results similar to those advocated here by means of a substantive
review of foreign governmental acts that are alleged to violate universal standards.

[114] See an excellent exposition of *lex situs* approach to foreign expropriation in
Baade, *Indonesian Nationalization Measures Before Foreign Courts—A Reply*,
54 AM. J. INT'L L. 801 (1960); for authoritative comparative treatment see 4
RABEL, THE CONFLICT OF LAWS, A COMPARATIVE STUDY 30–70 (1958).

[115] *Ricaud, supra* note 106.

[116] [1921] 3 K.B. 532.

[117] *In re* Helbert Wagg and Co., [1956] 1 Ch. 323, 247 (see also dictum at 349).

[118] Underhill v. Hernandez, 168 U.S. 250 (1897); see also Oetjen v. Central
Leather Co., 246 U.S. 297 (1918).

tension of review by an American domestic court. However, it runs counter to United States Supreme Court precedents. Also, such an argument overlooks the fact that domestic courts are not especially well equipped to carry on the technical inquiry into foreign law and may upset, by harassment, the chances for wider settlement by diplomatic methods. Most significantly, an activist role[119] is given to domestic courts in the property area where a legitimate diversity of policy from nation to nation exists. In general, domestic courts should respect the horizontal scheme of the international order by not reaching out to invalidate foreign governmental acts of territorial scope unless those acts violate universal standards of minimum decency.[120]

There are two points here. First, does the duty to apply international law *require* a domestic court to see whether foreign legislation conforms to substantive rules of international law? The answer seems clearly to be "no." A domestic court discharges its duty to apply international law if it invokes a conflicts rule that accords substantive deference. In fact, the traditional system of international law—faithful to its horizontal emphasis—stressed the development of allocational criteria more than the common substantive standards.[121] The main task was to delimit the respective spheres of national competence. The territorial principle of jurisdiction worked well so long as most of the subject matter could be identified as taking place and of concern to only one state; it is less easy to allocate competence under contemporary conditions of interdependence.[122]

[119] The distinction between "active" and "passive" intends to express the opposing postures of a domestic court toward substantive review.

[120] This attitude admirably pervades the review of the Iranian expropriation in the Rome Civil Court in 1954, *supra* note 71, especially at 39–42.

[121] There was far less consideration given to the formulation of common standards, except perhaps with regard to the administration of the high seas. For a survey of the substantive developments in recent years that make inaccurate this traditional image, see JENKS, THE COMMON LAW OF MANKIND 1–61 (1958).

[122] For the efforts to use "reasonableness" as a flexible criterion able to look at contextual variables, see McDougal & Burke, *Crisis in the Law of the Sea: Community Perspectives versus National Egoism,* in McDOUGAL, STUDIES IN WORLD PUBLIC ORDER, especially 871–89 (1960); *cf.* RESTATEMENT (SECOND) CONFLICT OF LAWS, Explanatory Notes § 42, comments *a–h* at 3–7, Reporter's Note at 8 (Tent. Draft No. 3, 1956); for a rejection of reasonableness as a criterion, see RESTATEMENT, FOREIGN RELATIONS §§ 6, 10 (Proposed Official Draft, 1962).

Second, a domestic court *must* apply international law. It *may* do this by looking at the validity of the foreign legislation under international law, but it is certainly not required to do so. In fact, the court is urged to refrain from such review on the basic ground that a domestic court in State B is not a convenient forum to examine the validity of the economic legislation passed in State A. "Convenient" should be understood as including considerations of international order, national interest, and judicial craftsmanship.

3. *The Act of State Doctrine.* Is a domestic court in the United States *bound* to accord deference to foreign economic legislation that confiscates property belonging to aliens? *May* it accord such deference? Does the public policy of the forum delineate the scope of deference? Or is it a matter of applying public international law to the foreign governmental acts? Does the scope of review depend upon prior authorization by the executive? These inquiries concern what has been said already about judicial responses to executive foreign policy and the meaning of the domestic duty to apply international law.[123]

Earlier American decisions on a Supreme Court level were quite unambiguous. They use broad language to describe the duty of deference that a domestic court owes to foreign governmental acts of a nonjudicial nature.[124] Several policies seem to explain the growth of this doctrine: the effort to avoid international friction, the judicial withdrawal from conduct that might conflict with executive preference, the reciprocal tolerance built into the basic concepts of territorial sovereignty and jurisdiction, the extension of respect for the sovereign character of governmental acts already present in the doctrine of sovereign immunity, the limited competence of a domestic court to pass judgment on the validity of official action performed in a foreign society, the inclination to avoid imposition of a provincial reading of public policy or international obligation, and the difficulties of enforcement.[125]

The act of state doctrine of strict deference, if reciprocally effec-

---

[123] Farther in the background is the shadowy presence of the criterion of "national interest."

[124] See especially *Underhill, Ricaud,* and *Oetjen, supra* notes 106 & 118.

[125] For a good summary, see Zander, *supra* note 108, at 834.

tive, seemed well designed to meet the needs of a legal order in a decentralized social system.[126] Specific injustices might result; but, given the deficiency of supranational institutions, the political benefits of self-restraint seemed overwhelming. The international atmosphere was greatly influenced by the dominance of investor countries in world affairs. Intervention and the procedures of diplomatic settlement were available to resist serious infringements of property rights; broad settlements could be coerced or negotiated on a diplomatic level.[127] Sporadic domestic judicial participation could not give adequate relief and might interfere with the broader techniques of executive settlement.

This nineteenth-century pattern has increasingly changed. Socialist nations possess considerable power and solidarity; revolutionary nations, with the might of the Soviet bloc behind them, initiate programs of radical social and economic reforms without any serious intention to compensate adequately the former alien property owners.[128] Less developed nations are sensitive to appearances of foreign exploitation and are quick to assert their own rights on the international stage. The dangers of nuclear war, the omnipresence of the Cold War, and the energies of nationalism all militate against protecting the interests of creditor nations by coercive means.[129] Intervention (at least in a dictatorial sense) to restore an economic *status quo* is obsolescent. Two factors are present: an increasing pressure to expropriate alien property in many parts of the world and a decreasing capacity to protect the owners of such property, even to the extent of compensation, by the former rather reliable political means of domination. This trend is slightly counteracted by the efforts of the newly developing countries to attract foreign private capital in order to hasten their development without

[126] Suppose there is no reciprocity? This is a probable supposition. See text *infra* for brief consideration.

[127] Today power is more evenly distributed between investor and noninvestor nations, and the use of force to compel satisfaction of economic claims is too dangerous. See the excellent earlier analysis by Dunn, *International Law and Private Property Rights*, 28 COLUM. L. REV. 166 (1928).

[128] Today there are emerging alternatives of minimum compensation and lump sum settlement. This trend is deplored by Becker, *Just Compensation in Expropriation Cases: Decline and Partial Recovery*, 53 ASIL PROCEEDINGS 336 (1959), and described by Baade, *supra* note 114, at 808–14.

[129] See general considerations *supra* in text.

endangering their national independence through acceptance of foreign public capital.[130]

A further relevant development resulted from cases passing upon the validity of the Nazi legislation that infringed Jewish property holdings as part of a program of racial persecution.[131] There was a tendency of United States domestic courts to extend deference uncritically to the economic effects of this abhorrent governmental activity. Courts were very unimaginative, and remain so, about creating a limited public policy exception to the standard practice of deference. Instead, the leading decision tended to exhibit this rigidity by interpreting the act of state doctrine to require absolute deference in the absence of explicit executive dispensation.[132] It is submitted, however, that it was unnecessary to consider the judiciary helpless and that it was improper to solicit executive guidance. The effect of this appeal for executive rescue was both to undermine the legitimate scope of the act of state doctrine by overextending it and to diminish the prospects for a growth of judicial independence for domestic courts confronted by international legislation. These difficulties stem partly from a dubious expansion of the *Pink* approach to executive-judicial relations in the foreign affairs realm.[133]

Out of this background arose, not unexpectedly, an ever widening flow of learned and less learned appeals for the curtailment of the act of state approach to foreign governmental acts.[134] Especially in Anglo-American literature, one finds critics struggling manfully to circumvent fairly unambiguous judicial interpretations of the act of state doctrine by arguing in behalf of artificial limitations. Great stress is put upon the fact that in most past cases the com-

---

[130] This point is stressed by commentators urging increased use of domestic courts to protect foreign investment, *e.g.*, Carlston, *supra* note 108; Domke, *Foreign Nationalization*, 55 Am. J. Int'l L. 585 (1961); Wortley, *The Protection of Property Situated Abroad*, 35 Tul. L. Rev. 739 (1961).

[131] It is "relevant" to the existing climate of opinion that is hostile to deference in the face of antagonistic foreign governmental acts.

[132] *Cf.* Bernstein v. Van Heyghen Frères, 163 F.2d 246 (2d Cir.), *cert. denied*, 332 U.S. 772 (1947).

[133] *Cf.* Latvian State Cargo & Passenger S.S. Line v. McGrath, *supra* note 93; Bank of China v. Wells Fargo Bank and Trust Co., 104 F. Supp. 59 (N.D. Cal. 1952).

[134] See citations, *supra* note 108; 1 Oppenheim, International Law 267–70 (Lauterpacht ed., 8th rev. ed. 1955). (Footnote 2 in Oppenheim, at 268 gives expression to the attitude taken by Judge Dimock in *Sabbatino* and is the primary basis for my criticism.)

plaining litigant was a national of the acting state and hence without an international claim. This is such an explicit disqualification of a claim, so useful as the basis for decision, that it is remarkable that courts resorted instead to elaborate formulations of the doctrine of deference and, in the *Ricaud* case, referred the alien (who had the standing to make an international claim) to diplomatic channels of protest or to the judicial system of the actor nations. The Restatement of Foreign Relations Law nevertheless finds that "no American case has raised the question of application of the doctrine" in a situation where the foreign governmental act is alleged to violate international law.[135] Thus, "in this absence of controlling precedent, courts of the United States would appear to be free to consider on its merits the act of a foreign state charged to be in violation of, or in conflict with, international law." [136] The Restatement urges review on its merits, and this review is not subject to executive "suspension in order to prevent embarrassment in the conduct of foreign affairs." [137] *Sabbatino* follows the Restatement approach, although it did assure itself that no executive embarrassment would follow from an inquiry into the status of the Cuban acts under international law.[138] However, *Sabbatino* does refuse to confine deference under the act of state doctrine to acts consistent with the public policy of the forum.[139]

This critical commentary depends upon two assumptions that seem to require very careful analysis. First, the duty to apply international law does not imply a correlative duty to refuse effect to foreign official acts that violate substantive norms of international law. As has been said, it is preferable on technical and policy grounds to consider the duty to apply international law to be discharged by use of the norm of deference contained in the act of state doctrine.

---

[135] RESTATEMENT, FOREIGN RELATIONS § 28(d), comment *e,* at 19 (Tent. Draft No. 4, 1960).

[136] *Id.* at 20.

[137] *Ibid.;* see Reporter's Note to § 28(d) at 21.

[138] The full test of the approach taken by the RESTATEMENT, FOREIGN RELATIONS must await a judicial inquiry undertaken in the face of executive embarrassment.

[139] *Sabbatino, supra* note 1, at 379–80; *cf.* Zander, *supra* note 108, at 834; but *cf.* RESTATEMENT, FOREIGN RELATIONS § 28(d) (1), (Tent. Draft No. 4, 1960), which extends a judicial veto to resist foreign governmental acts that violate forum public policy *without* violating substantive norms of international law.

There is a tendency on the part of those critical of the act of state doctrine to dismiss it as a "judicial invention" without supranational status.[140] However, the special qualities of the international legal system make "the requirements" of international law depend upon horizontal implementations of reciprocity.[141] Thus, a court applies international law when it accords deference to foreign acts of state.

The act of state doctrine gives to domestic courts a self-limiting criterion that satisfies the needs of the international legal system with respect to a subject matter that occasions legitimate diversity of national opinion. Rather than risk the bias of decentralized review, it is preferable to insist upon deference, relying upon diplomatic pressure and supranational review for the application of substantive standards of international law.

Second, the area of economic legislation, including the status of private property, is a dominant instance of *legitimate diversity* between social systems.[142] The assertion of "diversity" is a factual acknowledgment of the emergence of significant socialist states. The assertion of "legitimacy" is partly factual but mainly normative; it is a judgment based on considerations of international stability and ethical tolerance. This position throws doubt upon the existence of common substantive norms that might resolve a dispute as to property rights on a supranational level. But this presents a different issue. Our concern is with the alleged duty of domestic courts to *apply* substantive norms rather than with the issue of whether such substantive norms *exist*. It is true that the dubious character of the substantive norms—given the diversity of national policy—underscores the hazard of entrusting their application to domestic courts with a partisan orientation.

The ambiguity of the word "law" in the context of international transactions underlies much of the recent commentary on the act of state doctrine. For instance, according to Judge Philip Jessup, "if the courts of the leading power of the free world support by their silence or by their jurisprudential verbiage the notion that there is no international law, they certainly lend no support to the De-

---

[140] "[T]he doctrine [act of state] seems to be one of judicial invention designed to give the executive branch of government maximum flexibility in foreign affairs by precluding the possibility of international friction or disharmony as a result of judicial edict." Note, 35, N.Y.U. L. REV. 234, 237 (1960).

[141] *Cf.* text *supra*.

[142] This is, of course, widely and wildly contested by role actors in contending social systems.

partment of State when it seeks to protect American interests abroad"; [143] thus, he evidently identifies "law" with substantive norms dispositive of the dispute. But this view of law overlooks the distinctive quality of horizontal norms suitable for the international order. Norms of deference such as act of state or *lex rei sitae* are an essential aspect of "law" as adequately perceived in the international environment. A similar preoccupation with substantive norms intrudes upon Professor Baade's erudite and persuasive analysis of the treatment of Indonesian nationalization measures by foreign courts: "Since public international law does not contain any pertinent conflict of law rules, any court is free to disregard any foreign law affecting property, if authorized to do so by the forum's conflict of law rules." [144] The traditional distinction between public and private international law obscures the role of national institutions initiating and sustaining legal order in international affairs.[145] It also fails to fit national judges into the international legal system. A domestic court has a duty to act in behalf of this supranational reality. In the area of expropriation, as a consequence of legitimate diversity, a domestic court should emphasize deference. This appears paradoxical: law is best applied by the refusal to apply it. But judicial experience does not indicate the availability of objective norms in the expropriation areas. In fact, the Iranian and Indonesian cases evidence the tendency of courts to decide the outcome of the particular controversy in accordance with the national interest. Act of state guards judicial institutions from the temptation to act in a provincial manner.[146] The formal framework of allocation in areas of legitimate diversity appears to give more assurance of reaching a just result

[143] JESSUP, THE USE OF INTERNATIONAL LAW 85 (1959).

[144] Baade, *supra* note 114, at 833 n.200; see also *id.* at 802.

[145] This distinction tends to emphasize the discretionary quality of horizontal norms of international law. It depreciates the obligatory quality of the domestic function by using a word such as "comity." See, for instance, EHRENZWEIG, 1 CONFLICT OF LAWS 17–22 (1959); Ehrenzweig, *Interstate and International Conflicts Law: A Plea for Segregation,* 41 MINN. L. REV. 717 (1957).

[146] See the pattern of Indonesian and Iranian cases to discern links between the national forum and the quality of judicial review. This pattern emerges most clearly in Baade's treatment, *supra* note 114. We must not neglect the tendency of modern statecraft and communications technique to produce national truths. One aspect, thus, of the contemporary situation is a diminished capacity to perceive truly. We should take this into account by formal mechanisms such as deference. This guards against provincialism that deceives itself into the belief that it is universalism.

than does a spurious attempt to apply substantive standards in behalf of the world community.[147]

Professor Carlston profoundly challenges this kind of conclusion in a different way. He suggests that the interdependence of economic life in the modern world and the demise of the territorial state undermine the conceptual basis for deference in domestic courts.[148] The act of state doctrine, for instance, presupposes a territorial concept of national jurisdiction.[149] Carlston reasons that if one cannot discern limits upon the primary competence to make legal policy by reference to the traditional spatial criterion, then it becomes necessary to develop new methods to decide which national unit should prescribe controlling substantive norms. Carlston thus ties his criticism of judicial patterns of deference to the inadequacy of traditional delimitations of national jurisdiction. He proposes, instead, a flexible appraisal of relevant policies in light of "those interests and expectations of the parties which will best promote the viability of the international society." [150] Carlston suggests a flexible appraisal of competing interests and policies, giving the domestic court a wide creative role to define its own jurisdiction. This view overlooks the danger of giving enlarged responsibilities to domestic courts in this area of economic policy. It fails, as well, to appreciate that the participation of domestic courts in the international system presupposes their respect for radical social experiments going on throughout the world.

Carlston supports his plea for a more flexible delimitation of the jurisdiction of foreign states with an argument in favor of the existence of valid supranational substantive standards in the property area. Specifically, he adduces support for the requirement that a valid expropriation must give full, effective, and prompt compensation to former alien owners. Domestic courts should not defer to foreign governmental acts because events appear to take place abroad, nor should they hesitate to control the controversy by norms that protect private property. International society today depends

---

[147] "Form" is integral to a just order. I have tried to develop this point in the context of jurisprudence. Falk, *The Relations of Law to Culture, Power, and Justice,* 72 ETHICS 12, at 21–25 (1961).

[148] Carlston, *supra* note 108.

[149] For this reason, Carlston observes that "the act of state doctrine commits the fallacy of begging the question." *Id.* at 413.

[150] *Id.* at 412.

upon secure patterns of trade. Such security rests upon protection for the property owner and investor. This objective should guide the response of a domestic court to a foreign expropriation. The jurisdictional critique supports, then, an activist role for the domestic judiciary in the property area. Despite my admiration for Carlston's jurisdictional level of analysis,[151] I disagree with its use to implement a notion of international society that incorporates the capitalist ethic. It perverts the role of domestic courts, inhibits the growth of mutual tolerance, and insists wrongly upon the decentralized application of substantive norms in disputes between societies with antagonistic attitudes toward the institutions of private property.

If we look once more at *Sabbatino,* we see that the court conceded Cuban jurisdictional competence. The only genuine issue remaining is whether substantive norms exist and take precedence over the Cuban attempt to assert jurisdiction. Carlston would evidently agree with Judge Dimock's use of a substantive veto but might be expected to criticize the finding—by spatial criteria—that the expropriation was performed within Cuban governmental jurisdiction.[152] Presumably, for Carlston, the locus of the sugar in Cuba would not necessarily bring the expropriation within the orbit of Cuban governmental authority; that is, upon an analysis of the facts, it might be appropriate for an American court to disregard the Cuban claim by treating it as an extravagant assertion of jurisdiction.

Such jurisdictional sophistication is quite appealing, but its effect is to remove the limits from judicial review by domestic courts. Mechanical criteria of territory and nationality must be used to resist the provincial tendency of domestic courts to override foreign programs of radical internal reform. This is not fully satisfactory, but it is the only way to reenforce legitimate deference at a time when investor pressure seeks to make partisan use of our domestic courts in the current rivalry between economic systems.

4. *Substantive Standards.* The status of property in the modern international legal system is far too complex to discuss here, where

---

[151] I agree with the need to dissolve mechanical notions of independent space when one makes the effort to comprehend contemporary interdependence in world affairs.

[152] But what criterion is preferable? Especially when one wants maximum objectivity to guard against self-serving applications of rules in domestic courts.

the concern is with the role of domestic courts. However, for completeness, it seems useful to give brief consideration to the substantive issue posed by the *Sabbatino* decision. There are two relevant levels of analysis: first, the existence of supranational norms; second, their application by domestic courts. The first set of problems is outside the scope of this article, except to the extent of affirming the problematic status of property in the contemporary world and its resulting classification as a matter of legitimate diversity.

If a domestic court classifies an expropriation as being beyond the jurisdiction of the expropriating state,[153] or if it asserts a competence to validate the expropriation by reference to supranational norms, it then becomes necessary to discern and apply universal substantive standards.[154] *Sabbatino* invoked several substantive norms to support its refusal to allow the plaintiff's claim for the proceeds of the sugar sale: (1) an expropriation must be "reasonably related to a public purpose"; (2) the expropriation must take property on a nondiscriminatory basis; and (3) the expropriation must provide former property owners with adequate compensation. As has been described, *Sabbatino* found that the Cuban expropriation decree was unenforceable in an American court because it violated each of these three norms.[155]

The decision artificially denies a public purpose because the particular expropriation was decreed as a response to the American cut in the Cuban sugar quota.[156] Although this was the provoking influence, it is evident that the Cuban program of nationalization is part of a broad program of socialization that seeks to change the character of the domestic society.[157] Regardless of attitudes toward such a program, it fits well within the scope of governmental discretion to reorder the relations of men and property within the domestic social order. As such, it seems that *Sabbatino,* by judicial notice, should have attributed a public purpose to the Cuban expropriation.

The decree was discriminatory, since it expropriated only the property of American nationals. Here, respectable international au-

---

153 That is, the notion of extraterritoriality.

154 That is, *Sabbatino.*

155 *Cf.* text *supra.*

156 *Sabbatino, supra* note 1, at 384, and n.23.

157 See, *e.g.,* a depiction of the pervasive program of Cuban social reform under Castro by HUBERMAN & SWEEZY, CUBA. ANATOMY OF A REVOLUTION (1961); for a more skeptical appraisal see DRAPER, CASTRO'S REVOLUTION (1962).

thority supports the conclusion of invalidity drawn by Judge Dimock. In fact, if the discriminatory facts are used to classify the case in the first instance, then the expropriation no longer falls within the domain of legitimate diversity. This means that objections to substantive review disappear, and an American domestic court would be entitled to refuse recovery to the plaintiff. In other words, discriminatory economic legislation violates universal standards.

Also, it is generally agreed and appears to be good policy to allow a domestic court to refuse to enforce foreign confiscatory legislation. However, if, as here, provision is made for compensation, then it becomes undesirable to allow a domestic court to review its adequacy; the reasoning used to urge deference to foreign expropriation generally applies equally to specific disputes about the adequacy of compensation. The compensation provision is best contested by entry into foreign courts, by use of diplomatic remedies, and by seeking, where available, litigation in supranational tribunals.

But suppose that the plaintiff asks a domestic court to enforce a foreign expropriation law that allegedly fails to provide adequate compensation? Then a domestic court seems entitled to insist, especially if the plaintiff is a representative of the expropriating government, that the plaintiff's burden of proof include a demonstration of the adequacy of compensation. The affirmative use of a foreign expropriation decree in a domestic court gives the forum a certain right to qualify the claim by reference to supranational standards. Such an approach would perhaps permit a court to refuse relief without ever raising the complicated issue of deference to foreign governmental action.

There is, however, one problem. What constitutes adequate compensation? Is there a universal standard of adequacy? Behind the abstract formula of "prompt, adequate, and effective" lies a great diversity in practice and attitude among modern societies. If there is no universal standard, should a domestic court use local policy to supply the norm? In general, the role of a domestic court should be passive in an area where there is no consensus among national units. Thus, the reasonableness of putting the burden on the plaintiff must be balanced against the absence of an acceptable supranational norm to sustain the burden.

An adequate judicial compromise between forum policy and international order obviously requires an awareness of both dimensions of the problems posed for a domestic court. My purpose is to suggest an approach rather than to offer solutions for the concrete problems of the *Sabbatino* case. It should be restressed that this critique concerns the failure of the first *Sabbatino* decision to be sensitive to the role of a domestic court in the developing international legal system; this is not an argument about the proper substantive outcome in this kind of litigation.

THE ARGUMENT CONCLUDED

The conclusions of the argument are quite evident. Perhaps a simplified tabular contrast between domestic courts and supranational tribunals can best summarize the position.

Substantive Review

	Domestic Court	Supranational Tribunal
Legitimate Diversity	No	Yes
Universal Standards	Yes	Yes

Legitimate Diversity

	Domestic Court	Supranational Tribunal
Formal Deference	Yes	No
Substantive Respect	Yes	Yes

Universal Standards

	Domestic Court	Supranational Tribunal
Formal Deference	No	No
Substantive Respect	Some	No

Use of a Functional and Policy Approach to the Allocation of Jurisdiction

	Domestic Court	Supranational Tribunal
Legitimate Diversity	No	Yes
Universal Standards	Yes	Yes

This broad proposal has two objectives. First, it discourages judicial activism in areas of legitimate diversity; this is part of a plea to end both the participation of domestic courts in the Cold War and the other rivalries over the status of private property in diverse social orders. Second, it encourages judicial activism in areas of universality where independent action by domestic courts can implement and bear witness to legal standards of broad acceptance in the world today. This may lead to affirmative action such as the punishment of pirates or war criminals. More likely, it involves refusing effect to foreign governmental conduct that discriminates on the basis of race, creed, or nationality. Of course, this proposal has serious problems. How is a court to deal with facts that intertwine the two kinds of controversies? *Sabbatino* involves expropriation with a discriminatory feature. The preferred solution would be to distinguish carefully between the two aspects of the controversy, and to rest the decision upon a refusal to give effect in an American domestic court to a foreign decree that discriminated against United States nationals. It is important, however, to make evident that a domestic court will not apply substantive standards to expropriations of property subject to governmental control by a foreign state.

But what makes property subject to governmental control? We observe that the jurisdictional delimitation precedes the grant of formal deference. Suppose that Cuba purported to expropriate all the oil in Texas. What jurisdictional criteria should be used to resist the claim? Although a functional appraisal is generally preferable, it gives too much policy flexibility to domestic courts since what is reasonable is often quite subjective. The provincial tendencies would then be displaced from the level of deference to the level of jurisdiction. Instead of reviewing Cuban expropriation, a court could classify the property as beyond Cuban jurisdiction and therefore subject to forum policy. Thus, mechanical notions of situs seem preferable, despite the rigidity that comes from determining legal competence by exclusive relevance to spatial characteristics. Some flexibility exists even here, since a court can vary the legal consequences by manipulating the distinction between tangible and intangible property or can classify the foreign governmental activity as "fiscal" or "penal." However, the reenforcement of self-restraint at the jurisdictional and substantive level is as much as can be reasonably expected from domestic courts at present.

As was said at the outset, the primary hope is to persuade domestic courts to be sensitive to the bearing of the Cold War, nuclear weapons, and socialism upon the discharge of their function in international litigation. Of course, it is plausible to argue that domestic courts should become even more a part of our ideological arsenal and should defend where possible the Western belief in the link between private property and individual liberty. However, the overriding significance of achieving enduring accommodations between ourselves and our present political enemies leads me to develop a contrary image of ideal behavior for our domestic courts. Until further evidence compels reassessment, it appears prudent to devote our domestic courts to the task of reducing international tensions by carrying out judicial duties without assuming a partisan posture. My suggestions for a passive judicial role in the area of legitimate diversity seek this end. My criticism of the first *Sabbatino* decision is directed primarily at its insensitivity about the responsibility of a domestic court in an international law case of this kind.

Chapter VI

The Further Search for Principles in the *Sabbatino* Case

DEVELOPMENTS in the *Sabbatino* litigation subsequent to the decision in the District Court, considered in Chapter V, make the case even more interesting than it was for theory-building. The decision written by Judge Waterman of the Circuit Court of Appeals gives us two decisions to compare. Some commentators have expressed their praise or criticism of the two decisions. The United States government has expressed an unexpected and significant viewpoint in the form of an amicus brief to the Supreme Court. Yet the litigation is still in process. There is no final decision on the case by the Supreme Court, although it is awaited with growing suspense. No international law case in recent United States judicial practice has aroused such widespread interest among members of the legal profession.

The *Sabbatino* litigation concerns the validity in United States domestic courts of the expropriation laws enacted by the Castro government and applied to American property located in Cuba. Lower federal courts have ruled that the Cuban expropriation laws are void in American courts because they violate international law. This conclusion could be reached only because courts thought that the executive had given them permission to adjudicate the substantive issues in controversy. Such a determination has radical consequences both for the status of official acts of foreign governments in United States courts and for the distribution of functions between the executive and the courts in an international law case.

Several law issues are presented in *Sabbatino:* (1) the extent to which the judicial function in international law cases should be governed by executive discretion; (2) the extent to which the retention of the act of state doctrine serves national and international interests; (3) the extent to which a domestic court is competent to review the official acts of foreign governments that have been undertaken to carry out a new social program; (4) the extent to which widespread recourse by foreign governments to social programs that interfere with property rights have rendered indeterminate the standards of international law applicable to the treatment of foreign property; (5) the extent to which this indeterminacy makes it inappropriate to permit domestic courts to enforce as "international law" those traditional rules developed when international society was dominated by nations committed to the protection of private property.

Acute commentators on *Sabbatino* have had a tendency to concentrate upon the first issue and to cluster the rest into a single defense of Judge Dimock's holding that the act of state doctrine does not preclude an inquiry into whether a foreign governmental act violates international law. This emphasis had led these commentators to criticize harshly Judge Waterman's modified and narrower basis for deciding against the plaintiff in the Second Circuit Court of Appeals.[1]

An appraisal of the appellate decision is useful to highlight the two main branches of the argument about the role of domestic courts in the development of international legal order. Judge Waterman's opinion is a distinct improvement over Judge Dimock's opinion with regard to the external or foreign relations aspects of the case. Judge Waterman is very ready to concede the relevance of diverse economic systems to the stability of those rules of international law pertaining to private property that developed in a period when international society possessed a homogeneous character, that is, in a period prior to the emergence of socialism as the basis for the organization of many national societies. It will be recalled that Judge Dimock avoided reference to this diversity and thus did not find it difficult to conclude that old rules of international law applied with undiminished vigor in contemporary international society.

On the other hand, in the matter of the proper character of executive-judicial relations in an international law case—the internal aspect—Judge Waterman accentuates, rather than corrects, the failings of Judge Dimock. The ideal of judicial independence is shame-

---

[1] *Cf.* Lillich, *A Pyrrhic Victory at Foley Square: The Second Circuit and Sabbatino*, 8 VILL. L. R. 155 (1963) [hereinafter cited as Lillich]; Stevenson, *The Sabbatino Case—Three Steps Forward and Two Steps Back*, 57 AM. J. INT'L L. 97 (1963) [hereinafter cited as Stevenson]; see also Baade, *The Legal Effect of Cuban Expropriations in the United States*, 1963 DUKE L. J. 290 and Domke, *The Present American Attitude Towards Nationalization of Foreign-Owned Property, id.* at 281.

lessly sacrificed without any development of defensive or limiting principles. In other words, Judge Waterman concedes executive primacy as an outgrowth of executive responsibility for foreign relations without requiring either a formal intervention by the executive or a demonstration that judicial deference to executive will is a result of an established connection (not a presumed connection) between the conduct of foreign affairs and the controversy before it. As the amicus brief of the United States government now makes evident, the lower federal judges, who had explained the suspension of normal deference under the act of state doctrine as something that could (and perhaps should) be done to carry out the wishes of the executive, were in error. The executive did not want the act of state doctrine suspended. This discloses that the faulty notion of judicial subservience was also mistaken in fact, since the wrong message was received. The courts were not entitled and were certainly not requested, according to the executive, to examine the validity of these Cuban acts of state.

It should be pointed out that the issue of faulty communication is not the core of the problem. Our argument is that the judiciary should develop *its own principles* to determine when it will examine the validity of challenged foreign acts of states, and that these principles should express the distinction between legitimate diversity and universal standards developed in the previous chapter. This is much more radical than a criticism of the way Judge Dimock and Judge Waterman construed executive intention, for it asserts the irrelevance of executive intention to the litigation of an international law case in a domestic court. The ideal is to make the executive of State A as irrelevant to judicial process in State A as it is to judicial process in State B. No one would contend that a British court examination of Cuban acts of state should hinge upon the will of the executive in the United States. This objective is also in direct opposition to the government's position. The government is arguing in *Sabbatino* that the act of state doctrine should be suspended only after a formal executive mandate and that otherwise the act of state doctrine should be applied to assure executive control over the subject matter in diplomatic channels. There is no scope for judicial discretion, and there is a subordination of the judiciary to the executive in international law cases. The executive wants to prevent courts from presuming executive intention.

Judge Waterman's Opinion

Judge Waterman's decision relies upon elaborate research and extended analysis. A brief exposition will highlight its distinctive aspects.[2]

1. *What Is the Act of State Doctrine?* Is it a mandatory rule of international law or a discretionary rule of American conflict of laws? The act of state doctrine, according to Judge Waterman, "is one of the conflict of law rules applied in American courts; it is not itself a rule of international law." [3] This classification of the act of state doctrine has become almost standard now. The *Restatement,* Judge Dimock, and most commentators agree with Judge Waterman's conclusion. I would contend that the distinction between international law and conflict of laws has been drawn too sharply if, as a concomitant, the former category of rules is mandatory whereas the latter is discretionary. The act of state doctrine, however classified, attempts to allocate legal competence among nations. An adequate system of allocation is an essential element of minimum world legal order.

Judge Waterman does stress the long pattern of American adherence to the act of state doctrine. His examination of the main precedents suggests that the availability of the doctrine was not thought to depend upon the conformity of the act to international law. In fact, it is only after executive authorization that courts are entitled to suspend the operation of the act of state doctrine. This feature of Judge Waterman's opinion provokes, especially, his critics as they seek to confer upon courts the competence to determine, without any reliance upon executive guidance, when to suspend the doctrine. The content of act of state is treated by Judge Waterman as an issue of domestic law, but the teaching of American precedents is that the courts will defer to the foreign act unless and until the executive relieves them of this normal duty.

2. *The Nature of Executive Participation.* Judge Waterman uses a rather odd, but quite revealing formulation: "When the executive branch of our Government announces that it does not oppose inquiry by American courts into the legality of foreign acts, an exception to the judicial abnegation required by the act of state doctrine has

---

[2] *Cf. supra* Chapter V for a full exposition of the issues in controversy.
[3] Banco Nacional de Cuba v. Sabbatino, 307 F.2d 845, 855 (2d Cir., 1962).

arisen and has been recognized both in this circuit and elsewhere." [4]
That is, and this is not set forth clearly in the opinion, there are, in
effect, two act of state doctrines. If the executive stays completely
silent, then a domestic court cannot entertain any complaint whatsoever against the foreign official act.[5] However, if the executive says
anything, no matter to whom and no matter how coyly and obliquely,
then a court is permitted to construe these communications as in-
dicative of an executive's will not to be embarrassed if the courts
inquire into the validity of the foreign acts.[6] Evidently, courts must
consider potential embarrassment as foreclosing their inquiry until
there has been some executive utterance that can be construed as
being to the contrary. Once the possibility of embarrassment is removed, then it is unclear whether the act of state retains any significance.

It is evident, and also reassuring, that the executive is not inclined
to offer advice on the status of contested official foreign acts. The
Legal Adviser and other high government officials have been careful
to distinguish their protest against acts of foreign government in
diplomatic channels from the determination of the validity of these
acts in the national courts of the United States.[7] The issue of validity

[4] *Id.* at 857–58.

[5] See, *e.g.*, the approach taken by the majority in Pons v. Republic of Cuba,
294 F.2d 925 (1961).

[6] On this issue, see Lillich, especially at 170–75, and Kane v. National Institute of Agrarian Reform, 18 Fla. Supp. 116 (1961); a summary of authorities
on this issue of the relation between executive embarrassment and judicial conduct is found in Bilder, *The Office of the Legal Adviser: The State Department
Lawyer and Foreign Affairs*, 56 AM. J. INT'L L. 633, 673 (1962); see a defense
of act of state to assure nonembarrassment of executive by Professor Stanley
Metzger, *The Act of State Doctrine and Foreign Relations*, in METZGER, INTER-
NATIONAL LAW, TRADE AND FINANCE—REALITIES AND PROSPECTS 66–77 (1962);
cf. also comprehensive discussion in Cardozo, *Judicial Deference to State Department Suggestions: Recognition of Prerogative or Abdication to Usurper?*, 48
CORNELL L. Q. 461 (1963).

[7] See Memorandum on Behalf of the United States on Petition for a Writ of
Certiorari to the United States Court of Appeals for the Second Circuit, Banco
Nacional de Cuba v. Sabbatino, Appendix B, 14–43 (U.S. Supreme Court, Oct.
Term, No. 403, 1962) reprinted 2 INTERNATIONAL LEGAL MATERIALS 212 (1963);
Memorandum on Behalf of the United States, Filed with the U.S. Supreme
Court in Connection With an Application for a Stay Pending Action on Petition
for Writ of Certiorari in Rich v. Naviera Vacuba, S.A., 295 F.2d 24 (4th Cir.
1961), excerpted in 1 INTERNATIONAL LEGAL MATERIALS 288 (1962); and espe-
cially, Brief for the United States as *Amicus Curiae* in the United States Supreme
Court, No. 16 Banco Nacional de Cuba v. Sabbatino, 34–46, Oct. Term, 1963, reprinted in 2–3 INTERNATIONAL LEGAL MATERIALS 1009, 1020–23 (1963).

is regarded very explicitly as something the courts should decide for themselves.

3. *The Scope of Deference in the Absence of Executive Embarrassment.* Judge Waterman follows Judge Dimock in holding that the act of state doctrine contains sufficient deference to foreign law to foreclose arguments about the claim that the acts in question violate the municipal law of the actor or contravene the public policy of the forum. However, and this is critical, "if there is no good reason for abstention, a court should recognize and accept its fundamental responsibility to decide a case before it in accordance with whatever substantive norms may be relevant." [8] This "fundamental responsibility" governs Judge Waterman's consideration of the applicability of substantive rules of international law. The points in his argument are clearly set forth: [9] first, a court cannot possibly harm United States foreign policy by acting in this sort of a case; second, the rights of a foreign sovereign are limited by its duty to abide by international law; third, when the sovereign is the plaintiff, there is no reason to refrain from a determination of validity in order to protect the security of title enjoyed by purchasers for value from that sovereign; fourth, the court is familiar enough with the foreign setting of these contested acts to make a competent legal evaluation; and, fifth, the possibility of nationalistic prejudice is no greater than other biases that might exist but are nevertheless not regarded as disqualifying judges or courts. For these reasons Judge Waterman deemed it appropriate to examine the validity of these Cuban expropriations under international law.

4. *The Application of International Law.* Judge Waterman referred to international law as a "hazy concept" [10] and suggested that "anyone who undertakes a search for the principles of international law cannot help but be aware of the nebulous nature of the substance we call international law." [11] Despite this appearance of a negative approach, the opinion, as a whole, discloses a discerning and progressive attitude toward international law and took note, for instance, of the need to avoid the "pitfall" of regarding "as a fundamental principle of international law some principle which in truth

---

[8] 307 F.2d 845, 858.
[9] *Id.* at 859–60.
[10] *Id.* at 859.
[11] *Id.* at 860.

is only an aspect of the public policy of our own nation." [12] "We must," instead, "take a more cosmopolitan view of things and recognize that the rule of law which we municipally announce must be a rule applicable to sovereignties with social and economic patterns very different from our own." [13] This is reassuring rhetoric in an American decision that had to deal with an expropriation controversy having strong Cold War overtones.

5. *The Cuban Nationalization Measures.* The fact that over 90 per cent of the stockholders were Americans was held to overcome the Cuban nationality of the corporation that had owned the sugar. Judge Waterman examined whether international law presently contains a rule requiring the payment of adequate compensation. Impressive lists of authorities were assembled in support of compensation requirements, but the challenge directed by the modernizing countries was also considered: namely, that the right to carry out radical economic reforms takes precedence over a duty to pay for what one takes. The court, having raised appropriate doubts, wisely avoided a conclusion, regarding it as unnecessary for a resolution of the dispute before it. "Instead, we narrow the question for decision to the following: Is it a violation of international law for a country to fail to pay adequate compensation for the property it seizes from *a particular class of aliens, when the purpose for the seizure of the property is to retaliate against the homeland of those aliens and when the result of such seizure is to discriminate against them only.*" [14] This narrowing of the controversy is a crucial aspect of Judge Waterman's opinion, differentiating it from Judge Dimock's broad holding that clearly went beyond dispositive needs.

Once again, the opinion makes an impressive survey of available authorities, as well as characterizing the Cuban expropriation as a retaliation for the refusal of the United States to maintain the Cuban sugar quota. The conclusion reached was significant: "Unlike the situation presented by a failure to pay adequate compensation for expropriated property when the expropriation is part of a general social improvement, confiscation without compensation when the expropriation is an act of reprisal does not have significant support among disinterested international commentators from any country.

[12] *Id.* at 861.
[13] *Ibid.*
[14] *Id.* at 864 (original emphasis).

And despite our best efforts to deal fairly with political and social doctrines vastly different from our own, we also cannot find any reasonable justification for such procedure." [15] This language exhibits tolerance for diversity and admits the importance of a consensus supporting a disputed norm of international law. The decision holds that the nationalization of property of aliens resident in a particular country appears "contrary to the generally accepted principles of morality throughout the world." [16] The invocation of morality here is rather confusing. One wants to know the basis for the conclusion that "generally accepted principles of morality" exist. Furthermore, one questions the relevance of a moral violation to a determination of law. The passage seems to reveal that Judge Waterman's understanding of international law is "hazy" and "nebulous" and thereby reminds one of the common view that international law is a normative order situated somewhere between law and morality. It is unfortunate that a judicial official in the United States should give aid and comfort to those who denigrate international law as a legal order.

However, even here, it is easy to neglect the subtlety of Judge Waterman's analysis. The issue of what makes legislation discriminatory is dealt with in an impressive manner. To establish discrimination, one must look at the entire context of expropriating activity and not merely at the decree before the court. Judge Waterman acknowledges that "perhaps, international law is not violated when equal treatment is accorded aliens and natives, regardless of the quality of the treatment or the motives behind that treatment." [17] The opinion stresses the fact that, whereas American-owned sugar enterprises were expropriated on August 6, 1960, Cuban-owned sugar enterprises were not seized until October 13, 1960. This time lapse was considered sufficient both to prevent the inference of equal treatment of Cubans and Americans and to confirm the conclusion of discrimination against Americans. This degree of discrimination was held by Judge Waterman's court to be a violation of international law, especially when it was combined with a retaliatory purpose and a failure to provide adequate compensation.

This raises the question of a remedy: can a domestic court grant

[15] *Id*. at 866.
[16] *Ibid*.
[17] *Id*. at 867.

restitution to the former owner? Even though international courts have refrained from restitutionary remedies, Judge Waterman affirms the competence of domestic courts to grant them. Once again, Judge Waterman is extraordinarily sensitive to the issues at stake, emphasizing the distinctive contributions of domestic courts to the development of international law, as well as giving focus to the particular elements in the controversy under review; for example, the opinion notes that the Cuban decree "explicitly precludes review of the confiscation by the Cuban courts." [18]

A NOTE OF COMMENDATION

Judge Waterman's opinion is an excellent model, in many respects, of optimum behavior by a domestic court in an international law case. First, dispositive issues are delineated as narrowly as possible. Second, underlying and competing policies are explicitly acknowledged and set forth. Third, the status of the challenged acts is examined to the greatest extent possible from the perspective of the foreign actor as well as from that of the forum. Fourth, changes in the extralegal environment are recognized as casting doubt upon traditional rules of international law applicable to expropriation. Fifth, a maximum attempt is made to rest the decision upon bases that would be reasonable to any tribunal, wherever situated in the international system. Sixth, rhetoric, analysis, and holding all confirm the impression that this court is trying both to act like an agent of the international legal order and to serve as a municipal court in the American judicial system.

Several criticisms qualify this endorsement of Judge Waterman's opinion. First, there is the ambiguous and faulty notion, developed in the two *Bernstein* cases, that judicial competence to review foreign acts of state is wholly dependent upon some prior manifestation of executive nonembarrassment. The *Sabbatino* case aggravates *Bernstein* by resting executive authorization upon dubious collateral communications rather than by making the suspension of the act of state doctrine depend upon a formal and direct instruction from the executive to the judiciary. Judge Waterman's treatment of internal deference—executive-judicial relations in act of state cases— is, perhaps, the most objectionable part of his opinion.[19]

[18] *Id.* at 868.

[19] This is discussed with insight and precision by Lillich at 171.

Second, there is a failure to be clear about the policies of deference governing the scope of the act of state doctrine, once it has been established that no executive obstacle exists to thwart judicial inquiry. Third, a rather unfortunate image of international law as a source of normative authority is set forth. And fourth, there is some failure to demonstrate the significance of the discriminatory element in the Cuban expropriations; this could have been done if the treatment of American and other non-Cuban investment interests had been compared.

On balance, however, the decision is a model for the way a domestic court should do its job when litigation involves a claim that foreign law violates international law. How can one explain the preference of commentators for Judge Dimock's treatment of the *Sabbatino* controversy? Perhaps Mr. Stevenson's succinct condemnation can best disclose, partly because of its bluntness, the reasons why Judge Waterman's decision has been criticized so vigorously.[20] There are two principal attacks. First, the role and burden of executive authorization. Judge Waterman makes judicial inquiry into a challenged foreign act of state depend upon a prior expression of executive approval, regardless of an allegation that the act of state violates international law. Mr. Stevenson prefers Judge Dimock's analysis of the freedom of a court in the absence of executive objection to carry out its duty to determine whether allegations that a foreign act of state violates international law are well founded.[21] A requirement of nonobjection is less burdensome than is a requirement of express authorization. Mr. Stevenson would like to go beyond both decisions and presume judicial competence to evaluate acts of state under international law, unless there has been an executive request for judicial abstention. Lillich supplements this position by showing how unpersuasive Judge Waterman's inferences of executive authorization seem to be. Stevenson argues that a regular judicial duty to review foreign acts of state would spare the executive "the embarrassment of affirmatively authorizing review of a foreign sovereign's acts in a specific case."[22] This is, I think, a convincing and important criticism; the executive has not even claimed or sought

[20] Stevenson at 98–99.
[21] See also Lillich at 176.
[22] Stevenson at 98; see also RESTATEMENT, FOREIGN RELATIONS § 44 (Proposed Official Draft, 1962) [hereinafter cited as RESTATEMENT].

the supervisory competence that the courts have thrust upon it: "Whether or not these nationalizations will in the future be given effect in the United States is, of course, for the courts to determine." [23] Such a statement is an interesting, if easily misunderstood, confirmation of the Stevenson-Lillich approach.[24] For the word "determine" is not inconsistent with an acceptance of validity through deference, that is, by an application of the act of state doctrine. It does not clearly mean, nor should it be taken automatically to mean, a substantive determination.

This leads to the second, and more dubious, line of attack: the use of international law to prevent uncompensated expropriations. Mr. Stevenson maintains that "however important the security of individual commercial transactions may be, of far greater concern is the maintenance of those minimum standards of *civilized conduct* on which the general security of all such transactions ultimately rests." [25] Thus, here it is in the open—the identification of civilized conduct, international law, and the sanctity of private property—the linkage that one suspects but rarely confronts quite so directly. Mr. Stevenson is here contending that it is better to invalidate the title of a purchaser for value of "illegally" expropriated property than it is to unsettle the standards that govern the expropriation process itself. But who sets these standards? And how are these standards to be changed in order to reflect the new character of international society? Can one achieve stability or merely underscore perceptions of conflict and hostility by insisting on describing one's own position as "civilized," despite the challenge of socialism and despite the assorted plights of the newly independent states?

Perhaps this digression is somewhat unfair, as Mr. Stevenson's main critical point is more modest: why cast unnecessary doubt upon the requirement of adequate compensation? The issue was not relevant for decision in view of the fact that the discriminatory feature of the Cuban expropriation made it illegal, without any wider consideration of the duties of the expropriator. But even here, it is not necessary to search for esoteric meanings to uncover a policy bias

[23] Letter of Chayes to Laylin, October 18, 1961, reprinted in 2 International Legal Materials 212 at 220–21 (1963).

[24] This is especially true if the sentence quoted in the text is read together with the sentence following it in Chayes' letter: "As you yourself point out statements by the executive branch are highly susceptible of misconstruction."

[25] Stevenson at 99 (emphasis added).

that fastens itself onto Mr. Stevenson's otherwise reasonable criticisms of Judge Waterman from the perspective of judicial craftsmanship.[26] Judge Waterman is chastized because "by reviewing the relevant authorities in its opinion and, in effect, concluding . . . that the question was a difficult one, the court tends to suggest the uncertainty of international law in an area of fundamental importance to private international investment abroad." [27] It is as though such an acknowledgment of uncertainty is a betrayal. However, the uncertainty that exists (for confirmation, consult the Sixth Committee debates in recent sessions of the United Nations) will not disappear because American courts refuse to acknowledge it.[28] In fact, Judge Waterman displays wisdom and insight by his willingness to concede the reality of those challenges Mr. Stevenson would have him deny. If a domestic court perceives international law from a nationalistic viewpoint it confirms the most cynical image of international law, an image that Western commentators self-righteously, albeit accurately, ascribe to the communist states.

A further line of criticism—that substantive norms of international law are applicable—is a consequence of a narrow conception of the judicial function. Of course, if one assumes that a domestic court exists primarily to provide individuals with extra remedies and to prevent abuses of the alien property-owner, then the proper focus for judicial decision-making is easily attained or, if not attained, at least easily scorned. But is this a desirable conception? This question, for all its inquiring innocence, is meant to raise a fundamental issue of priorities: do we primarily want international law to protect national values and interests or to help construct a more stable world

[26] If Judge Waterman is guilty of hazarding opinions about relevant matters that were nondispositive, then Judge Dimock is even more guilty, for Judge Dimock raises questions about the status of foreign acts of state that went far beyond a denial of effect to Cuba's discriminatory and confiscatory decrees. Why has not Judge Dimock's extravagance disturbed the critics of Judge Waterman? The temptation is to explain this selective tolerance by noting both the agreement of Judge Waterman's critics with Judge Dimock's ends and their disagreement with Judge Waterman's ends. Thus, the distinction becomes one of substantive outlook rather than judicial craftsmanship.

[27] *Ibid.*

[28] Falk, *International Jurisdiction: Horizontal and Vertical Conceptions of Legal Order*, 32 TEMP. L. Q. 295 (1959); *id.*, *Jurisdiction, Immunities, and Act of State: Suggestions for a Modified Approach*, in ESSAYS ON INTERNATIONAL JURISDICTION 1–20 (1961).

order? There is no necessary incompatibility between what is good for the United States and what is good for world order; but, just as surely, there is no necessary compatibility. Judge Waterman's style of inquiry tries to make a domestic court sensitive to changes in the international environment that may make the old rules obsolete or cast doubt upon the continuing validity of national preferences. This spirit of adaptation should guide a domestic court, especially when it is dealing with an issue falling within the area of legitimate diversity.[29] Therefore, it is desirable both to rest a decision upon rules that most closely command a universal respect and to eschew consciously a basis of decision that could be reasonably construed as imposing our special interpretations of international law merely because the litigation happened to find its way into our courts. The United States is a precedent-creating state in the application of international law; this is especially true for negative precedents. No other nation can be expected to treat the system with any greater respect than that which we are prepared to demonstrate. Thus, we recommend broad judicially created rules of substantive deference for disputes involving a clash between social orders. It is more important to depoliticize the treatment of international law than it is to make the world safe once more for private investment abroad—a futile quest, in any event.

An even broader argument exists against a provincial interpretation of the norms of international law. A court influences the whole climate of attitudes that form around a legal obligation. The manipulation of property norms, in order to support narrow interests, encourages revisionist powers that would themselves manipulate self-defense and aggression norms. What the United States does in *Sabbatino* is not completely severed from what India does in Goa or what the African states do to the Republic of South Africa. In a decentralized social system that maintains peace amid conflict by means of a delicate equilibrium mechanism, it is essential to cultivate habits of restraint and to foster impartial limits appealing to common standards that can serve competing states as an approximation of

---

[29] "Legitimate diversity" is a phrase used to suggest that there is no global consensus in favor of making universal a single substantive standard. Therefore, states are at liberty to adopt diverse national standards. Such diversity is legitimate, in this sense, with respect to the practice of either socialism or capitalism, but not for the choice between upholding civil liberties or practicing genocide.

objective reality. Anything that either weakens these habits or self-interestedly manipulates these limits endangers peace, despite the short-term gain made by any one country with respect to its values and its interests. Therefore, it is important to oppose those who advance adversary approaches to international law, and this includes any form of policy science that regards normative restraints as never so inflexible as to hamper our side's security, wealth, and dignity.[30]

In this context, Judge Waterman's astronomical adjectives "hazy" and "nebulous," as applied to international law, strike me as unfortunate, especially since they do not appear to reflect his fundamental understanding. I would hazard a limiting interpretation. If authoritative and universal guidance about the status of the claims of an expropriated foreign investor is sought in international law, then it will indeed appear to consist of vague, confusing, and contradictory mandates. For this reason, each sovereign state has broad, although not unrestricted, discretion to make effective its own views about the protection of private property located within its territory. It is akin to the discretion vested in states by the dramatic notion of permanent sovereignty over natural resources. This wide allocation of discretion, familiar in the domain of recognition of foreign governments and states, is not incompatible with the upholding of law unless it is misunderstood, as when a state denies the presence of discretion in a domain where it would seem to exist. The limits placed upon discretion are closely tied to the distinction between legitimate diversity and universal standards that I have set forth earlier. It rests most insecurely upon the simultaneous availability of a substantive *and a political* consensus. The requirement of a political consensus is a natural consequence of decentralization: one cannot expect to coerce the same compliance with human rights in the Soviet Union as in the Republic of South Africa. But this is a characteristic of horizontal legal order; it is not an occasion for a

---

[30] An adversary approach to international law implies an emphasis upon legal arguments favorable to "our side" without a corresponding effort to examine the arguments favorable to "their side." It also suggests the orientation of an adversary in the sense of a partisan as distinct from a judge in the sense of an impartial observer. The Legal Adviser for the United States may be expected to play the role of adversary; in contrast, legal scholars may be expected to provide a corrective impression. For this reason, scholars serve neither their country nor the cause of international law by stepping forward in periods of crisis and conflict to give a one-sided account of the relevance of international law.

cynical denial of international law. It is dangerous to have illusions about the role of legal restraint in world affairs, but it is equally dangerous to move from a discernment of defects to a denial of legal restraint altogether.

Sabbatino AND THE RESTATEMENT

The Proposed Official Draft of the Restatement "takes no position" [31] on whether the act of state doctrine permits a domestic court to review the challenged foreign act by reference to international law; however, "it calls attention to the fact that in such situations there is no precedent expressly contrary" to the authorization of such an inquiry. Then, in a Reporters' Note, precedents are reviewed, including the *Ricaud* case: "It seems fairer to regard the *Ricaud* case . . . as one in which the attention of the Court was not directed to the international law issue." [32] The opinion is ventured that "the Reporters do not regard either *The Fortitude* or *Ricaud* as presenting major obstacles to the development by the Supreme Court of an exception to the act of state doctrine." [33] Are these precedents, then, a minor obstacle? If so, of what stature is it? Although no hint is given, it is said that the development of a doctrine that permitted limited review of foreign acts of state would help national courts to vindicate international law and that it would grant relief to injured parties in situations in which either the complainant is a private party or the defendant refuses to submit the controversy to an international tribunal. Judge Dimock's decision is cited as one that "tends to support" the exception allowing foreign acts of states to be challenged as violative of international law.[34]

This Restatement presentation is one-sided. It gives no mention of the argument against the exception; it lightly discards precedents [35] (an attitude, that is, incidentally, quite inimical to maintaining the authority of shaky international precedents in the substantive

---

[31] *Cf.* RESTATEMENT § 43, Caveat and Reporters' Notes at 141–43.

[32] See *id.* at 143; also *The Fortitude* 11 U.S. (7 Cranch) 423 (1813); *cf.* RESTATEMENT, FOREIGN RELATIONS § 28d, comment *e* at 19–20 (Tent. Draft No. 4, 1960).

[33] RESTATEMENT 143.

[34] The Proposed Final Draft of the Restatement was published before Judge Waterman's *Sabbatino* opinion was available.

[35] *E.g.*, Pons v. Republic of Cuba, 294 F. 925 (D.C. Cir. 1961) is not cited in the RESTATEMENT discussion, which had a publication date of May 1962.

law of expropriation); [36] and it takes no notice of the unavoidable
ambiguity of the conception of "applying" international law in this
context. This is certainly an odd way to take "no position!"

Section 44 states the more easily explained version of "the exception": if the executive indicates that it has no objection to a judicial
determination of the validity of a foreign act of state, then the court
can go ahead. The difference between Section 44 and the Caveat to
Section 43 hinges upon the need for an expression of lack of objection.[37] In view of Judge Waterman's use of the second *Bernstein*
case as an analogue, it is probably accurate to say that the Section
44 version of the exception is as far as *Sabbatino* presently goes.
No consideration is given to what form the executive communication
should take.

Which is preferable: Section 43, Caveat (no need for executive
authorization) or Section 44 (when executive expresses "no objection")? In order to achieve maximum judicial independence for
domestic courts, the Section 43 approach is far better; it also tends
to keep foreign relations out of litigation. Section 44 is sporadic,
ad hoc, and invites strained inferences of executive authorization.
On the other hand, nationalistic courts with the grant of competence
made in Section 43 could prove quite disruptive; but if an executive
veto existed, then part of *this* danger could be met.

[36] See RESTATEMENT §§ 190–97.

[37] The relevant provisions of the RESTATEMENT are as follows:

§ 43. *Act of Foreign State Contrary to Public Policy Of United States.*
     Under the foreign relations law of the United States, the rule stated in
§ 41 prevents examination of the validity of an act of a foreign state of
the type described in § 41 even though it is attacked on the ground that it
violates the public policy of the United States.

. . .

Caveat: Act of a foreign state in violation of international law
     The Institute takes no position whether, in situations not governed by
the rule stated in § 44, the rule stated in § 41 permits examination in the
United States of the validity of an act of a foreign state challenged as in
conflict with international law but calls attention to the fact that in such
situations there is no precedent expressly contrary to the possibility that an
act so challenged could be examined. See Reporters' Note 3 to this Section.

. . .

§ 44 *Effect of Expression of Lack of Objection by Executive Branch
of United States Government*
     Under the foreign relations law of the United States the rule stated in
§ 41 does not prevent the examination of the validity of the act of a
foreign state if the executive branch states that it has no objection to the
examination.

Is Section 43 an improvement upon a more unrestricted act of state doctrine? The answer here depends upon whether domestic courts can be trusted to conclude that foreign official acts are "valid" if they are reasonably classified as "legitimately diverse." The designation of what is legitimately diverse must itself proceed from a world, rather than a national, outlook. Can this degree of detachment be expected in domestic courts in periods of political tension at the present stage of international relations? The evidence, although inconclusive, does not indicate a willingness by domestic courts to internationalize their orientation when dealing with litigation that affects "a political enemy" of the United States. For this reason, it is hoped that neither Section 43 nor Section 44 will be allowed to compromise the traditional scope of the act of state doctrine.

Sabbatino AND THE "SOLICITOR GENERAL'S MEMORANDUM RECOMMENDING U.S. SUPREME COURT REVIEW"

By order of the Supreme Court, the Solicitor General was invited to express the views of the United States on the *Sabbatino* litigation.[38] He recommended that the court grant a writ of *certiorari* on two grounds: first, to determine the extent of reviewability of a foreign act of state and, second, assuming some measure of reviewability in domestic courts, to decide what international standards are available to govern nationalization of alien property. "Neither of these questions has been recently examined by this Court, and, in our view, both have substantial public importance." [39]

Reviewing the precedents, the Solicitor General "takes no position at this time" on whether the *Bernstein* approach is "a permissible or desirable limitation on the Act of State doctrine." [40] The memorandum goes on to examine various executive communications in *Sabbatino* and in *Bahía de Nipe* and concludes that no executive opinion has yet been given as to whether or not Cuban nationalizations should have effect in United States' courts, although the Solicitor General expresses a willingness "to present a full statement of the Executive Branch and supporting argument upon the merits." [41]

Only then will it become clear whether the state-to-state protest against Cuba's nationalization program will be coupled with an

[38] See *supra* note 7 (first citation).
[39] *Id.* at 4.
[40] *Id.* at 6.
[41] *Id.* at 10; *cf.* memo filed in Rich v. Naviera Vacuba, S.A., *supra* note 7.

exception to the act of state doctrine, thereby permitting an American court to declare the nationalization to be illegal under international law. In this connection, it should be recalled that in the *Rich* case, when the executive was eager for dismissal, the Solicitor General presented a view flatly opposed to judicial inquiry. The act of state doctrine "applies with full force to preclude judicial review, in domestic courts, even where the act of the foreign state is asserted, as here, to be in conflict with or in violation of international law." [42] It is very hard to reconcile such a contention, except on a case-by-case analysis of United States interests, with executive encouragement of judicial encroachment upon the act of state doctrine. But it is equally hard to reconcile the *Bernstein* approach with an absolute act of state doctrine. There is great confusion here. What does the Legal Adviser mean when he says that it is up to the courts, "of course," to determine whether the Cuban nationalizations are valid? How can it be up to the courts unless inroads are made on the act of state doctrine? It is unlikely that the Legal Adviser meant to affirm the "determination" by deference to the validity of the foreign acts; he would have made explicit this subtle but important point.

THE *Sabbatino* BRIEF FOR THE UNITED STATES AS AMICUS CURIAE

In certain respects, this brief [43] is welcome and useful, although its fundamental tendency is, unfortunately, to emphasize executive functions at the expense of the national judiciary in matters of foreign relations law. I will first indicate the contributions made by the brief, and then suggest why I dislike its principal rationale.

The amicus brief, first of all, gives us in a coherent and persuasive form an authoritative statement of executive outlook on the crucial issues raised by the *Sabbatino* litigation; significantly, the brief is signed by the Solicitor General, the Deputy Attorney General, and the Assistant Legal Adviser for Economic Affairs, that is, by representatives of each of the principal executive departments concerned with international law.

---

[42] Quoted from Brief for Petitioner, pp. 26–27, Banco Nacional de Cuba v. Sabbatino—U.S.—(1963), reprinted in 2 International Legal Materials 1142, 1147 (1963).

[43] "Brief for the United States as *Amicus Curiae* in Banco Nacional de Cuba v. Sabbatino," filed September 10, 1963, conveniently reprinted in 2 INTERNATIONAL LEGAL MATERIALS 1009 (1963) [hereinafter cited as "Brief"].

Second, the brief both demonstrates beyond doubt the extent to which domestic courts have misconstrued executive intentions in the course of *Sabbatino* and, more generally, points out the hazards of allowing courts to act on the basis of what they presume the executive to intend.[44]

Third, the amicus brief treats the second *Bernstein* case as a narrow, atypical precedent that can be understood only by reference to its exceptional circumstances.[45] This interpretation of *Bernstein* resists the growing judicial tendency to assume that the policy supporting act of state deference is undercut whenever the United States finds itself at odds with a foreign country. The amicus brief explains why courts should not attempt to construe executive intentions on the basis of indirect evidence such as letters to counsel, protests to foreign governments, communications to other courts faced with similar litigation, or the general drift of foreign policy.

Fourth, the brief relies upon policy and precedent to argue against an interpretation of the act of state doctrine that permits judicial exceptions to deference whenever it can be shown that the foreign act violated international law.[46] And, fifth, a strong general argument is advanced to support the retention of the act of state doctrine in undiluted form.[47]

The argument developed in the amicus brief proceeds mainly from a conception of executive function in foreign relations. The

[44] *Id.* at 43–46.

[45] *Id.* at 33–43.

[46] *Id.* at 10, citing Oetjen v. Central Leather Co., 246 U.S. 297, 304 (1918); Shapleigh v. Mier, 299 U.S. 468, 471 (1937).

[47] *Id.* at 25–33, although the endorsement is restricted to *domestic* acts of a *recognized* foreign government. This leaves undisturbed the precedents that suggest that the act of state doctrine is unavailable for extraterritorial acts ("Brief," ns. 5, 12 & 13) and, possibly, for the domestic acts of an unrecognized government. If nonrecognition is allowed to suspend the act of state doctrine, then executive policy, not objective standards, is allowed to control the application of international law in domestic courts. The United States now pursues a political approach, withholding recognition either because it disapproves of a new government or state or because it seeks to bargain concessions in exchange for recognition. At the same time, arguments against recognition often stress the failure of the unrecognized government to obey international law. But why should such a state accept its duties under international law when it is unrecognized and when it is denied its rights? This digression seems warranted because recognition doctrine in the period since the *Pink* case (United States v. Pink, 315 U.S. 203 [1942]), raises the same kind of issues that are presented by the *Bernstein* exception to act of state. The amicus brief reserves judgment as to "whether a different rule should prevail in case of an unrecognized foreign government," at note 4, 9.

idea of executive function concentrates upon, but is not limited to, the protection of American public and private interests. Upon this basis, the act of state doctrine is endorsed as a way to assure that the executive enjoys the kind of flexibility needed to work out the best national responses in a variety of situations in which foreign acts of state affect United States' interests.

Similar considerations accounted for executive opposition to a liberal interpretation of the *Bernstein* suspension of deference. It must be understood that suspension is not appropriate merely because the executive is hostile to a foreign government and its policies. The brief takes pains to depict the special *Bernstein* context: "The governmental acts there were part of a monstrous program of crimes against humanity; the acts had been condemned by an international tribunal after a cataclysmic world war which was caused, at least in part, by acts such as those involved in the litigation, and the German state no longer existed at the time of [*sic*] State Department's letter. Moreover, the principle of payment of reparations had already been imposed, at the time of the 'Bernstein letter,' upon the successor government so that there was no chance that a suspension of the act of state doctrine would affect the negotiation of a reparations settlement." [48]

Therefore, the *Bernstein* exception to act of state requires an affirmative executive decision, formally conveyed to the courts, that a judicial resolution of the substantive issues in dispute is all right with the executive branch. Even then, as the brief makes clear, the court itself might decide for independent reasons that the act of state doctrine continues to apply to the litigation.[49]

It would appear that two main positions are taken by the executive. First, the act of state doctrine continues to serve well the executive interests in the vast majority of circumstances. Second, in the rare instance in which the executive department wishes to urge the judiciary to suspend deference, then a very explicit and formal statement to that effect will be made to the court.[50] The brief devotes a long section to explaining that executive silence should never be construed by a court as an equivalent to a "Bernstein letter." "[I]t

[48] "Brief," 38; Bernstein v. N.V. Nederlandsche-Amerikaansche Stoomvaart-Maatschappij, 210 F.2d 375 (2d Cir. 1949).

[49] *Ibid.* (by reference to the "conflict-of-law" rules of the forum).

[50] *Id.* at 46.

may be of the utmost importance to preserve silence or at least to refrain from issuing official documents upon the legal status of the act of a foreign government." [51]

It is easy to agree with certain parts of the executive argument, such as its stout defense of the act of state doctrine and its restrictive view of executive communications. Nevertheless, I find myself in sharp disagreement with the underlying rationale of the amicus brief that develops a strong argument for what amounts to the subordination of law to diplomacy in the resolution of international disputes involving foreign acts of state: "The primary and most satisfactory way to deal with foreign acts of state which violate international law is the exercise of diplomacy." [52] This is persuasive reasoning if confined to subject matter for which there is no consensus supporting a universal norm, but not otherwise. The courts, as independent judicial institutions, should invoke the act of state doctrine whenever the legitimate diversity of social systems casts doubt upon the availability of universal legal standards. But where this doubt is absent, as in the *Eichmann* case, then a domestic court promotes the development of world law by making a substantive judgment. Deference should be primarily a consequence of diversity and understood as such, and should only secondarily justify itself by foreign policy considerations or by the efficacy of diplomatic settlement techniques.

The brief develops a theory of the proper distribution of internal legal functions for the United States' political system. It largely neglects the need for a parallel theory that considers what would be an optimum distribution of legal functions within the global[53] political system. From this perspective, domestic courts provide a useful means to overcome the failure of the global system to develop adequate judicial institutions of its own. A domestic court confronted by an international law controversy is in a position to display the seriousness with which it regards international law.[54] Furthermore,

[51] *Id.* at 44.

[52] *Id.* at 28.

[53] The term "global law" is used, despite its awkwardness, to suggest that more is involved than the regulation of the relations among states.

[54] Prominent international lawyers as dissimilar as Quincy Wright and Myres S. McDougal have stressed the extent to which the growth of international law depends upon the formation of more constructive public and elite opinion. See, *e.g.*, Wright, *The Strengthening of International Law*, 98 RECUEIL DES COURS 1, 32 (1959); McDOUGAL & FELICIANO, LAW AND MINIMUM WORLD PUBLIC ORDER 376 (1961).

an opportunity is given to demonstrate the reality of a national commitment to a conception of international law that is broad enough to embrace antagonistic social and economic systems.[55] From the viewpoint of world legal order, this is a far more constructive rationale for act of state deference than is the stress of the amicus brief upon the primacy of foreign affairs and the superior pragmatics of executive settlement. Judicial opinions manifesting this spirit of deference as a functioning part of international law could serve as educational documents, especially if they disclosed a sensitivity to the character and limits of universal law in a divided world. Such a disclosure is far more meaingful than is a general admission that domestic judicial institutions are more inept than is the executive in matters of foreign relations law.

Furthermore, courts should be encouraged to operate as independent institutions deciding for themselves when the circumstances do not warrant deference: that is, when the diverse character of foreign official acts do not deserve respect because they contravene those fundamental norms resting upon a firm consensus among dominant nations. Where such consensus exists, then domestic courts can operate as active agents to apply and develop the substantive norms of the global legal order. Where such consensus is absent, then the act of state doctrine, without prejudging the substantive issue in other forums, permits domestic courts to apply and develop the jurisdictional norms of the global legal order.

This view of judicial function tries to develop principles that govern deference and its denial, without any reliance upon executive guidance. It seeks to make foreign relations irrelevant to the application of international law in domestic courts. As such, it runs against the current of American judicial practice that has tended to treat international law issues almost as if they were political questions and thus more suitable for executive than judicial settlement. The *Bernstein* approach to the suspension of deference, no matter how narrow, confers an *ad hoc* competence upon the executive that is not restricted by principles enunciated in advance. It thus reinforces a deprecating impression of international law as a weak legal system

[55] For a forceful expression of a view opposed to the present reliance upon a universal legal order, see McDougal & Lasswell, *The Identification and Appraisal of Diverse Systems of Public Order*, in McDougal & Associates, Studies in World Public Order 1–43 (1960).

rather than trying as a matter of national policy to counter such an unfortunate impression. These considerations lead me to oppose the adoption by the Supreme Court of the kind of rationale for the act of state doctrine that has been argued so clearly in the executive branch's amicus brief.

CONCLUSION

The Supreme Court has a momentous opportunity to clarify the proper role for domestic courts in international law cases. In addition, it can clarify the status of the act of state doctrine, as well as respecify the independence of courts from executive interference. The reasoning and rhetoric used to affirm judicial autonomy might also improve the domestic comprehension of the current limits of international law, especially if approval is given to Judge Waterman's insistence that the international environment is relevant to the authority of international substantive standards. The Supreme Court has also an opportunity to repudiate the implication of the *Pink* case that foreign policy considerations, when present, take precedence over the normal application of international law. This is part of a larger opportunity to denationalize courts and to emphasize the need to strengthen respect for international law. This is only accomplished by denying to its substantive rules a dispositive character in areas of legitimate diversity and, at the same time, by affirming their dispositive character in the areas where a substantive and political consensus exists, in order to assure that a legal standard has universal backing.

However, the Supreme Court decision is of secondary interest in the context of this book. The purpose of this extended critique of the *Sabbatino* case is to develop a theory about the role of domestic courts in international law cases. The theory is, in effect, a proposal that is based upon an interpretation of international society. Its relevance is neither established nor eliminated by a single decision of a domestic court, even if it is a celebrated case in a dominant nation. One reason that the case has attracted so much attention is that it is evidently perceived as a symbolic case.

It is symbolic because it raises such fundamental issues concerning the degree of judicial independence in litigation involving rules of international law. It is also symbolic because the decision reflects the extent to which domestic courts are prepared to give valid effect to acts performed by other social systems committed to values incompatible with their own. Tolerance for incompatible values is a precondition for harmony in a world composed of diverse social systems. Judicial awareness of this need for tolerance is itself an important step in the direction of adapting international law to changes in international environment. These issues are present in many contexts of interaction other than *Sabbatino*. The reasoning used here is transferable. No decision by the Supreme Court will settle these problems, for they go to the heart of the management of international conflict in our times. My analysis of *Sabbatino* seeks to develop some principles of general applicability.

Chapter VII

Sovereign Immunity: A Discourse on Recent Havoc

SOVEREIGN IMMUNITY AND ACT OF STATE: A POLICY CONTRAST

ALTHOUGH it is not generally acknowledged, criticism of the doctrine of sovereign immunity rests upon far less provincial grounds than does the attack upon the act of state doctrine. Whereas exemption by immunity is a consequence of the status of the defendant or his property, deference by act of state arises from an attempt to restrain domestic courts from adjudicating matters with a foreign locus in accord with the controverted policies of the forum. Thus, if applied in areas within which a legitimate policy diversity exists, the act of state doctrine safeguards a rational allocation of jurisdictional competencies among national courts. As has been already argued, the form of deference decreed by the act of state doctrine is an application of international law on the horizontal level, for international law *is applied* either when a rule of deference leads a national court to decline substantive jurisdiction or when substantive norms are used to settle the controversy between the litigants. Thus, criticism of the act of state doctrine expressed in the form of an invocation of the dictum from *Paquete Habana* is, as has been said, beside the point.[1]

But why decline jurisdiction simply because the defendant is a foreign sovereign or because the subject of the suit is sovereign property? It is the contention of this chapter that diplomatic immunity together with minimum rules of specific deference (applying, for example to acts of state or to warships) provides the sovereign with all the protection that is proper, given the character of international

---

[1] *Cf. supra* Chapter V, pp. 96–102; *but see* the tendency to cite *Paquete Habana*, 175 U.S. 677, 700 (1900) without any evidence that deference under the act of state doctrine may, in fact, be one way to apply international law; *e.g.,* Stevenson, *The Sabbatino Case—Three Steps Forward and Two Steps Back,* 57 AM. J. INT'L L. 97 (1963). In RESTATEMENT, FOREIGN RELATIONS § 41, Reporters' Note, at 136–38 (Proposed Official Draft, 1962) [hereinafter cited as RESTATEMENT], the act of state doctrine is not treated as a doctrine of international law.

disputes and national sovereignty in the contemporary world. Such a diminution of exemption by status, as distinct from deference by function, also helps to maximize the role of national courts as agents of an emerging international legal order.

In a sense, this is a relatively uncontroversial recommendation. Various commentators have urged either the drastic curtailment or the abandonment of the so-called absolute doctrine of sovereign immunity.[2] Two sets of arguments, somewhat similar to those found in the act of state literature, predominate. First, there is the stress on improving the remedial potentialities for participants in international commercial life. Restricting or eliminating sovereign immunity opens up national courts to those plaintiffs with contract or tort claims against sovereigns and their property.[3] Especially if combined with an annihilation of the act of state doctrine,[4] domestic remedies are made available to victims of the most controversial class of foreign acts, the allegedly confiscatory expropriations of private property, as soon as an instrumentality or ship of the foreign state dares to enter national territory. The position taken here makes the sovereign subject to the jurisidiction of a domestic court, but it retains the status of nonreviewability for official acts performed within the territory of the defendant sovereign.

The second ground for an attack on immunity arises in response to the changed character of international life. The notion of sovereign immunity was developed in the nineteenth century when a *laissez-faire* economic philosophy resulted in a clear functional differentiation between private and public spheres of activity. Thus, the sovereign did not go into business or enter into commercial trans-

---

[2] Among the most significant accounts are the following: Weiss, *Compétence ou l'incompétence des tribunaux à l'égard des Etats étrangers*, 1 RECUEIL DES COURS 525 (1923); H. Lauterpacht, *The Problem of Jurisdictional Immunities of Foreign States*, 28 BRIT. YB. INT'L L. 220 (1951); ALLEN, THE POSITION OF FOREIGN STATES BEFORE NATIONAL COURTS (1933).

[3] M. H. Cardozo, *Sovereign Immunity: The Plaintiff Deserves a Day in Court*, 67 HARV. L. REV. 608 (1954); Timberg, *Sovereign Immunity, State Trading, Socialism and Self-Deception*, in ESSAYS ON INTERNATIONAL JURISDICTION 40 (1961); Comment, *The Jurisdictional Immunity of Foreign Sovereigns*, 63 YALE L. J. 1148 (1954).

[4] *E.g.*, report, A RECONSIDERATION OF THE ACT OF STATE DOCTRINE IN UNITED STATES COURTS, ASSOCIATION OF THE BAR OF THE CITY OF NEW YORK (May 1959); Hyde, *The Act of State Doctrine and the Rule of Law*, 53 AM. J. INT'L L. 635 (1959).

actions, and the role of government was far more limited than it is today. Sovereign immunity was a convenient way to assure states that domestic courts would not obstruct their discharge of governmental duties. The simplicity of a rule of absolute deference assured uniform application, thereby encouraging the development of a universal standard without requiring a multilateral convention or supranational machinery. But the gradual expansion of state functions in the economic realm and, especially, the emergence of socialist states with state trading companies led to an increasing dissatisfaction with a solution of the problem of jurisdictional competence achieved by mere reference to the presence or absence of sovereign status.[5] It was thought that traditional patterns of immunity gave socialist or socialist-inclined states an unfair advantage. And, as a consequence of the expansion of economic activities by nonsocialist states, it was thought to be unfair to private interests to make them subject to legal responsibility while giving a governmental buyer or seller immunity in the same transaction. These reactions led to a variety of proposals to restrict the scope of immunity along functional lines that took account of the difference between governmental and "nongovernmental" acts by the foreign state. In what contexts should the foreign state be amenable to domestic jurisdiction? Although much of the original rationale for immunity, such as the irreproachable dignity of the state,[6] has been rejected, national courts, espe-

---

[5] In addition to the references given in notes 2 through 4, see Aron, *State Trading, Commercial Immunity, and The Jurisdictional Risks of International Trade,* in ESSAYS ON INTERNATIONAL JURISDICTION 21 (1961); Friedmann, *The Growth of State Control over the Individual and its Effect upon the Rules of International State Responsibility,* 19 BRIT. YB. INT'L L. 118 (1938); *cf.* also Brussels Convention: Convention for the Unification of Certain Rules relating to the Immunity of State-owned Vessels, Articles 1, 2 (1926), reprinted HUDSON, 3 INTERNATIONAL LEGISLATION 1837 (1931); Draft Convention, Competence of Courts in Regard to Foreign States, Article 11, Harvard Research 26, AM. J. INT'L L. (Supp.) 451, 597 (1932); 1958 Geneva Convention on the Territorial Sea and Contiguous Zone, U.N. Doc. No. A/Conf. 13/L. 52 [1958], reprinted 52 AM. J. INT'L L. 834 (1958); and, of course, The Tate Letter, reprinted as *Changed Policy Concerning the Granting of Sovereign Immunity to Foreign Governments,* 26 DEP'T STATE BULL. 984 (1952). *But see* Fensterwald, *United States Policies Toward State Trading,* 24 LAW AND CONTEMP. PROB. 369 (1959), for some suggestion of American ambivalence about the curtailment of the scope of sovereign immunity.

[6] See, *e.g.,* leading English cases: The Prins Frederick, 2 DOD. R. 451; *The Parlement Belge,* 5 P. 197, 205–06 (1880); *The Cristina,* [1938] 1 ALL E.R. 719.

cially in Great Britian and the United States, have found it difficult
to withdraw from their adherence to the doctrine of absolute immunity.[7]

In addition to reasons of the plaintiff's justice and to the changed
situation of the sovereign defendant, I would add three further reasons for discarding immunity. First, the determination of immunity
has too often been made by reference to executive policy toward
the particular sovereign. This invites politics into the resolution of
legal disputes situated in national courts and causes the outlook of
these courts to become nationalized. This, in turn, prevents the fulfillment of their role as impartial agents and undermines the credi-
bility of their claim to uphold international law. There is not any
necessary connection between sovereign immunity and executive
deference, but the actual connection made in American practice
makes it desirable to destroy immunity as a policy instrument in the
conduct of foreign relations. A discussion of recent cases discloses, I
think, the extent of the problem.[8]

My second argument against the doctrine of sovereign immunity
is that it interferes with the optimum performance of domestic
courts in the international system. The satisfaction of this objective
requires the gradual transformation of national courts into international institutions or at least into quasi-international institutions.
To reach such a goal, it is essential to curtail as much as possible
the executive interference in domestic judicial process. But this also
requires, and this is more radical, an insistence upon international
law as the primary source of regulative authority in the context of
transnational relationships. Therefore, it is desirable to simulate the
perspective of a supranational tribunal, at least to the extent of assuming competence on the basis of the nature of the transaction
rather than by reference to the character of the participating parties.
There is no longer any reason to accord states the special status of
being exempt from law observance. This attitude is part of an effort
to use national courts to hasten the process of supranational inte-
gration, a process whereby the relation between law and behavior
must not be subject to the requirement of national consent. In this

[7] Cf. e.g., the uncertainty expressed in *The Cristina* and in the Republic of
Mexico v. Hoffmann, 324 U.S. 31, especially Mr. Justice Frankfurter's concur-
rence at 38 (1945).

[8] Cf. *infra* at pp. 145–58.

respect, advocacy of the abandonment of sovereign immunity is a more ambitious equivalent to the argument in favor of repealing the Connally Amendment; [9] both proposals attempt to make the state subject to compulsory jurisdiction when its acts are challenged as giving rise to duties and liabilities. In the domestic context, the violation may thus be called into question directly by the aggrieved party (without awaiting the unreliable adoption of the cause by the party's state as plaintiff), and this applies to violations of any legal obligation, not just to violations of international law.

A third ground for urging the abandonment of sovereign immunity is that it is a crude rule incapable of sensibly differentiating between the proper occasion for restraint and the proper occasion for assertion of national judicial competence. Whereas the act of state doctrine can be correlated meaningfully with the distinction between legitimate diversity and universal standards, there is no comparable way to manipulate the applicability of the immunity concept. The status of the defendant is not a functional ingredient in typical jurisdictional decisions. For reasons that will be shown later, the concept of qualified immunity, especially if the qualifications are determined *ad hoc* by the executive department, provides neither uniform and predictable grants of immunity nor lines of inclusion and exclusion that are functionally persuasive. In fact, I would maintain that the ideal qualification of the immunity concept would make it almost a redundant invocation of the act of state doctrine, with its availability subject to the same considerations. Perhaps it does make sense to grant immunity to foreign warships, but even here the determination is one of fact (that is, the nature of a warship), or at least it should be treated as an issue of fact that can be left to the courts, thereby promoting ideas of judicial independence. It

[9] The Connally Reservation refers generally to the second of the three reservations attached by the United States to its acceptance of the compulsory jurisdiction of the International Court of Justice:

> Provided, that this declaration shall not apply to (b) Disputes with regard to matters which are essentially within the domestic jurisdiction of the United States of America as determined by the United States of America. (Res. 196, exception b, 79th Cong., 2d Sess., 1946).

For useful commentary, see Briggs, *Reservations to the Acceptance of Compulsory Jurisdiction of the International Court of Justice,* 93 RECUEIL DES COURS 230 (1958); Goldie, *The Connally Reservation; A Shield For an Adversary,* 9 U.C.L.A. L. Rev. 277 (1962).

must be admitted that recent tendencies toward unlimited judicial deference to executive policy seem to frustrate any attempt to transform national courts into quasi-international institutions.

A source of confusion has undoubtedly been created. This apparent championship of an activist role for domestic courts may seem to contradict the defense of the deference caught up in the act of state doctrine. However, it does not, since rules of deference are essential to guard against certain negative tendencies that would be encouraged by an expanding role for domestic courts. These courts, by virtue of their national outlook, are not yet competent to appraise substantive issues upon which major national societies disagree. Therefore, it is more in keeping with peace and order for domestic courts to express a pattern of respect and tolerance when the subject-matter of the dispute can be characterized as being within the scope of "legitimate diversity" and when the controverted acts were performed as official acts of a foreign sovereign acting within its jurisdiction. The problem is to reconcile judicial activism with the obstacles to the growth of a universal legal order in a divided world.[10] Sovereign immunity can be discarded, it is felt, without imperiling the presently fragile support for international law; but act of state is needed to discourage national courts from becoming partisans in the cold war and from championing national causes that lack an authoritative international imprimatur.

Perhaps this formulation puts the argument in an extreme form. There remain good grounds for exempting foreign diplomatic and military activity from normal national judicial process. This exemption may be most effectively achieved by a mechanical rule of exemption rather than by a substantive rule of deference. Hence, the immunity concept is functionally sound for cases involving the official representatives of foreign states, as well as military planes or ships. What makes something "official" or "military" seems to be an issue within judicial competence, although the possibility in international relations of a crisis arising from a delay or an adverse judgment supports the argument that the executive branch requires an extraordinary, as distinct from a routine, power to intervene in judicial proceedings. But the primary point remains: if we wish to reconcile nation-states with the growth of a reliable international

[10] For a general discussion see Lissitzyn. *International Law in a Divided World*, INT'L CONC. No. 542 (March 1963); see also Chapter III.

order, we must become accustomed to the partial denationalization of judicial institutions. In this sense, what is proposed is a reconsideration of the main rationale of the *Pink* majority.[11]

Rich v. Naviera Vacuba, S.A.: THE STATUS OF SOVEREIGN IMMUNITY IN DOMESTIC COURTS TODAY

Although it may be misleading, it is tempting and useful to search for explanations of the contradictory outcomes reached by those United States federal courts that have been asked to decide controversies arising from the expropriation policies of Castro's Cuba. The cases seem to agree about the illegality of the expropriations, but they grant or deny relief partly on the basis of whether or not the *res* of the controversy is free from actual sovereign possession. The result of this pattern is to inform expropriating states that they are able to ship expropriated cargoes abroad, or at least to American ports, if they expropriate the ship as well as the cargo or if they ensure that only state-owned merchant vessels are employed to deliver their expropriated goods. The irony is obvious: it is more dangerous to expropriate only the cargoes than to expropriate both the cargo and the instrumentality of carriage. This observation is supported by a comparison of *Sabbatino* with the *Bahía de Nipe* litigation.[12]

This irony is actually the more constructive perception of the comparison. It is also possible to relegate the whole subject matter to the vagaries of executive policy. Thus, if we want to release a ship in return for a particular favor from Cuba, then a suggestion of immunity or executive embarrassment is forwarded to the court, its acquiescence being accurately presumed.[13] Such *ad hoc* reciproc-

---

[11] United States v. Pink, 315 U.S. 203 (1942).

[12] Rich v. Naviera Vacuba, S.A., 197 F. Supp. 710 (E.D.A. 1961); 295 F.2d 24 (4th Cir. 1961); see also State *ex rel.* National Institute of Agrarian Reform v. Dekle, 137 So. 2d 581 (Fla. 1962); Dade Drydock Corp. v. The M/T Mar Caribe, 199 F. Supp. 871 (S.D. Texas 1961).

[13] Among the most important comments on the *Bahía de Nipe* litigation are M. H. Cardozo, *Judicial Deference to State Department Suggestions: Recognition of Prerogative or Abdication to Usurper,* 48 CORNELL L. Q. 461, 464–68 (1963); Lillich, *A Pyrrhic Victory at Foley Square: The Second Circuit and Sabbatino,* 8 VILL. L. R. 155, at note 75 (1963); see also Baade, *The Validity of Foreign Confiscations: An Addendum,* 56 AM. J. INT'L L. 504 (1962); Rabinowitz, *Immunity of State-Owned Ships and Barratry,* 1962 JOURNAL OF BUSINESS LAW 89.

ity [14] dissolves all stable expectations, undermines the authority of legal rules, and tends to destroy the confidence of the judiciary in its capacity to act as an independent institution in controversies involving the application of international law. Whether one views the recent extreme doctrine of executive deference as an indication of the priority of diplomacy over law or as a confirmation of the centripetal dynamics of the modern state, the doctrine is antipathetic to the growth of world legal order.

Either of two explanations is available to account for the difference in disposition in act of state and immunity cases: one involves the consequences of judicial analysis, and the other, those of executive discretion. Either the courts have concluded that the policies underlying act of state are less valid now than at the time of their original formulation and that the policies justifying the immunity doctrine continue to hold, or the courts have agreed to follow expressions of executive will, regardless of doctrinal consistency or policy justification. The nature of the choice and the consequence of choosing one way rather than the other are clarified, it is felt, by a scrutiny of the *Bahía de Nipe* litigation.

The S.S. Bahía de Nipe was sailing from Cuba in August 1961 to the Soviet Union with a cargo of sugar. Both the ship and the cargo had been acquired by the Castro government as part of its program of nationalization. While on the high seas, the master and ten of the crew held the rest of the crew in restraint, departed from their sailing orders by heading the ship toward the United States, and informed the U.S. Coast Guard of their desire to enter United States waters and there to seek political asylum from Castro. The ship was duly met by the Coast Guard at the three-mile limit and taken to anchorage near Lynnhaven, Virginia. Shortly afterwards, four sets of libels were filed: first, two longshoremen filed a libel against the vessel to recover judgments previously held against the Republic of Cuba and Naviera Vacuba, S.A. (the prenationalization owner of the vessel); second, a libel was filed by Mayan Lines, S.A. on the basis of its previous recovery of a judgment in a Louisiana state court of $500,000 against the Republic of Cuba (which had

[14] There is a difference between policies adopted by our courts in light of reciprocity as an ordering force (see Chapter II) and policies adopted in a specific case to get something in exchange from a foreign government. It is this latter behavior that we describe as *ad hoc* reciprocity.

consented to be sued); third, a libel was filed against the cargo by the United Fruit Company, allegedly its prenationalization owner; and fourth, libels for wages were filed by the defecting master and ten crewmen.

At this point, some rather odd complications originated. The clerk of the district court sought to have service of process delivered to the ship by a United States marshal. The Coast Guard refused to allow the marshal to enter the area of the ship, basing its action upon a statute authorizing the government to take precautionary steps to avoid danger and destruction; thus, it was claimed that it was necessary to deny service in order to assure the safety of the marshal. The district judge, upon discovering this interference, issued an order to the captain of the port and the commander of the Coast Guard to show cause why an order should not be entered permitting the marshal to serve his papers. At the hearing on this issue, the United States attorney advised the court that a communication from the Department of State would be forthcoming by telephone. A one-sentence letter from Secretary of State Dean Rusk to Attorney General Robert F. Kennedy was received in evidence. It read: "In response to your inquiry to the Department of State concerning the Cuban motor vessel Bahía de Nipe, now at anchor at Norfolk, this is to inform you that it has been determined that the release of this vessel would avoid further disturbance to our international relations in the premises." [15] This curiously worded note was supplemented by another dated August 20, 1961 in which the Secretary of State said, "I understand that the ship and cargo are owned by and are the property of the Government of Cuba." [16] Even more surprisingly, the note continued: "heretofore, assurances were given by the United States that the vessel would be released in the event that the Government of Cuba declared the vessel to be its property, requested its return, and provided sufficient properly identified personnel to replace those electing to remain in the United States. These conditions have now been fulfilled." The letter ends by concluding, without setting forth its reasons for so doing, that "in the circumstances, it is my opinion that the prompt release of the vessel is

[15] 197 F. Supp. 710, 714.

[16] The Solicitor General, when opposing United Fruit's application for a stay in the Supreme Court, gave views that he stated were shared by the State Department and the Justice Department. See text at note 40 *infra* p. 153.

necessary to secure the observance of the rights and obligations of the United States." [17] It also was made explicit that the Department of State had specifically instructed the Coast Guard Commander to forbid the marshal on board the vessel to serve process.

The opinion of Judge Walter E. Hoffmann strongly opposes the interference by the executive with the marshal's service of judicial process, although its holding leaves the basic allocation of competence somewhat uncertain. The president, it is asserted, has the authority to prevent our foreign relations from becoming "endangered by action deemed by him inconsistent with a due neutrality," and he may use any executive agent that "appears adapted to effectuate the desired end" so long as he is acting *in the absence of any statutory restrictions.*" [18] And the opinion suggests that "the difficulty here presented is that Congress has enacted legislation on the subject."[19] The president possesses extensive authority to act in periods of national emergency. The reasoning of the court is not very clear, but it emphasizes that the executive claim to bar service is a very extreme form of interference with judicial activities. The opinion observes that "there is no statute expressly authorizing the Executive to effectively destroy the judicial process for, without the ability to serve the court process, the doors of the court may be forever closed." [20] This produces "the conclusion that the Executive has exceeded his power in the present situation." [21] The question of whether the power, if conferred, would be constitutional is expressly reserved. Presumably, what is meant here is that a legislative enactment on the general subject of supervising the presence of foreign flag vessels in United States waters, prohibits additional executive claims except in the reserved case of a national emergency. The statute authorizes action to prevent a deterioration of foreign relations, but it does not indicate that a service of judicial process is a basis for invoking the statute, nor is there in the facts any suggestion that the prevention of service in this case was essential "to secure the observance of rights and obligations of the United States." [22] In view of the separation of powers, an executive prerogative to prevent judicial service

[17] 197 F. Supp. 710, 714–15.
[18] *Id.* at 717.
[19] *Ibid.;* statutory provision: 50 USC § 151.
[20] *Id.* at 718.
[21] *Ibid.*
[22] *Id.* at 713.

was held to be contrary to legislative intent. As Judge Hoffmann puts it:

> In our system of law, a dangerous precedent may be established under the urgency of the existing system. The separation of the three great powers of our government—Executive, Legislative, and Judicial—is essential to the preservation of a democracy. The several rights of our respective powers should be zealously safeguarded in upholding these constitutional powers.[23]

What is peculiarly interesting about this issue, otherwise tangential to our inquiry and raised by the denial of access to the marshal, is that the court expresses great concern about the preservation of the formal prerogatives of judicial independence [24] and yet manifests a willingness to sacrifice the functional prerogatives of judicial action in the immunity context. The courts seem far more ready to countenance an erosion of their role by accepting the expanding claims of the executive acting within the province of foreign relations than they are to tolerate the symbolic humiliation of an executive attempt to block a service of judicial process.

The first issue confronting Judge Hoffmann was the need to interpret a prior waiver of immunity by Cuba in a Louisiana state court, a waiver that had been entered with respect to the claim of Mayan Lines, S.A. The private plaintiff, in apparent exchange for Cuba's waiver of immunity, had compromised its claim against Cuba from an original $1,006,551.81 to $500,000. As a result of this compromise, it "is forever precluded from recovering in excess of the agreed amount of the state court judgment," and thus it is fair to conclude that its rights "have been substantially diminished." [25] In Cuba's Louisiana stipulation in April, 1961, the waiver was extended beyond the original entry of judgment to apply to subsequent action against all Cuban property, wherever located, and to extend to actions by Mayan to enforce or execute the Louisiana judgment. The Cuban request for recognition of sovereign immunity for the Bahía de Nipe and its cargo was not construed as "a *specific* repudiation" of the

---

[23] *Id.* at 718.

[24] 295 F.2d 24, 25: "We likewise do not condone the Coast Guard's refusal to permit the Marshal to serve the process and find no authority therefore in section 191."

[25] 197 F. Supp. 710, 721; *cf.* the language of the stipulation of waiver, at 719–20.

prior waiver of immunity.[26] The crucial issue, once the court held the Louisiana judgment entitled to full faith and credit, was whether "the waiver of immunity" was "of such a continuing nature that it cannot be repudiated as to a special item of personal property seized under attachment." [27] The court interpreted itself as bound by the *Dexter & Carpenter* [28] precedent to accept the subsequent claim of immunity as an effective repudiation of the waiver. "Cuba has breached its contractual agreement not to plead immunity in the enforcement of a judgment"; and "the law says this may be done." [29] What is odd here is that the court was so quick to accept the authority of the judgment of the Court of Appeals in *Dexter & Carpenter* [30] and to discount the relevance of the Supreme Court decision in the *Republic of China* [31] case. In this latter case, the Supreme Court held that when a sovereign initiates a claim as plaintiff in a court it is vulnerable to a counterclaim that reduces the sovereign's recovery; but the rationale was broad, based upon a "chilly feeling against sovereign immunity" that the court felt could be traced back as far as 1795.[32] It was noted by Mr. Justice Frankfurter that in domestic law and in executive policy (reflected principally through the advocacy of restrictive immunity) there has been a continual narrowing of the scope of immunity in United States practice based upon an overriding concern for fairness to litigants and upon a sense of public morality. In *Bahía de Nipe*, *Republic of China* was discounted because "it can hardly be said that Cuba, when it appeared in the Louisiana proceeding, was the party originally invoking the jurisdiction of that court. The limited scope in *Republic of China* does not permit the expansion of the 'fair play' doctrine in the absence of more implicit approval of our highest court." [33] But the guidance given by the Supreme Court seems to suggest an orientation for interpreting sovereign immunity, and this orientation is less concerned with the specifics of the adjudicative

---

[26] *Id*. at 720.

[27] *Id*. at 722.

[28] Dexter & Carpenter v. Runglig Jarnvagestyrelsen, 43 F.2d 705 (2d Cir. 1930), *cert. denied*, 282 U.S. 896 (1931).

[29] 197 F. Supp. 710, 723.

[30] Consider the relevance of *Dexter*.

[31] National Bank v. Republic of China, 348 U.S. 356 (1955).

[32] *Id*. at 359; *cf*. also 361–62.

[33] 197 F. Supp. 710, 723; contrast the judicial conservatism here with the display of judicial radicalism (innovativeness in the face of contrary legal authority developed by higher courts) in the first *Sabbatino* case.

context than with an insistence that the sovereign refrain from using its immunity to frustrate reasonable expectations that it has itself helped to create. An explicit waiver by a state would seem to illustrate this kind of situation. The Circuit Court of Appeals subsumed the waiver issue under an overarching willingness to defer to the executive. The doctrine of separation of powers is invoked to foreclose, rather than make mandatory, judicial inquiry—for the doctrine "requires us to assume that all pertinent considerations have been taken into account by the Secretary of State in reaching his conclusion." [34] The word "assume" is important as there is no indication whatsoever that, in fact, all considerations were taken into account by the Secretary of State. It is the emptiness of this assurance of executive inquiry that makes it more plausible to complain about shutting off the plaintiff and shutting out the judiciary.[35] The circuit court, unlike the district court, linked the waiver to the issue of deference in a case where the executive has spoken; thus, at least the effect of the waiver is held to be irrelevant because it is subordinate to executive discretion, rather than nullified by reference to the teaching of *Dexter & Carpenter.*

The district court considered the other allegations of the libellants, all of whom argued for disregard of immunity, either because the suggestion was insufficiently forwarded to the court or because the character of judicial independence enabled a court to determine for itself whether immunity has been appropriately given. The fact that the ship came within the jurisdiction of the court as a consequence of barratry is given great stress by the court. The relationship between the immune status and barratry is not examined; thus, would jurisdiction be accepted if the barratry was committed by the master of a privately owned ship? [36] It would seem that barratry by itself gives the court a policy basis for declining to act, although, at least in the criminal context, the illegality of the facts surrounding the acquisition of control over the defendant has not been normally allowed to interfere with the validity of a subsequent prosecution.[37] Should

[34] 295 F.2d 24, 26.

[35] *E.g.,* see articles cited in note 3.

[36] If the answer is affirmative, then the claim of immunity could have been kept irrelevant from the outcome in *Bahía de Nipe.*

[37] *Cf.* the separation of the means of acquiring jurisdiction from the subsequent application of criminal law in The Attorney General of the Government of Israel v. Eichmann, Criminal Case No. 40/61, District Court of Jerusalem, De-

a civil action be governed by contrary considerations? It is, admittedly, an artificial acquisition of jurisdiction, but it is also artificial to defeat a plaintiff's claim merely because a prospective defendant has been able to stay outside of the forum.[38] There is an aspect of foreign relations in all of this, but it has little to do with the immunity of the ship. If, in conditions of tension between states, the fruits of barratry are realized, then it does stimulate a retaliation and a worsening of relations. This is especially true if, as in the case of *Bahía de Nipe,* the United States is offering political asylum to those hostile to the foreign state that owned the vessel. But is it not a gross confusion to explain the refusal to subject the ship and its cargo to judicial action by reference to its sovereign status? Would we be prepared to tolerate Cuban judicial proceedings against highjacked planes owned by private airlines in the United States simply because the *res* was private rather than public? The crucial variable seems to be that neither side wants to allow interstate hostilities to interfere with normal transactions of trade and transporation. The United States does not want to encourage the kind of instability that would probably result if it appeared that we were prepared to accept a jurisdiction over Cuban property, whether public or private, that could not have been obtained except by barratry, especially if the instance of barratry is itself a political act. Such a rationale for a refusal to act, if based upon explicit statements to this effect from the executive, would illustrate a claim properly within the foreign relations domain that could be usefully accepted by the judiciary. In fact, it should not matter whether the ship brought in was Cuban or French or whether the court to which it was brought was American or Dutch. It can be argued with considerable reason that barratry should never be ratified as a basis for jurisdiction in a horizontal legal order.[39] Such a dis-

---

cember 11, 1961 (excerpted in 56 AM. J. INT'L L. 805, 835–45 [1962]); *cf.* the leading United States case of Ker v. Illinois, 119 U.S. 436 (1886).

[38] However, it is important not to separate this equity from the more fundamental equities involving the rules of deference that prevail in the forum. Thus, the repudiation of the act of state in those controversies where one party alleges a violation of international law affects negatively a proposal to curb immunities. Immunity is a crude instrument to achieve deference, for a greater functional clarity and a more convincing policy justification can be achieved by means of the act of state doctrine.

[39] Mutuality of tolerance and respect, as well as stability of specific transactions, is promoted by refraining from using individual defections from hostile regimes as a means to acquire jurisdiction, especially if the litigation concerns a matter within the realm of legitimate diversity.

position would avoid giving the impression that whatever the executive maintains is binding on the judiciary, even in the absence of any demonstration of executive reasoning or application of prior standards.

As it is, the opinion is ambiguous about the matter of Cuban ownership of expropriated property. Judge Hoffmann observes that "the Court would, if permitted to do so, find that title to the cargo of sugar remains in the United Fruit Company." He goes on, however, to say, "Unfortunately this is not sufficient as the decided cases tend to the view that vessels *and cargo* expropriated by, and *in possession of*, a foreign sovereign are immune from suit upon suggestion of immunity." [40] But how is this view to be reconciled with *Sabbatino?* As to the cargo, the only difference, besides the suggestion itself, is the fact that in *Bahía de Nipe* the Cuban government "possessed" the sugar.[41] In opposing United Fruit's application for a stay in the Supreme Court, the Solicitor General wrote in a memorandum that was said to incorporate the views of both the State Department and the Justice Department:

> It may be assumed that the confiscation is unlawful under international law, *i.e.,* so far as relations between the Governments of the United States and Cuba are concerned. But that does not mean that Cuba, as between itself and petitioner, does not have valid title to the expropriated property so far as our courts are concerned.[42]

Note that the policy supporting this conclusion would also tend to support deference in *Sabbatino:* that is, a recognition in domestic courts of the conclusiveness of official acts transferring title to property located within territory. This interpretation follows clearly from the Solicitor General's further statement that "it would not be inconsistent for the State Department to challenge the validity of the Cuban expropriation under international law, and at the same time to accept the validity of the confiscation of American property located

[40] 197 F. Supp. 710, 724 (citing three cases). Emphasis added.

[41] But see Mexico v. Hoffmann, 324 U.S. 30, 39–40 (1945) (Frankfurter, J. concurring).

[42] Memorandum of the United States in Opposition to Application for a Stay of United Fruit Sugar Company, Sept., 1961, reprinted in 1 INTERNATIONAL LEGAL MATERIALS 302 (1962). This issue of distinguishing between internal and international validity is never clearly perceived in the *Sabbatino* litigation, although it is glimpsed in Judge Waterman's opinion. See Chapter VI.

in Cuba, so far as our domestic courts are concerned." [43] Here again, as with barratry, a persuasive rationale for deference exists, but its basis is the act of state doctrine not sovereign immunity.[44] It is possible, I suppose, that United Fruit lost in the Supreme Court on grounds of act of state; in this event, the Supreme Court disposition of the *Sabbatino* case should be especially helpful for a resolution of the issue of whether a domestic court is entitled to satisfy itself that foreign acts of state are in accord with substantive rules of international law.

In *Bahía de Nipe,* the court was also faced with the argument that the grant of immunity would be inconsistent with the executive department's own doctrine of qualified immunity as expressed in the Tate Letter of 1952.[45] The *Bahía de Nipe* was, at best, a government-owned vessel engaged in commercial activities; without any indication of a reversal in the government's attitude toward the proper scope of immunity,[46] the *Bahía de Nipe* case stands forth as a precedent for the availability of immunity for state-owned and possessed ships engaged in trade. Judge Hoffmann explained the retreat from the Tate Letter by saying "that no policy with respect to international relations is so fixed that it cannot be varied in the wisdom of the Executive. Flexibility, not uniformity, must be the controlling factor in time of strained international relations." [47]

Thus, the long struggle of law to be relevant to international relations, particularly in periods of strain, is abruptly cast aside by the self-denying action of a judge.[48] The word "flexibility" is a euphemism for the liberation of the executive from standards and rules, even those of his own fashioning. What is worse, a departure from prior

---

[43] *Ibid.*

[44] Cf. discussion of government brief in the *Sabbatino* case, Chapter VI, pp. 132–37. The relationship between executive will and judicial action was obviously misunderstood by Judge Dimock and Judge Waterman.

[45] As cited in note 5; see a useful interpretation by Bishop, *New United States Policy Limiting Sovereign Immunity,* 47 AM. J. INT'L L. 93 (1953).

[46] For record of consistent United States support for the restrictive theory of immunity, see references in note 5.

[47] 197 F. Supp. 710, 724.

[48] The self-flagellating irony is that the executive has been more willing to affirm the court's competence than the court has been to accept it. See the appendix containing executive correspondence printed in the Solicitor General's Memorandum for the United States in the *Sabbatino* Case, No. 403, October 1963, reprinted in 2 International Legal Materials 212.

standards apparently does not have to be explained or defended by
the executive. It is merely done by executive fiat, transformed in the
process of transmission to and reception by the courts to emerge in
the form of a "suggestion." When the matter somehow touches upon
international relations, then "it is not for a court to question such
matters of policy, the reasons for action taken in specific instances,
the alleged inconsistent positions asserted and the 'findings' of the
Executive." [49] It is at this point, and not in the *Sabbatino* context,
that it seems apt to recall and insist upon the *Paquete Habana* dictum
accepting for American courts the obligation to apply international
law as often as it is relevant.[50]

This general endorsement of executive competence operates as
the premise for complete deference to the executive's request for immunity. This avoids any consideration of Cuban ownership and possession, as well as of the extent to which immunity can be conferred
in excess of the doctrine of qualified immunity. In principal reliance
upon *Ex parte Peru*,[51] an opinion written ten years before the Tate
Letter, the court concludes that the executive suggestion of immunity
"is final and binding upon the courts." [52] Conceding conflict on the
issue, "the conclusion of this Court is predicated upon what the Court
believes to be the principles set forth by the United States Supreme
Court." [53] The equivocal character of authoritative Supreme Court
guidance is neglected in the short *per curiam* insistence in the Circuit
Court of Appeals that when the Secretary of State has spoken, the
courts must heed the advice that has been given. The District Court
tries, somewhat unconvincingly, to refute each line of plaintiff's attack on immunity in this case, whereas the Circuit Court is content

---

[49] A study of the interpretation of the legal significance of various kinds of
semiformal advice is badly needed: for example, in executive suggestions, Advisory Opinions of the International Court of Justice, and Resolutions by the
General Assembly.

[50] See note 1 and Chapter V for the dictum and commentary upon its relevance.

[51] 318 U.S. 578 (1942); *e.g.* at 587: "When the Secretary elects, as he may
and as he appears to have done in this case, to settle claims against the vessel by
diplomatic negotiations between the two countries rather than by continued
litigation in the courts, it is of public importance that the action of the political
arm of the Government taken within its appropriate sphere be promptly recognized, and that the delay and inconvenience of a prolonged litigation be avoided
by a prompt termination of the proceedings in the district court."

[52] 197 F. Supp. 710, 725.

[53] *Id.* at 726.

to determine that the appropriateness of an exercise of executive discretion makes irrelevant any kind of disagreement with the executive's suggestion of immunity. Once the executive has been vested
with authority, the judiciary has no function other than to manifest
its accession.

Bahía de Nipe is an illustration of and an introduction to a more
general consideration of the proper province of sovereign immunity
in the contemporary judicial practice of the United States. An assessment of the case is consistent with a strong interest in the principles.
The opinion in *Bahía de Nipe* illuminates several dimensions of the
immunity problem. First, there is the problem of allocating competence between the judiciary and the executive in the immunity context. Does the executive have the preliminary competence to make
the allocation? According to *Bahía de Nipe*, there are no discernible
limits to what the executive may regard to be within executive competence, except perhaps the authority to foreclose judicial service of
judicial process upon a vessel or a person claiming to be immune.

Second, the executive is given absolute discretion to confer or
withhold a suggestion of immunity. There is evidently no obligation
either to explain why immunity is conferred or withheld or to abide
by principles pertaining to immunity that have been enunciated in
advance. Thus, for instance, the Tate Letter, adopting a policy of
qualified immunity so as to withhold immunity from state-owned
commercial enterprises and vessels, is evidently relevant for a court
when the State Department does not suggest immunity, but not relevant to the construction of an executive grant of immunity. Apparently the District Court, with Circuit Court approval and Supreme Court tolerance, has now given to the executive the same kind
of unrestricted authority to promote *ad hoc* government policy in the
immunity context as it has long had in the area of nonrecognition of
foreign governments.[54] One suspects that if a desire to normalize re-

---

[54] For a recent opinion that subordinates sovereign status to recognition (or
diplomatic) status, see Dade Drydock Corp v. The M/T Mar Caribe, 199 F. Supp.
871 (1961); this holding is directly contrary to Wulfsohn v. Russian Socialist
Federated Republic, 234 N.Y. 372, 138 N.E. 24 (1923), which had been assumed
to be an authoritative decision. Nonrecognition as a criterion to determine amenability to suit is more arbitrary and ephemeral than is nonavailability via sovereign
immunity. The atmosphere is so political that *Dade Drydock* does not even refer
to *Wulfsohn*. This is a very significant further subordination of the judiciary to
the executive policy of the moment, especially as applied to Cuba. The court

lations with respect to transport facilities had not dominated the executive imagination at the time of *Bahía de Nipe,* then hostility to Castro might have generated a contrary expression of executive policy.

Third, when the executive chooses to speak, there is no role for the judiciary; when the executive fails to speak, then a wholly distinct style of evaluating claims for and against immunity would presumably be adopted. In such situations, one would imagine a gradual erosion of immunity by a combined recourse to the equity rationale of *Republic of China* and the *Tate Letter,* the latter relying upon patterns of international practice shifting away from absolute immunity and indicating a muted intention to place private and state traders in the same position with regard to commercial litigation in national courts.

It is important to appreciate the extent to which executive encroachment is incompatible with the development of international law by domestic courts. This is emphatically the case if the executive is given license by the judiciary to exercise discretion without even manifesting a relationship to precedents or general principles. It is one thing to determine that the executive is in the best position to apply "the law"; it is another to approve of a process for executive decision that does not enable the observer or the participant to determine or challenge the reasons for the decision or to distinguish between a principled decision and an arbitrary one. Thus, it is the *form* of executive communication, as well as the extent of executive discretion, that constitutes the grounds for criticism. It forms part of a more general criticism of the willingness, in times of international stress, to allow political institutions of the modern state to displace legal institutions in matters of foreign affairs. At the very time when events seem to be making the state increasingly obsolete in external relations, we are building up that part of the state system that most favors the promotion of exclusive and immediate interests at the expense of the longer term benefits of increasing world legal order.[55] The outlook of *Bahía de Nipe* is profoundly inconsistent with the

---

makes the rupture of diplomatic relations equivalent to nonrecognition and suggests, among other things, how political and normative the general understanding of recognition has become under the impact of the cold war.

[55] For an interesting recent discussion, see Etzioni, *European Unification and Perspectives on Sovereignty,* DAEDALUS 498 (Summer, 1963).

development of an independent judiciary in the foreign relations field; it applies norms and settles controversies by looking at the relation between law and facts rather than by accepting a judicial outcome that happens to be most in harmony with the immediate national interests of the forum state, as determined by a harassed executive.

SOME COMMENTS ON THE COMMERCIAL EXCEPTION TO THE RULE OF IMMUNITY: DOCTRINE AND POLICY

There are, it should be emphasized, two centers of inquiry. First, the allocation of function between executive and judiciary in the event of a claim of immunity in a domestic court. Second, the delineation of the proper scope of sovereign immunity in contemporary practice, as a matter of law and as a matter of discretion. The *Bahía de Nipe* litigation was described at length to illustrate the confusion that exists in both areas. In the present section, some attempt will be made to perceive the American understanding of the scope of sovereign immunity. Here also, considerable confusion exists on a doctrinal and policy level; part of this confusion, unhealthy for the development of community standards, arises because courts have been unsure about the definition of their own role. The nature of the problems can be grasped most easily, it is felt, by looking first at the recent effort of the American Law Institute to formulate the law of sovereign immunity in its Restatement of Foreign Relations Law.[56]

Section 72 states the following rather confident rule:

> The immunity of a state under the rule stated in § 68 does not apply to proceedings arising out of commercial activities that the state carries on outside its own territory. Such proceedings, however, may not be the basis of ancillary legal process against the property of the foreign state located in the territory of the state exercising jurisdiction.[57]

This formulation is somewhat surprising for a document denominated a "Restatement." For, as the Reporters' Notes indicate, "the only decision in point holds to the contrary" [58] of the rule set forth in Section 72. What is referred to as "the only decision" was the 1925

[56] RESTATEMENT 212–50.
[57] *Id.* at 230.
[58] *Id.* at 232.

United States Supreme Court case of *Berizzi Bros. Co. v. S. S. Pesaro.*[59] The opinion was delivered by Mr. Justice Vandeventar in principal reliance upon Chief Justice Marshall's classic rationale for the immunity of public ships in *The Schooner Exchange v. McFaddan.*[60] Although it was noted that *The Exchange* dealt with the immunity of a foreign warship, it was felt that the justification for granting immunity was broad enough to be available "to all ships held and used by a government for a public purpose." Berizzi goes on to explain that a ship used "for the purpose of advancing the trade of its people or providing revenue for its treasury" is a public ship "in the same sense that war ships are"; furthermore, it avers that "[w]e know of no international usage which regards the maintenance and advancement of the economic welfare of a people in time of peace as any less a public purpose than the maintenance and training of a naval force." [61]

As the Reporters' Notes to the Restatement recognize,[62] reliance upon an executive suggestion of immunity was used as the principal basis for the subsequent decision in *Ex parte Peru*. "When the Secretary elects, as he may and as he appears to have done in this case, to settle claims against the vessel by diplomatic negotiation between the two countries rather than by continued litigation in the courts" then it is up to the courts to recognize this executive claim by accepting the suggestion of immunity.[63] The decision by Chief Justice Stone formu-

[59] 271 U.S. 562 (1925).

[60] 11 U.S. (7 Cranch) 116 (1812).

[61] 271 U.S. 562, 574 (1926); see also *The Maipo*, 252 Fed. 627 (S.D.N.Y. 1918) and 259 Fed. 367, 368 (S.D.N.Y. 1919):

> If the Republic of Chile considers it a governmental function to go into the carrying trade, as would appear to be the case here, that is the business of the Republic of Chile; and if we do not approve it, if we do not wish any longer to accord that respect to the property so engaged, which has hitherto been accorded to government property, then we must say so through diplomatic channels and not through the judiciary. Otherwise the judiciary are contributing to what might become, under conceivable circumstances, a *casus belli*.

But see *The Pesaro*, 277 Fed. 473, 482 (S.D.N.Y. 1921): "[I]n my opinion a government ship should not be immune from seizure as such, but only by reason of the nature of the service in which she is engaged." And, at 483: "So it may be said that the Italian government, by giving to the Pesaro the capacity to be sued in the Italian courts voluntarily strips the Pesaro of its sovereign character and waives all privileges of that character. . . ."

[62] RESTATEMENT 234.

[63] 318 U.S. 578, 587 (1942).

lates no accompanying duty by the Secretary either to disclose the reasoning underlying its suggestion or to adhere to criteria enunciated in advance.[64] This enables the executive department to assimilate decisions about immunities into the fluctuating framework of foreign policy. The result is to eliminate predictability and uniformity from the law. This kind of use of the courts as a conduit for political decision-making reached its culmination in the holding and dicta of *Bahía de Nipe*. The latter decision ran contrary to prevailing policy guides for the limits of immunity (*e.g.*, The Tate Letter) and offends basic equity notions (by overlooking the specific waiver by the Cuban government). The result in *Bahía* could, and probably should, have been reached by a stress upon the barratry aspects of the case. But just as the politicalization of the judicial process led the lower court in *Sabbatino* away from an emphasis upon the discriminatory feature of the expropriation, so now with respect to immunities the court agrees to play dead whenever the executive chooses to act.

But this also means that the judiciary is likely to act awkwardly when the executive is quiet, as in *Republic of Mexico,* where there was a certification of public ownership but no suggestion on immunity one way or the other.[65] Here also, the court was faced with a libel of a publicly owned ship engaged in commercial operations. The opinion, once again by Chief Justice Stone, achieved clarity about the absence of judicial function in working toward a formulation of a doctrine of absolute deference.[66] In the beginning, the decision held that "it is a guiding principle in such cases, that the courts should not so act as to embarrass the executive arm in its conduct of foreign affairs." Furthermore, "it is therefore not for the courts to deny an immunity which our government has seen fit to allow, or allow an immunity on new grounds which the government has not seen fit to recognize." [67] The notion of international "embarrassment," not an especially attractive idea to make prominent in a legal order, is advanced as the proper basis on which to decide whether immunity should be extended or withheld. This affirms the willingness to cast aside doctrine or substantive policy, in favor of a case-by-case inquiry into what

[64] United States v. Pink, 315 U.S. 203 (1942); see especially Chief Justice Stone dissent at 242.

[65] 324 U.S. 30 (1945).

[66] There is a double absolute here: first, the unrestricted view of immunity; second, the complete subjection to executive suggestion.

[67] 324 U.S. 30, 35.

would embarrass the United States in its foreign relations. It sounds like a notion developed by men who are skeptical about the role of law as a regulator of international matters, for what could be more embarrassing to the development of the habits of law than a bland endorsement of an inconsistent pattern of disposition? And, as *Bahía* also helps to show, what branch of government is less equipped or prepared than the executive to uphold consistent principles of response? Judge Mack, in an earlier version of the *Pesaro* litigation that eventually ended up in the Supreme Court, made a remark that admirably formulates this view of the subject: "Indeed, it would seem that foreign relations are much less likely to be disturbed if the rights and obligations of foreign states growing out of their ordinary civil transactions were dealt with by the established rules of law, than if they were made a matter of diplomatic concern." [68]

Hoffmann criticizes, in an interesting footnote,[69] the *Berizzi* decision, but only because it failed to act on the basis of executive guidance.[70] There was no consideration given to whether the distinction between governmental and commercial functions should guide the decision on immunity. Although it would take a courageous jurist to rehabilitate the general reputation of Mr. Justice Van Devanter by praising the wisdom of his reasoning in *Berizzi,* I think he raises an interesting doubt about deciding what is and what is not a governmental act of a foreign state. Since the advent of state-trading and socialism, commenators in the West have almost unanimously favored abridging immunity by referring to the characteristics of the activity for which the exemption is claimed and by relying heavily upon the capacity of a court to distinguish between governmental and nongovernmental activities.[71] Abundant foreign practice supports this approach, although the considerable inconsistency of the characterizations that have been given to activity by courts fails to establish

[68] 277 Fed. 473, 485 (S.D.N.Y. 1921); *cf.* also Jessup, *Has the Supreme Court Abdicated One of Its Functions?*, 40 AM. J. INT'L L. 168, 170 (1946); *cf.* also FISHER in INTERNATIONAL LAW IN NATIONAL COURTS 14 (Third Cornell Summer Conference on Int'l Law 1960).

[69] 324 U.S. 30, 35, n.1.

[70] A further irony, suggested by the RESTATEMENT at 233–34, is that in *Ex parte Peru* the executive suggested immunity in principal reliance upon the judicial authority of *Berizzi.*

[71] For discussions of this distinction, see the authorities cited in notes 2 & 3; *cf.* also García-Mora, *The Doctrine Sovereign Immunity of Foreign States and its Recent Modifications*, 42 VA. L. REV. 335 (1956).

anything close to a uniform approach based on predictable standards.[72] Thus, the outcome of a claim of immunity is uncertain even if one adopts the judicially developed and applied criteria for distinguishing the immune from the non-immune; the outcome varies, partly in reflecting the location of the foreign forum in which the litigation happens to take place. It has been suggested that uniform standards be fixed by the enactment of national legislation or by the negotiation of a multilateral international treaty.[73]

The United States has seemed to favor this restrictive approach to immunity, although it has never been able to translate it into effective and prevailing practice. As early as 1918, there was a disposition on the part of Secretary of State Lansing to advise courts to curtail unlimited immunity. Attorney General Gregory refused the suggestion on the principal ground that the law as it stood favored absolute immunity and that it was not up to the executive to urge the courts to make a fundamental change in law.[74] It is not entirely clear from the Attorney General's remarks whether his view of immunity is based upon a reading of the requirements of international law or is a recognition of an established tradition of domestic law; also, it may have been conditioned by the interest of the Justice Department in safeguarding the claim of immunity for assertion on behalf of United States activities abroad.[75] The *Berizzi* case adopted the Attorney General's view as authoritative law. Respect for this precedent, in turn, influenced the formulation of subsequent suggestions by the State Department and served as an explanation of its adherence to immunity in later cases. Finally, when the State Department decided to abandon *its* policy of recommending immunity in accord with the absolute form of the doctrine, it did so in a letter written by the Legal Adviser to the Attorney General: the Tate Letter.[76] The shift of doctrine in 1952 was explained mainly in terms of dominant patterns of practice by foreign states with a minimum reliance upon policy and equity considerations, although the growth of state trading, the failure of the United States to claim immunity in foreign jurisdictions, and the importance of providing remedies

[72] For surveys of the inconsistency found in practice, see Harvard Research, *op. cit. supra* note 5, at 609–11.

[73] Lauterpacht, *supra* note 2, at 227, 237–39, 247; García-Mora, *supra* note 71, at 359.

[74] 2 HACKWORTH, DIGEST OF INTERNATIONAL LAW 429–30 (1941).

[75] See Timberg, *supra* note 3; Fensterwald, *supra* note 5.

[76] See note 5 *supra*.

for people who do business with governments were all enumerated as additional reasons for the adoption of the restrictive theory.

What status would this new doctrine of qualified immunity acquire with respect to the future suggestions of the State Department? *Bahía de Nipe* illustrates a willingness to abandon the restrictive theory in the event that a wider concept of immunity is deemed desirable in order to achieve a particular result in foreign relations. What is more interesting is that the State Department felt no need to account for its departure from restrictive immunity, nor did the court feel inclined to request an explanation, at least no such evidence exists.

What effect does the Tate Letter have upon the behavior of the judiciary? If *Ex parte Peru* is truly declaratory of the allocation of competence between executive and judiciary, then the courts are bound to follow right along after the State Department. The Tate Letter itself is more cautious about its effect on the discharge of judicial function: "It is realized that a shift in policy by the executive cannot control the courts but it is felt that the courts are less likely to allow a plea of sovereign immunity where the executive has declined to do so." [77] No Supreme Court case has tested the scope of judicial function in situations where the State Department either declines to act or has been challenged by the court in a case where it has chosen to act. But we have the interesting phenomenon that the executive uses language that indicates a recognition of judicial function, whereas the judiciary abdicates this function by emphasizing the extent of executive discretion.

The Restatement is probably correct when it predicts judicial adherence to restrictive immunity in the event that the State Department declines to recommend one way or the other on the issue of immunity. But even here, a residual ambiguity exists. Does the failure to suggest immunity indicate a prior executive determination that the foreign government was engaged in private, as distinct from public, operations? In other words, is it tantamount to a refusal, such as the *Hoffmann* dictum that it is not up to the courts to recognize "new grounds" for immunity? [78] The characterization by a court independent of an executive suggestion that a given

[77] The Tate Letter, reprinted as *Changed Policy Concerning the Granting of Sovereign Immunity to Foreign Goverments*, 26 DEP'T STATE BULL. 984, 985 (1952).
[78] 324 U.S. 30, 35.

activity is "public" or "governmental" is thus understood to be a new ground. There is an alternative reading, although it is incompatible with the spirit of judicial abdication that prevails in *Hoffmann;* [79] but it is logically consistent with the holding: namely, that the courts adopt the restrictive doctrine but decide for themselves how it should be applied. Such an exercise of judicial function would be consistent with foreign judicial practice,[80] with the absence of classificatory criteria in the Tate Letter, and with a normal appreciation of judicial competence. However, there is no indication that courts are willing to participate in this activity in immunity cases.

One can summarize the situation of immunity claims in United States courts by observing that the subject is governed by executive decision. Furthermore, the exercise of executive discretion apparently involves a free interplay between general policy and *ad hoc* considerations, and courts appear quite content to implement an executive decision that is based upon *ad hoc* grounds without even requesting an explanation for the departure from general policy. A study of *Bahía de Nipe* confirms these conclusions and illustrates the problems presented.

PERSONS, THINGS, AND CLAIMS

The retention of an absolute doctrine of diplomatic immunity seems reasonable. It gives some assurance that the security of diplomatic contact will not be impaired by private or public harassment in periods of tension. Even though such immunity results in individual injustices, as when an ambassador causes an injury to private citizens by reckless driving, it is probably the most effective way to keep diplomatic channels open under all conditions, including those of crisis and hostility. Limited abridgements of diplomatic immunity, by the development of a restrictive concept that limits immunity to acts performed in the course of diplomatic duty, could never be undertaken with the confidence that courts and executive officials would not yield or seem to yield to political pressure when their decision was to refuse immunity. Therefore, it is best to foreclose such lines of interpretation by confining inquiry to the personal status of the defendant. Once the person is found immune, juris-

---

[79] *Cf.* Jessup, *supra* note 68.

[80] *Ibid.* See H. Lauterpacht, *supra* note 2, at 250–72, for review of multinational judicial practice.

diction is defeated. There is, however, no reason to extend immunity to members of a diplomatic entourage or, for that matter, to anyone that is not accredited diplomatic status upon entry.

The same kind of reasoning applies to things that are sought to be attached either to establish *in rem* jurisdiction or when the effort is made to proceed from judgment to satisfaction. Thus, places designated for the conduct of diplomatic activity should be protected by absolute rules of immunity. Similarly, foreign warships and military aircraft should be immune from attachment; the distinction between a warship and a merchantman may not be easy to make if, for instance, the ship has hybrid functions. Here, as with most issues relating to status, the executive could be properly entrusted with the job of classification, although it would be beneficial to require that general policy criteria be announced in advance as the basis for particular decisions. A law-oriented approach has always emphasized the advance disclosure of standards for decision. Just as the courts are urged to accept as one role among several the task of acting as an international institution, so also might the argument be made with respect to the behavior of the foreign relations office in the executive branch. To play such a role requires the adoption of a style of behavior that is characteristic for a legal system and especially for the quest for a uniform application of visible rules.

A rule-oriented approach cannot do away with judgment and interpretation of borderline cases. There is also the need to heed Mr. Justice Frankfurter's advice in his *Hoffmann* dissent in order to avoid resting decisions on distinctions that are too tenuous. It may be possible, as a first step, to bring United States claims of immunity into harmony with the grant of immunity to foreign claimants in United States courts. A more ambitious plan would involve an advance definition of what constituted an immune public vessel.

In general, it would be desirable to allow the plaintiffs with contract and tort claims arising out of transactions with a foreign government to proceed without concern for the identity of the defendant. Difficulties are presented, however, by the attempt to serve process or attach property. How would one identify a public vessel that is properly exempt from *in rem* jurisdiction? Even a warship should be made to pay for its provisions, but not by being forced into a domestic court against its will.

Why should assets, merely because they are owned by a foreign government, be made exempt from attachment or made unavailable for the satisfaction of a judgment? The same equity considerations that led the Supreme Court in *Republic of China* to allow a counterclaim against a sovereign plaintiff should also allow enforcement against a sovereign defendant that has consented, or has been found subject, to prosecution. Immunity, as a modern concept, should be correlated with functions, not with status. The conduct of diplomacy and the noninterference with military operations require some method in order to withdraw litigation from the courts. Perhaps this result would be achieved with greater clarity of purpose if the executive branch were entrusted with the explicit task of applying these two exceptions.

How relevant is international law? Can it be said that, regardless of policy, customary rules of international law require that the doctrine of sovereign immunity be upheld? The abridgement of immunity in many foreign courts confirms the existence of broad discretion possessed by states in this realm; this discretion is further confirmed by the absence of protest against diverse patterns of practice. Certainly, states have the authority to reformulate the basis for jurisdictional exemptions by relying upon functional rather than status concepts. It is also quite clear that, from the viewpoint of the international system, a state may distribute its internal competencies between the two parts of government as it sees fit; the allocation of competence between judiciary and executive is a matter of domestic jurisdiction, although its exercise, as this book maintains, is closely related to the growth of international law. So long as the minimum duties to safeguard the security of diplomatic and military contact are carried out, the choice of legal rationale adopted by national courts would not offend duties to uphold international law.

Abandonment of the rhetoric of immunity would accord with efforts to downgrade the state as the ultimate repository of authority in world affairs. With the virtual disappearance of monarchies, the state has become a political abstraction for a vast bureaucratic apparatus administered by a variety of ordinary men. It is inconsistent with the development of a rule of law community to consider that these men are outside the realm of law when they are performing governmental functions; an insistence upon norm-oriented behavior is an increasing characteristic of the relations between a government and its own nationals. There is no reason why a foreign government should be any less liable for the negligent injury of an individual than is a foreign corporation. And there is no reason to perceive this kind of controversy as a matter of foreign relations. Rather, it is a matter of governing transactions by law—and this means allowing parties to receive legal relief for breaches of faith or violations of duty.

Immunity is a concept appropriate only for a society in which, as a matter of policy, certain acts and actors are placed outside the law. Immunity is hostile to the policy of extending law to cover in an orderly and a just fashion as many controversies involving international law as possible. An argument in favor of a minimum doctrine of immunity is part of a program for bolstering the independence of courts in litigation involving foreign facts and actors. Independence is not enough. There must also be a strong insistence on an impartiality that depends upon a detachment of courts from foreign policy. A sovereign defendant should be confident that its participation in litigation is not influenced by conditions of hostility between itself and the forum state. Nonimmunity raises quite different issues than does a refusal to defer to foreign official acts. In one case, an impediment to conventional judicial inquiry is removed; in the other, a judgment must be made about the compatibility of a foreign government's social policy with international law. Sovereign immunity and act of state are well suited to disclose the arguments that favor judicial activism in one context and judicial deference in the other.

SOVEREIGN IMMUNITY AND WORLD ORDER

There is an extensive critical literature that argues for a narrower doctrine of sovereign immunity.[81] The arguments characteristically stress the plaintiff's remedies, a reliability in commercial practice, and the elimination of advantages for state trading or socialist operations and economies. The realization of these objectives is said to be frustrated by a broad immunity doctrine because the government is today so often an important participant in commercial life; the argument is bolstered by a reference to the decline of "internal" immunity, that is, immunity of a government in its own courts, and by the asymmetrical practice of states with respect to claiming immunity abroad. The United States, for instance, neither claims immunity for its commercial acts *(jure gestionis)* nor seeks to exempt

[81] *Cf. supra* notes 2 through 5.

its public nonmilitary vessels from foreign *in rem* jurisdiction. The argument is also connected with the movement to desanctify the state; this favors treating a foreign government more as a bureaucratic abstraction than as an earthly embodiment of the divine. In functional terms, it is hard to distinguish the impact of state activity upon private lives through negligence and breach of contract from a similar detriment inflicted by any other kind of corporate entity. The same reasoning would suggest that international institutions should be made legally responsible for their nondiplomatic activities.

These sovereign immunity cases do not depend upon judgments about whether a foreign state's social and economic policy conforms to international law. They involve routine application of noncontroversial substantive norms to human activity, allowing for relatively insignificant variations both in standards of recovery and liability and in the criteria used to choose the applicable law. Although a particular outcome may be unfair, it will not likely entail anything more fundamental than an obligation to pay some money to an "injured" party. For instance, the claims made in the *Bahía* litigation by United Fruit, the pre-nationalization owner of the cargo, should be foreclosed, but by rules of deference (act of state) not by a status exemption (sovereign immunity). These rules of deference, if applied to uphold legitimate diversity among states, are a more precise instrument for keeping out of domestic courts the kind of litigation for which it is not yet suited. The amenability of foreign sovereigns to private litigation is a reasonable burden to place upon a government that serves its interests by entering into foreign transactions. The same reasoning that makes foreign individuals and corporations subject to the claims of the territorial legal system applies to actors with governmental status. It is part of the general effort to extend the coverage of law as far as possible. Furthermore, the reduction of the scope of immunity makes a more appropriate use of domestic courts in a decentralized social system.

For the reasons outlined above, it is important to routinize litigation involving a foreign sovereign. This counsels against a stress upon the links between foreign policy and domestic litigation and thus against the use of executive intervention, except to assure the security of diplomatic action and military property. Immunity should not be available as a bargaining counter; it makes impossible a prediction of the outcome, it undermines judicial independence, and it makes law subordinate to politics.

These problems have been analyzed for decades, but not from the perspective of optimalizing the use of domestic courts as agents of an emerging international system of order. It is this perspective that governs the conclusions set forth here. And, from this perspective, it is essential to stress the dependence of our critique of sovereign immunity upon the acceptance of our defense of act of state. If deference rules are overcome as recommended by the *Restatement* and followed as in *Sabbatino,* then immunity exemptions should probably be retained at maximum breadth, so as to have some way left to indicate respect for the diverse sovereign. Our principal assertion, however, is that respect for diverse policy is appropriate, whereas respect for the sovereign, as expressed through the immunity concept, is unnecessary, oblique, and detrimental. In conclusion, act of state finds an adequate functional justification; sovereign immunity does not.

Chapter VIII

Domestic Courts and World Legal Order: Concluding Comments

A DOMESTIC COURT operates at that peculiarly sensitive point where national and international authority intersect. The character of this intersection is closely connected with the role that can be given to law in world politics. The classical argument is between monist and dualist conceptions of international law—that is, between those who assert the supremacy of international law and those who maintain a theory of dual sovereignty to explain the connection between the state and the international legal system. This traditional controversy was waged primarily by European scholars contending for inconsistent applications of doctrinal logic. These inconsistencies centered upon interpretations of the proper way to fuse the idea of national sovereignty with the idea of an obligatory international law.[1]

The relationship between national and international authority remains at the core of my inquiry into the proper functioning of domestic courts. However, the relationship is not conceived of as a problem calling for doctrinal reconciliation. It is instead approached as a matter of social and political dynamics—as a search for a conception of domestic judicial function that is broad enough both to acknowledge the national setting and to explain the duty of upholding international law. This conception of judicial function is based upon an interpretation of international society: its values, conflicts, participants, structure, and requirements for minimum order. Importance is especially attached to the weakness of central or international institutions, as well as to the evidence of diversity and consensus that is found when one compares the policies both prevailing and advocated within separate national societies. The

[1] KELSEN, PRINCIPLES OF INTERNATIONAL LAW 401–47 (1952); a useful short summary of the issues is found in BRIGGS, THE LAW OF NATIONS 17–24 (2d. ed. 1952). See also McDougal, *The Impact of International Law upon National Law: A Policy-Oriented Perspective,* in McDOUGAL & ASSOCIATES, STUDIES IN WORLD PUBLIC ORDER 157–236 (1960).

supremacy of national law within national territory is regarded as an established reality, except in those instances in which there is among states a strong consensus either affirmative or negative, and this consensus must include the most powerful states. Where diversity exists, common standards are both ineffective and inappropriate, at least so long as the enunciation, the application, and the enforcement of international standards cannot be entrusted reliably to central institutions; there is no evidence that such centralization is forthcoming. In contrast, where uniformity exists to support political majorities in international institutions, there is a basis for effective and appropriate common standards, even in the event that such standards override the fundamental policies of the national governments. This general distinction serves to identify the domain within which substantive rules of international law can and should be made to operate, as well as to suggest the domain within which the diversity of national policies can and should determine "the law." Within this context of diversity, the role of international law is confined to the tasks of making rules of deference explicit and uniform and of formulating mutually acceptable ways to delimit the domain of national competence. This general relationship between national authority and international consensus should guide and dominate the analysis of what domestic courts should and should not do.

This is tantamount to urging that the general will of the international community, as it is formalized in the recommendations and decisions of the principal organs of the United Nations, is a formal source of international law. It should be noted that this is a radical contention. For one thing, the requirement of consent—either expressed (conventional international law) or presumed (customary international law)—is dropped. For another, no limit is introduced to confine the claims of the political majority of nations within the domain of reason, fairness, or common expectations. Instead, law develops or fails to develop depending upon the presence or absence of a consensus that is available to transform its policy into effective action. This limitlessness of the authorization points to the need for, but not the existence of, a global constitution that specifies procedural and substantive restrictions governing the implementation of a global consensus. Until World War I, the idea of national sovereignty provided international society with the functional equivalent of a constitution. Today, the doctrine of sovereignty expresses the national claim to be autonomous in a form that is too absolute for the realities of present international society. Instead of the rude insistence upon over-all autonomy, a set of specific restraints is needed. The Charter of the United Nations incorporates the doctrine of national sovereignty into the formal structure of the organization; however, the history of the United Nations suggests that the idea of sovereignty possesses no political content and generates no predictable restraints upon the assertion of supranational authority. This situation creates a serious weakness in international relations that undermines the authoritative status of international law and seems to inhibit its development. In consequence, the lawmaking institutions are formally restrained by a doctrine that is almost without practical significance.

Another general observation is closely associated with the national status of domestic courts. States continue to be unwilling to entrust international tribunals with reliable and regular adjudicatory competence; the result is that domestic courts are often the only judicial institution likely to adjudge the legality of important controversies about the application of international law. If national courts are going to help fill the institutional vacuum, then it is essential to work toward a common methodology that would enable any national court to act within a uniform pattern of outcomes and explanations. Obviously, the stress upon diversity and deference means that the same controversy will yield different *substantive* results depending upon which national law is chosen as predominant.

Unless some fairly common method for the choice of applicable national law can be formulated and made acceptable to most states, a system of law based on decentralization either breaks down or operates in a marginal manner. Therefore, the subject of jurisdiction is a critical focus of inquiry. One seeks rules of deference and delimitation that are themselves supported by a consensus broad enough to include the main representatives of the diverse positions.[2]

---

[2] I have tried to deal with the significance of diversity, especially if it involves an encounter between revolutionary and anti-revolutionary outlooks, in a series of essays: *Revolutionary Nations and the Quality of International Legal Order*, in THE REVOLUTION IN WORLD POLITICS (Kaplan ed. 1962); *Historical Tendencies, Modernizing and Revolutionary Nations, and the International Legal Order*, 8 How. L. J. 128 (1962); *Revolution and International Order*, a paper presented to the American Society for Political and Legal Philosophy in Sept. 1963, and to be published in the NOMOS volume VIII on REVOLUTION.

Suppose, however, that some states accept this method of allocating legal competence between national law and international standards and that others merely maximize the extent of national policy by refusing to defer to diverse foreign standards. This, it may be assumed, is the way in which the revolutionary states in the Sino-Soviet orbit and certain ardently nationalistic new states are likely to behave. Is there any reason to encourage domestic courts in the United States to abet the policies of nationalistic and communist states by rules of deference? The response to this question is quite crucial to the process of forming a theory about the optimum participation of a nation in the present system of international relations. It depends upon the extent to which it is regarded as possible and necessary to influence the behavior of other actors in the decade or so ahead by a policy of explicated self-restraint. This is partly a matter of predicting how other states will behave and partly a matter of suggesting how they should behave in view of an interpretation of certain objective circumstances. If, as argued in this book, nuclear weapons have established a novel boundary upon international conflict, then certain adjustments of self-interested behavior are essential, regardless of ideology or objectives, in order to guard against the risks of nuclear war. Among the most pervasive of these adjustments is a recognition in theory and practice that coercive conflict among states with access to nuclear weapons is self-destructive; [3] thus, one way to reduce the incidence of coercive conflict is to improve the method by which areas and subjects of policy-supremacy are allocated among states with different social systems. Domestic courts have extensive experience with problems of balancing the claims of the forum against the claims of foreign states that have an interest in the outcome of a legal dispute. The judicial arena is an appropriate place for an articulation of a general view of international relations in which doctrines of reciprocal deference govern areas of significant diversity and in which common efforts at enforcement govern areas of significant consensus. Such an orientation seems consistent with the objective interests of all na-

[3] The interpretation of what kinds of interstate conflict are now too dangerous to be undertaken is at the center of the ideological aspect of the Sino-Soviet dispute. China contends that force can be used to help foreign revolutionary struggles without raising the risks of nuclear war to unacceptable levels; the Soviet Union disagrees. Some of the disagreement undoubtedly concerns what level is regarded as unacceptable.

tional actors in a nuclear age. In order to communicate the argument in favor of such a pattern of behavior, it would seem appropriate for the United States to seize the initiative, as it is a leading nuclear state and the dominant member of a conservative coalition in world politics. Therefore, the argument of this book is directed primarily at the judicial behavior of courts in the United States, although the rationale is applicable to the participation of any national actor in the international system. To adopt this position would undoubtedly lead courts in the United States to resolve certain issues altruistically at a time when foreign courts were resolving them egoistically. This would probably involve some sacrifice of American positions as narrowly conceived, but it seems a trivial sacrifice compared to those that we appear ardently ready to make in order to uphold our obligations of collective self-defense or of foreign aid. The willingness to sacrifice is well established in the military context of defense and in the political context of anticommunism. In contrast, the recommendation that a nation sacrifice its policies to serve the cause of improving the system of world order continues to sound unrealistic. "Why?" never occurs to those who are willing to permit the death of thousands upon remote battlefields.[4]

There is a pressing present need for a deeper understanding of certain common interests among nations—interests so important that they take precedence over differences in ideology, wealth, culture, and power. The United States, as a dominant actor with an obvious interest in preserving a stable international environment, has a special opportunity and responsibility to clarify the area of common interests. The settlement of controversies involving applications of international law in domestic courts provides the occasion. These courts are presented with the choice between decisions based upon the particular concerns of that nation in which the court is located and decisions emphasizing a community perspective identified and realized by resort to universal criteria. It would bear persuasive witness to a nation's commitment to world order if it encouraged its courts to behave more like international than national institutions, if

---

[4] It is an aspect of the domination of means over ends, of short-run considerations over long-term interests, and of immediate concerns over the more far-reaching aspirations throughout man's social and political life. This pattern makes change occur at an exceedingly slow pace unless it is induced by coercion or trauma.

it accepted the prospect that the rules of law impartially applied might give legal comfort to political enemies, and if it demonstrated a greater preference for the growth of law in world affairs than for the coordination of domestic judicial behavior with the day-to-day pursuits of foreign policy. Decision-making in the fields of economic policy and human rights provides exactly the right opportunity for demonstrating a national willingness to accept social diversity for some matters and to insist upon solidarity for others.

It may be difficult for the United States to persuade revisionist and revolutionary nations to share this kind of constructive approach to world affairs; these states, by history and ideology, have deep convictions about the need to alter the present system of international relations in certain drastic respects. The ex-colonial states are particularly reluctant to subordinate the immediate satisfaction of selfish interest to the more remote causes of world order and peace. There is a need for a new understanding, both of what their future interests really are and of the degree to which former imperialists and former colonies risk a shared doom by continuing to permit international relations to proceed within traditional parameters of conflict. The effort to induce a new orientation of nations should be understood in the light of these bleak prospects. Immediate results cannot be expected, but patient and articulate leadership by the nations favored by history, circumstance, and resources may create an awareness of the extent to which self-interest has come to be identical with mutual welfare in international relations.[5] Domestic courts in the United States are both excellently endowed and excellently situated to widen the subjective appreciation of these facts of solidarity in world affairs.

This objective has certain implications for judicial method. The development of common standards of deference by courts situated throughout so heterodox a community as the international social system requires rules that are based upon easily visible standards or delimiting boundaries. This leads to somewhat mechanical judicial behavior that may defeat the maximization of social policy in many

[5] This analysis is well developed by McDougal & Feliciano in Chapter IV of Law and Minimum World Public Order—The Legal Regulation of International Coercion 261–383 (1961); see also the very suggestive *Introduction* in Stone, Legal Controls of International Conflict XXXI–LV (1954).

specific cases. There is a need for objective standards, for relating activity to a single national polity, and for eschewing the sophistication of a policy-science approach to the interpretation of legal rules.[6] Thus, the old-fashioned notions of territoriality and nationality seem to be well adapted to contemporary needs. It is essential to realize that such a strategy arises from the distinctive needs of a decentralized and heterodox social system for the development of common rules. It is a special jurisdictional case that makes less applicable the kind of jurisdictional sophistication that has been developing in centralized and relatively homogeneous domestic societies. Before courts can advance community policy in international relations, there must be a more widespread appreciation that a community exists.

Judicial self-restraint is a favorite topic of the day. It is at the center of the present controversy about how the courts or the Congress should allocate responsibility for the development of civil rights. The case for judicial activism or judicial self-restraint is not usefully decided by an appeal to hallowed dogma. Rather, an evaluation depends upon the tradition of the community, the structure of the social system, the character of the issue, and the extent to which the values underlying applicable rules are shared. The argument of this book is that particular attention must be given to the horizontal structure of international society, to a dominant convergence of values in the human rights area, and to a dominant divergence in the area of economic policy.

Rational analysis must also take account of the costs of a military settlement of international conflict, especially in view of the radical advances in the technology of war. If this were done, there would be a much greater incentive for all participants in a situation of international conflict to seek an outcome compatible with the maintenance of nuclear peace, even if this compatibility can only be achieved by

[6] There is a crucial difference between the perspective of the scholar-observer and that of the authoritative decision-maker that is often overlooked. Sophistication about the fluidity of the legal order contributes depth to an "outsider's" understanding of the legal system, but it may undermine the stability of law if it is adopted by the "insider." This is especially true with respect to a horizontal legal order threatened with disruption by conflict and distrust; thus, there is a need to emphasize the objectivity of the system in the course of authoritative communication among officials in various states. Judicial opinions offer an excellent medium for communication.

the sacrifice of political and economic objectives either by those states seeking to maintain the old order or by those striving to create a new one. This can be illustrated as follows. Prior to World War II, it was still plausible to seek strategic goals by recourse to warfare or to threat of warfare; today it is not. Even the preparation for nuclear war undertaken by powerful states hostile to one another is dangerous over an extended period. Therefore, a sufficient reconciliation between international antagonists must be sought in order to minimize the dangers of nuclear war.

This has consequences for the role of the judiciary. The subordination of judicial practice to national policy made sense in relation to Nazi Germany; it does not make similar sense with respect to the Soviet Union.[7] The costs of war are now too high, the prospects for an eventual reconciliation too good. This sociopolitical interpretation leads to a reversal of priorities in the judicial context. It now seems more important to make domestic courts agents of world order than to instruct them to be servants of national policy. The development of law in world affairs depends upon convincing all major actors that a strong legal order, rather than its absence, serves their interests. This goal can be advanced by denationalizing courts in the United States, so as to encourage the application of impartial standards of international law formed without reference to the distinctive content of either public policy or foreign policy of the United States. The main suggestions for achieving this kind of judicial independence in international law cases are (1) development of rules of deference for subject matter in which there is a significant diversity of outlook among major nations and (2) encouragement of judicial activism for subject matter upon which major nations have formed a significant consensus. Such a distinction entails a judicial orientation. It is not possible or desirable to classify issues in one category or the other, although the areas of human rights and economic policy have been used to illustrate the character of the separation recommended.

There are, then, two steps in this theory of the role of domestic courts: first, as complete an independence of executive policy as is possible; second, an extensive deference in areas of diversity, together with a considerable aggressiveness in areas of consensus.

[7] *Cf.* Chapter IV for an argument in favor of using courts to promote national policy in the context of relations between the United States and Nazi Germany.

TABLE OF CASES

American Banana Co. v. United Fruit Co., 213 U.S. 347 (1909) . 34, 35, 37, 41, 99

Anderson v. N.V. Transandine Handelmaatschappij, 289 N.Y. 9, 43 N.E. 2d 502 (1942) 79

Anglo-Iranian Oil Co. v. Idemitu Kosan Kabushiki Kaisha, [1953] INT'L L. REP. 305 (Dist. Ct. Tokyo, *aff'd* by High Court Tokyo) 88

Anglo-Iranian Oil Co. v. Jaffrate, (The Rose Mary), [1953] 1 WEEKLY L.R. 246; 1953 INT'L L. REP. 316 .... 83, 87, 96, 100

Anglo-Iranian Oil Co. v. S.U.P.O.R. Co. [1955] INT'L L. REP. 19 (1953) (Ct. of Venice) 88

Anglo-Iranian Oil Co. v. S.U.P.O.R. Co. [1955] INT'L L. REP. 23 (1954) (Civil Ct. Rome) 88

The Attorney General of the Government of Israel v. Eichmann, Criminal Case No. 40/61, District Court of Jerusalem, December 11, 1961 (excerpted in 56 AM. J. INT'L L. 805) [1962]) 151

Bahía de Nipe . 145, 146, 150, 151, 152, 153, 154, 156, 157, 158, 160, 161, 163, 164

Banco Nacional de Cuba v. Sabbatino, 193 F. Supp. 375 (S.D.N.Y. 1961), *aff'd,* 307 F. 2d 845 (2d Cir. 1962), *rev'd* 11, 64–138, 145, 153–55, 169

Bank of China v. Wells Fargo Bank and Trust Co., 104 F. Supp. 59 (N.D. Cal. 1952) 104

Berizzi Bros. Co. v. S.S. Pesaro, 271 U.S. 562 (1925) 159, 161, 162

Bernstein v. N.V. Nederlandsche-Amerikaanshe Stoomvaart-Maattschappij, 173 F. 2d 71 (2d Cir. 1949); 210 F. 2d 375 (2d Cir. 1954) 11, 61, 90, 134

Bernstein v. Van Heyghen Freres Societe Anonyme, 163 F. 2d 246 (2d Cir.), *cert. denied,* 332 U.S. 772 (1947) 61, 89, 90, 104

Blackmer v. United States, 284 U.S. 421 (1937) 43

British Nylon Spinners, Ltd. v. Imperial Chemical Industries, Ltd., [1952] 2 ALL E.R. 780 .... 31, 38

British Nylon Spinners v. I.C.I., Ltd., [1954] ALL E.R. 88 31

Case of the Monetary Gold Removed from Rome in 1943 (Preliminary Question), [1954] I.C.J. Rep. 19 25

Case of the S.S. "Lotus," P.C.I.J., ser. A, No. 10 (1927) . 25, 27, 35, 39, 47, 53, 54

The Cristina, [1938] 1 ALL E.R. 719 .... 141, 142

Dade Drydock Corp. v. The M/T Mar Caribe, 199 F. Supp. 871 (S.D. Tex. 1961) 11, 145, 156

DeBeers Consolidated Mines, Ltd. v. United States, 325 U.S. 212 (1945) . 44

Dexter & Carpenter v. Runglig Jarnvagestyrelsen, 43 F. 2d 705 (2d Cir. 1930), *cert. denied,* 282 U.S. 896 (1931) 150, 151

Ex parte Peru, 318 U.S. 578 (1942) 155, 159, 161, 163

Fisheries Case, [1951] I.C.J. Rep. 116 .... 26, 53

The Fortitude, 11 U.S. (7 Cranch), 423 (1813) 129

In re Grand Jury Subpoena Duces Tecum Addressed to Canadian International Paper Co., 72 F. Supp. 1013 (S.D.N.Y. 1947) 43

Harris & Co. Advertising v. Republic of Cuba, 127 So. 2d 687 (Fla., 1961) . 11

Home Insurance Co. v. Dick, 281 U.S. 397 (1930) 41, 48

International Shoe Co. v. Washington, 326 U.S. 310 (1945) 41, 48

Interpretation of Peace Treaties, Advisory Opinion, [1950] I.C.J. Rep. 65 . 24
In re Investigation of World Arrangements with Relation . . . Petroleum, 13
    F.R.D. 280 (D.D.C. 1952) 43
Jorge v. Antonio Co., 19 Fla. Supp. 101 (1961) 11
Joyce v. Director of Public Prosecutions, [1946] A.C. 347 28
Kane v. National Institute of Agrarian Reform, 18 Fla. Supp. 116 (1961) 11, 119
Ker v. Illinois, 119 U.S. 436 (1886) 152
Latvian State Cargo & Passenger S.S. Line v. McGrath, 188 F. 2d 1000 (D.C.
    Cir. 1951) 45, 60, 94, 104
Luther V. Sagor, [1921] 3 K.B. 532 100
Magnolia Petroleum Co. v. Hunt 320 U.S. 430 (1943) 22
The Maipo, 252 Fed. 627 (S.D.N.Y. 1918) and 259 Fed. 367 (S.D.N.Y. 1919) 159
The Nailsea Meadow v. Bantham S.S. Co. Ltd. 55 T.L.R. 503 (1939) 91
National Bank v. Republic of China, 348 U.S. 356 (1955) 150, 157, 166
Nottebohm Case (second phase), [1955] I.C.J. Rep. 4 .... 27, 28
Oetjen v. Central Leather Co., 246 U.S. 297 (1918) 100, 102, 133
Paquete Habana, 175 U.S. 677 (1900) 139, 155
The Parlement Belge, 5 P. 197 (1880) 141
The Pesaro, 277 Fed. 473 (S.D.N.Y. 1921) 159, 161
Pons v. Republic of Cuba, 294 F. 2d 925 (1961) 11, 119, 129
The Prins Frederick, 2 Dod. R. 451 141
Ramirez and Feraud Chili Co. v. Las Palmas Food Co., 146 F. Supp. 594 (S.D.
    Cal. 1956), *aff'd per curiam*, 245 F. 2d 874 (9th Cir. 1957) 33
Ray v. Pan American Life Insurance Co., 19 Fla. Supp. 167 (1962) 11
The Republic of Mexico v. Hoffmann, 324 U.S. 31 (1945) 142, 153, 160
Request for Advisory Opinion Concerning the Status of Eastern Carelia, P.C.I.J.,
    ser. B, No. 5 (1923) 24
Ricaud v. American Metal Co., 246 U.S. 304 (1918) .. 75, 98, 100, 102, 105, 129
Rich v. Naviera Vacuba, S.A., 197 F. Supp. 710 (E.D. Va. 1961), *aff'd*, 295 F.
    2d 24 (4th Cir. 1961) 11, 145–46, 150–54, 156–58, 160–61, 163–64
Rodriquez v. Pan American Life Co., 311 F. 2d 429 (5th Cir. 1962), *rev'd*, 84
    Sup. Ct. 1130 (1964) 11
M. Salimoff & Co. v. Standard Oil Co. of New York, 262 N.Y. 220, 186 N.E.
    679 (1933) 95
The Schooner Exchange v. McFadden, 11 U.S. (7 Cranch) 116 (1812) 29, 30, 159
Shapleigh v. Mier, 299 U.S. 468 (1937) 98, 133
Société Internationale pour Participations Industrielles et Commerciales, S.A.
    v. Rogers, 357 U.S. 197 (1958) 38
State *ex rel.* National Institute of Agrarian Reform v. Dekle, 137 So. 2d 581
    (Fla. 1962) 145
Steele v. Bulova Watch Co., 344 U.S. 280 (1952) 33
Sulyok v. Penzintezeti Kozpont Budapest, 279 App. Div. 528, 111 N.Y.S. 2d
    75 (1st Dep't), *modified per curiam*, 304 N.Y. 704, 107 N.E.2d 604 (1952) 98
Underhill v. Hernandez, 168 U.S. 250 (1897) 100, 102
United States v. Aluminum Co. of America, 148 F. 2d 416 (2d Cir. 1945) 28, 37
United States v. American Tobacco Co., 221 U.S. 106 (1911) 41
United States v. Amsterdamsche Chininefabriek, C.C.H., Fed. Trade Reg. Serv.
    4186 (S.D.N.Y. 1928) 39
United States v. Diekelman, 92 U.S. 520 (1876) 98
United States v. Holophane Co., Inc., 119 F. Supp. 114 (S.D. Ohio 1954), *aff'd*,
    352 U.S. 903 (1956) 36, 43

United States v. Imperial Chemical Industries, 100 F. Supp. 504 (S.D.N.Y. 1951),
    decree, 105 F. Supp. 215 (S.D.N.Y. 1952) 31, 38
United States v. Nord Deutscher Lloyd, 223 U.S. 512 (1912) 41
United States v. Pink, 315 U.S. 203
    (1942) 11, 45, 60, 61, 62, 91, 94, 95, 104, 133, 137, 145, 160
United States v. Scophony Corp. of America, 333 U.S. 795 (1948) 48
United States v. Sisal Sales Corp., 274 U.S. 268 (1927) 32, 41
United States v. Timken Roller Bearing Co., 341 U.S. 593 (1951) 36
Vanity Fair Mills v. T. Eaton Co., Ltd., 234 F. 2d 633 (2d Cir. 1946) *cert. de-
    nied*, 352 U.S. 871 (1956) 33, 41
Vladikabkazsky Ry. v. New York Trust Co., 263 N.Y. 369, 189 N.E. 456
    (1934) 79, 91
Wilson, Secretary of Defense v. William S. Girard, U.S. Army Specialist, 31C,
    354 U.S. 524 (1957) 48
Wulfsohn v. Russian Socialist Federated Republic, 234 N.Y. 372, 138 N.E. 24
    (1923) 156

INDEX

Act of state doctrine, 7, 80–81, 95, 97–
109, 118, 129, 132, 134, 139–45
Antitrust regulation, 32–39, 57
Asylum, 152

Bernstein letter, 89–92, 123, 131–36
Bipolarity, 16

Cartels, 56–58
Civil strife, 15
Cold war, 65–72, 93, 113–14
Conflict of laws, 60, 87–88, 96, 99–101
Consensus, 8, 10, 12, 15, 18, 128, 136,
170, 172–73
Consent, 25

Decentralization, 8, 21–22, 27, 42–45,
65–66, 70–71, 106, 168, 172, 176
Deference, 160–61, 169; external aspect, 8–9, 34, 97–98, 102–06, 144,
175–76; internal aspect, 9, 10–11,
86–96, 118–21, 136–37, 143–44, 153–
58; its objective, 11; restrictions
upon, 9
Diplomatic immunity, 164–65
Diversity. See Legitimate diversity
Domestic courts, 123–24, 142–45, 165,
170–77; contribution to world order,
71–77; craftsmanship, 84–86; deference to executive policy, 86–96;
development of international law, 12;
and foreign policy, 11–12; function,
19–20; jurisdiction, 21–52; role, 19–
20; totalitarian public order, 19–20
Domestic jurisdiction, 22

Executive branch: embarrassment, 81,
89, 91, 105, 119, 124–25; foreign
relations, 105–06, 116–17, 119–20,
133–37
Executive-judicial relations, 60–62
Expropriation, 11, 46–47, 64, 80–81,
82–84, 87–96, 102–04, 107–12, 121–
23, 131–32, 153–54; duty to compensate, 83–84, 110–12, 125–26

Force, 50
Foreign investment, 46–47
Foreign relations, 105–06, 116–17, 119–
20, 160–61

Illegitimate diversity, 73–74
International agreements, 48–49
International claims, 97–98
International Court of Justice, 55, 93
International courts, 24–27
International law: and the character of
legal obligation, 17–18, 127; and the
cold war, 7–8; the duty to apply, 82,
96–102, 120–21; effectiveness, 18–19;
and foreign policy, 11–12; horizontal
legal order, 21–52, 101, 106–07, 128;
impartial application thereof, 93–94;
nature of, 1–7, 22–24, 166–67, 170,
171–72; and power, 17; Soviet view
of, 56; United States attitude toward,
69–70; violations, 27
International legal order, 65–66, 126–
29
International organization, 17; Soviet
attitude toward, 69; global, 14; regional, 14
International system, 15
Intervention, 17–46, 58–59
Investment abroad. See Foreign investment.

Judicial deference to Executive Branch.
See Deference: internal aspect
Judicial independence, 10–13, 95, 116–
17, 136–37, 157–58, 165–69, 172–77
Jurisdiction, 21–52, 53–63, 113–14, 172;
Carlston's view of, 108–09; terri-
torial principle, 28–32

Legal obligation, 17–18
Legitimate diversity, 72–73, 74–77, 85–
86, 101, 106–09, 111–14, 116–17, 131,
137–38, 143–44, 170–72
Lex loci, 34

National interest, 31, 35–36, 65–66, 72, 92, 126–27
Nationalism, 16
Nationalization. *See* Expropriation
Nation-state, 14–20, 172–75
New states, 16, 103–04, 125, 173, 175
Nonintervention. *See* Intervention
Nuclear testing, 27, 70–71
Nuclear war, 67–77
Nuclear weapons, 16, 67–77, 173

Peace, 23
Power, 29, 44–45, 50

Reasonableness, 33, 39–40, 42, 47
Reciprocity, 25, 32, 37, 39–40, 45–47, 51–52, 53, 102–03
Regionalism, 58–59
Remedies, 96–98

Self-help, 22
Self-restraint, 26–27, 36–37, 39–42, 46, 70–71, 103, 173, 176
Separation of powers, 19, 76–77, 131–37
Sino-Soviet dispute, 20
Sovereign immunity, 62, 139–69; executive suspension, 154–58
Sovereignty, 29–30
State. *See* Nation-state
State responsibility, 17
State system. *See* Nation-state
Supranational tribunal, 111–14

Universal legal standards, 73–74

War, 134, 176–77; technology of, 14–15
World legal order, 170–77